THE STOIC LIFE

The Stoic Life
Emotions, Duties, and Fate

Tad Brennan

CLARENDON PRESS · OXFORD

OXFORD
UNIVERSITY PRESS

Great Clarendon Street, Oxford OX2 6DP

Oxford University Press is a department of the University of Oxford.
It furthers the University's objective of excellence in research, scholarship,
and education by publishing worldwide in

Oxford New York

Auckland Cape Town Dar es Salaam Hong Kong Karachi
Kuala Lumpur Madrid Melbourne Mexico City Nairobi
New Delhi Shanghai Taipei Toronto

With offices in

Argentina Austria Brazil Chile Czech Republic France Greece
Guatemala Hungary Italy Japan Poland Portugal Singapore
South Korea Switzerland Thailand Turkey Ukraine Vietnam

Oxford is a registered trade mark of Oxford University Press
in the UK and in certain other countries

Published in the United States
by Oxford University Press Inc., New York

© Tad Brennan 2005

The moral rights of the author have been asserted
Database right Oxford University Press (maker)

First published 2005

British Library Cataloguing in Publication Data

Data available

Library of Congress Cataloging in Publication Data

Data available

Typeset by SPI Publisher Services, Pondicherry, India
Printed in Great Britain
on acid-free paper by
Biddles Ltd,
King's Lynn, Norfolk

ISBN 0-19-925626-8   978-0-19-925626-6

1 3 5 7 9 10 8 6 4 2

ACKNOWLEDGMENTS

I wish to thank the following people:

From my years at Princeton: David Furley, Michael Frede, John Cooper.

My former colleagues at King's College and the University of London: Richard Sorabji, M. M. McCabe, Bob Sharples, Verity Harte.

My former colleagues at Yale: Bob Adams, Marilyn Adams, Michael Della Rocca, Shelly Kagan, Susanne Bobzien, Pat Slatter.

My friends and mentors in the Symposium Hellenisticum: Keimpe Algra, Julia Annas, Jonathan Barnes, Jacques Brunschwig, Myles Burnyeat, Dorothea Frede, Brad Inwood, Tony Long, David Sedley, and Gisela Striker.

My closest intellectual associates: Charles Brittain, Rachel Barney, Stephen Menn.

Friends: Bill Buick, Pat Lambo, Jim and Jean Peters, Jon and Jean Blue.

Family: Anne S. Brennan, James Charles Brennan, Lexi Karns Brennan, and Lincoln Karns Brennan.

And as always, my deepest thanks go to Liz Karns.

To the memory of my beloved father
James Girard Brennan
30 August 1927–23 January 2002

and

my beloved nephew
Henry Swimmer Brennan
23 January 2000–25 February 2000

Sunt lacrimae

CONTENTS

ABBREVIATIONS

SE PH   Mutschmann, H. and Mau, J. (eds.) (1962) *Sexti Empirici Opera, vol. I Pyrrhoniae hypotyposes* (Leipzig: Teubner)

PART I

Introduction

I

Why be a Stoic?

What is it to be a Stoic, that is, to live as the Stoic philosophers told us we should live? And why would one want to live like that—why be a Stoic? In the central sections of this book I offer my answers to those questions, or rather, I offer what I take to have been the Stoics' answers. But in this chapter, I want to offer some other answers to it—answers that I think are incomplete, or misleading, or false, or completely hopeless. My view will be clearer by contrast with these other pictures. These pictures—or rather, caricatures—are derived from miscellaneous popular notions of what it is to be a Stoic, or what it is to be stoical about something.

We all know roughly what it means to be stoical or stoic—they are English words, fully naturalized from the Greek. Being stoic means being unemotional, indifferent to pleasure and pain, resigned to fate. The Victorian man of letters William Earnest Henley wrote a poem that is sometimes thought to encapsulate a stoic outlook on life:

> *Invictus*
> Out of the night that covers me
> Black as the pit from pole to pole
> I thank whatever gods may be
> For my unconquerable soul.

In the fell clutch of circumstance
I have not winced nor cried aloud;
Under the bludgeonings of Chance
My head is bloodied but unbowed.

Beyond this place of wrath and tears
Looms but the horror of the shade
And yet the menace of the years
Finds, and shall find, me unafraid.

It matters not how strait the gate
How charged with punishments the scroll
I am the master of my fate
I am the captain of my soul.

Now there's a stoic for you—tough, resigned, unemotional, indifferent. Unconquerable, unafraid, suffering the 'bludgeonings of Chance', without wincing or crying aloud.

But it is hard to put this picture together with the idea that being stoical means accepting fate—Henley's hero claims to be the master of his fate, not merely the patient recipient of its dictates.[1] The poem as a whole seems more like a boastful defiance of destiny; he is master and captain, unconquered and unbowed—hardly an attitude of resignation. And how unemotional is he, for that matter? It is true he prides himself on having neither 'winced nor cried aloud', but there is the clear implication that the whole ordeal hurt horribly. This is not a breezy indifference to pain, but a teeth-gritting struggle not to give pain any outward expression. But was the point of Stoicism not to have the emotions, or merely not to express them? Perhaps Stoicism does not counsel us to get rid of our emotions, but simply to repress them: the Stoic does not feel any less, he or she simply keeps it bottled up. The aim is to keep from crying aloud, no matter how much it hurts inside—and indeed, if it didn't hurt inside, there would be no particular glory in the mask of indifference.

But what is the point of this charade? If it is all done for looks—all done to convey a certain outward appearance, at odds with the inward experience—then Stoicism looks like an exaggerated obsession with the opinions of others. Of course, being called a crybaby is embarrassing, and it hurts your feelings. But if that is my reason for stoically concealing my feelings, then it seems I am doing it all in order to avoid a kind of hurt or pain, namely the hurt of humiliation, the pain of being publicly seen to express emotions. And this is surely not consistent with the idea that the Stoic treats pain as indifferent.

Or is it rather that the Stoic treats one kind of pain—physical pain, say—as indifferent, because he is so concerned about another kind of pain—the pain of being laughed at? That would be a logically consistent picture, at least, but it is hard to see what rationale lies behind it except for an arbitrary preference for one pain over another. Most of us, when we see a football hurtling towards our heads, put up our hands to protect our face. One can imagine an exceptionally ugly concert pianist who would put his face in the way to protect his fingers. On this model, the Stoic feels pain just as deeply as you or I do, and works just as hard to avoid it. The difference is simply in our tender spots; he has a less sensitive body and a more sensitive ego.

The philosopher David Hume, no Stoic himself, also thought that Stoics were caught up in an emotion, though a different one:

[The Stoic philosophy is] founded on this erroneous maxim, that what a man can perform sometimes, and in some dispositions, he can perform always and in every disposition. When the mind, by Stoical reflections, is elevated into a sublime enthusiasm of virtue and strongly smit with any *species* [i.e. appearance] of honour or public good, the utmost bodily pain and sufferings will not prevail over such a high sense of duty; and it is possible, perhaps, by its means, even to smile and exult in the midst of tortures. If this sometimes may be the case in fact and reality, much more may a philosopher, in his school or even in his closet, work himself up to such an enthusiasm, and support, in imagination, the acutest pain or most calamitous event which he can possible conceive.[2]

In Hume's view, Stoicism is a misguided attempt to model a whole way of life on a fleeting feeling. Anyone can be moved and uplifted by thoughts of heroic virtue—we can be temporarily transported into an ecstatic state in which the glories of virtue and honor are magnified a hundredfold, and the disadvantages of death are disregarded. It may be the result of 'Stoical reflections', or of a patriotic speech, or a John Philips Sousa march—anything that stirs and rouses the blood. Hume concedes that this sort of temporary ecstasy can work wonders, making it possible for the person in its grip 'even to smile and exult in the midst of tortures'.

What he denies is that any such condition can endure—it is necessarily transient, a brief flight that must inevitably be followed by a return to the solid earth of ordinary, undistorted concerns. Enthusiasms wane; conventional values reassert themselves; last night's ardent Stoic has cold morning thoughts about the glories of self-sacrifice. Hume's Stoic is a mood-junky, surfing a wave of bio-chemical exhilaration that will soon subside. Like Henley's Stoic, he is just as much the plaything of emotions as anyone else, even if the emotions are unusual ones.

But what about the idea that Stoics simply don't have emotions—not that they conceal or repress them, or exaggerate some to subdue others, but that they simply don't feel any? This Stoic is no hypocrite; the reason that he neither winced nor cried aloud is that it simply didn't hurt.

The puzzle here is simply why we would want to live this way. Stoicism in this picture is a sort of lobotomy, or at least a general anesthetic. Being a Stoic means being a zombie, or a robot. In Shakespeare's only use of the word, one character says it's like being a 'stock', that is, a lifeless stump or senseless block of wood (he doubtless chose the word for its punning resemblance as well):

> Only (good master) while we do admire
> this vertue and this moral discipline,
> let's be no Stoics, nor no stocks, I pray!
>
> (*Taming of the Shrew*, I.i.30)

Why be a zombie, or a stock? Why be a Stoic, if this is what it means? True, sometimes life can be very painful. If someone offered to teach you a system that would leave you without any emotions for the rest of your life—a life of numb detachment—you might be tempted to try it, if you were in great pain. Then again, you might prefer to take a tranquilizer instead. At least the Valium will wear off, and then you can reassess whether to continue the dosage or to return to normal.

Perhaps you would make the assessment based on the ratio of pleasures to pains. At a painful time in your life, when the pains far outweigh the joys, numbness looks like a bargain. But when joys preponderate, who'd be a Stoic? This line of thought may suggest a kind of historicizing interpretation of Stoicism, that grants it a certain validity in its day, but denies it any current relevance. Here's how it goes: living conditions in antiquity were sufficiently severe that an active engagement in life really was a bad bargain, and Stoicism really was the wisest course. To us now, of course, it seems barbaric not to feel anything at the death of your own baby, but infant mortality rates back then surely counseled emotional insulation. Who would want to become too attached to any particular infant, when ten live births in a family might yield one surviving toddler?

On the other hand, anyone in this decade who said that they were unwilling to marry, or have children, because of the possibility that their child or spouse might die, would be widely considered to be in need of psychological assistance. At the very least, one would want to say to them that things are really not that bleak and grim; that they have drastically over-estimated the chances for personal tragedy.

If Stoicism is an anesthetic, then, it is a good bargain for bad times, but a bad bargain in good times—the value of Stoicism will vary by the era, and this, happily, is not an era for Stoics. But even if the ratio of pains to pleasures were much greater than it is now, what would be so admirable about choosing Stoicism on those grounds? If someone said that they were willing to play a game provided that they got to win nine out of every ten matches, but that they would quit and take their ball home if they lost more than half the time, we would not think they were brave or tough. We would think that they gave the losses too much significance, that they were too averse to failure—so averse, indeed, that by opting out of the game altogether they were passing up a worthwhile pleasure that they might have had. Once again, the Stoic seems to have turned into someone who cares too much about feelings—someone who experiences the pain of frustrated desire as so overwhelmingly painful that they have opted out of desiring altogether.

And speaking of opting out—one thing that we all know about the historical Stoics, like Cato and Seneca, is that they permitted suicide. Indeed, one sometimes gets the impression that the ancient Stoics killed themselves frequently (though not more than once per Stoic), as if it were a fairly common response to provocation. Seneca sometimes makes it sound as though suicide is the sovereign remedy for every ailment. Are you persecuted by a tyrant? Commit suicide. Is someone forcing you to act dishonorably? Commit suicide. Is your backache troubling you again? Commit suicide. Somehow, this constant meditation on suicide is supposed to make one tranquil instead of morose and maudlin, but it is not clear how. It looks, to any sane person, like a morbid melancholy more than a strong and healthy attitude to life. It seems no surprise that people who are obsessed with suicide as a way out of life's difficulties will also advocate the extinction of the emotions—in both cases, it seems, a policy built on an extreme desire to avoid the possibility of negatives leads you permanently to forgo the possibility of positives.

And why place so much value on tranquility, in any case? Tranquility is a nicer word than numbness, and presumably it describes a different thing: not an absence of feeling, but a particular feeling; a perceptible awareness of the lack of conflict and turmoil. It sounds nice, of course. But so do many other feelings, for that matter. The feeling of excited exhilaration can be very pleasant, too, though it is inconsistent with tranquility; the feeling of having narrowly won an unlikely victory can be a very pleasant feeling, or the feeling of having persevered through initial frustrations to secure finally a hard-fought achievement. I cannot have those pleasant feelings if I make tranquility my constant aim; and yet who is to say that those feelings are not as pleasant as tranquility is? And even if someone said it, wouldn't it merely be another arbitrary preference?

These are the kinds of puzzles and perversities that struck me some years ago when I first met Stoic ethical doctrines, largely at second hand. The whole thing seemed perplexing, perverse, and even puerile—a mixture of tough-guy bravado, hypocrisy, and heartless-ness, neither personally compelling nor philosophically interesting. It seemed to me then—and seems to me now—that if being Stoic meant being stoic, then there would be little reason to study their philosophy.

A closer acquaintance has convinced me that being Stoic is very different from being stoic, and that the Stoic system is very much worth studying. But the best way to make their acquaintance is by seeing them in their ancient context. First, we should look at the Stoics themselves, and how we know about them: that is the job of the next chapter. Then, in the third chapter we will look at the philosophical context in which their system arose.

NOTES

1. It may be relevant that the phrase comes from a speech in Shakespeare that is *not* spoken by a Stoic. It is Cassius the Epicurean who in urging Brutus to join the plot to kill Julius Caesar says, 'men at some time are masters of their fates' (1.ii.139). The Epicureans were vehemently opposed to the Stoic doctrine of fate and determinism.
2. David Hume, *Dialogues Concerning Natural Religion, Part 1.*

2

The Ancient Stoics: People and Sources

This chapter is intended to help you get your bearings in an unfamiliar period, by introducing you to the major figures in the history of Ancient Stoicism, and also describing the sources of our knowledge of Stoic philosophy.

A Gallery of Stoic Philosophers

Philosophy deals in ideas, but to understand the origin and evolution of the ideas it helps to know something of the people who thought them up and wrote them down. The Stoic school got its start a little before 300 BC, and reached its highest degree of theoretical elaboration in the next century. It was an active school until sometime in the 200s AD; thereafter its membership dwindled, through inattention and the greater popularity of other schools. Stoic writings were still read for a few centuries, by Platonists and by Christians interested in philosophy. But the active life of the school lasted a mere six hundred years.

This book has two heroes, Chrysippus and Epictetus. The first is one of the greatest thinkers of all time; the second one of the greatest talkers. Chrysippus (*c.* 280–208 BC) did not start the Stoic school, but his far-reaching logical and philosophical abilities elevated it from the second rank of philosophical systems to the first rank. The philosophy that comes down to us as Stoicism is generally the work of Chrysippus, even when it is attributed merely to 'the Stoics'. Very little of his writing is left—not one of his seven-hundred-plus books survives complete. But from quotations, summaries, and reports, his brilliance still shines through. Among the ancients, only Plato and Aristotle surpass him as philosophers.

Epictetus (*c.* 50–120 AD) never wrote any books at all, and yet we are fortunate in possessing quite a number of his words. He taught public classes, and held long conversations with anyone who wanted to speak with him, and these talks were written down by one of his students, Arrian, who published them in eight books. Four of these books still remain, enough to fill a medium-sized paperback book. Epictetus was not a great theoretical innovator, and indeed I do not believe there is anything of philosophical substance in his works that we would not have found in Chrysippus' works. But the records of his conversations bring Stoicism to life better than any other writings do. He spoke easily, rapidly, without pretense or pomposity, and poked fun at himself as often as at others. The Greek he spoke was the ordinary, unsophisticated Greek of his day, and to my ear it sounds more like real speech than any other author in antiquity—there is more realistic dialogue in this philosopher than in all of the playwrights. He liked a clear example better than a complicated theory, and liked practical application better than either. He constantly reminds his students that the point of philosophy is to put the theory into practice, to change one's life.

The other figures it is worth knowing include, to begin with, the founder of the school, Zeno of Citium (*c.* 335–262 BC). Zeno the Stoic (so-called to distinguish him from Zeno the Eleatic, famous for paradoxes) came to Athens as a young man and studied with several of the best philosophers of the day, especially Plato's successors at the Academy, Xenocrates, Polemo, and Crantor. He seems to have been deeply influenced by Plato's dialogues, and by the picture of Socrates' life that Plato constructed. There were other schools active besides

The Ancient Stoics: People and Sources ~ 11

the Academy, and Zeno studied with several of the minor ones, too, including the Cynics, followers of the tub-dwelling Diogenes. The Cynics were deeply influenced by Socrates' unorthodox lifestyle—the simplicity and asceticism of his life, the unflinching honesty with which he lived by his philosophical beliefs, and his uncompromising disregard for appearances and conventional niceties. They developed this aspect of Socrates' legacy into a view that many of our ordinary beliefs about morality have no basis in nature and are only the result of custom, and they became famous for the outrageousness with which they flouted Greek customs for the sake of living according to nature.

When Zeno began his own teaching career he took up the habit of meeting his students in a stoa or portico, of which there were several in Athens at the time—long, open, colonnaded walk-ways where people came to do their shopping and transact business, to talk about politics and news—and philosophy. His students were first known as 'Zenonians'—rather in the way that Platonists, Aristotelians, and Epicureans all took their school-affiliation from their founder's name. Later, they came to be called Stoics—it may be that this habit dates to the period when Chrysippus was thoroughly remaking the school, transforming Zeno's rudiments into a real system, and thereby rendering the old name less appropriate.[1] Zeno was known during his lifetime for the virtue and austerity of his life, and the Athenians voted to grant him several honors, both during his life and in connection with his burial.

He was succeeded in 262 BC by one of the odder characters in antiquity, an ex-boxer and ditch-digger named Cleanthes. The opinion of all ancient reporters is unanimous: Cleanthes was not a genius. But he won admirers through the simplicity of his life, his capacity for hard work, and his gentle decency. He wrote over fifty treatises, but all that is left are a few scraps of verse, most notable for their religious fervor. Ancient sources seem puzzled that Zeno chose him to carry on the school, but we are also told that he compared himself to a writing-tablet made of bronze: difficult to make an impression on, but very retentive of whatever it receives.[2] Zeno may have felt that his

teachings were safe in Cleanthes' unimaginative hands; when someone accused him of being cowardly, Cleanthes replied, 'that's why I so
seldom make a mistake'.[3] He led the school until 232 BC.

Chrysippus was his pupil, his successor, and his intellectual opposite. Mercurial and lightning-fast, Chrysippus would sometimes step in
to defend his more stolid teacher from clever opponents. When a
logic-chopping visitor was setting up Cleanthes to fall for a fallacy,
Chrysippus interrupted him by saying, 'Stop distracting your elder
from more important things, and leave these trivialities to us young-
sters.'[4] He also told Cleanthes that he only needed to be taught the
doctrines; he himself would work out the proofs.[5]

And he seems to have done very nearly that: while keeping, as far
as we can tell, to the main lines of Stoic doctrine as laid down by
Zeno, he completely revised its theoretical underpinnings, connect-
ing up all the parts, providing new arguments, and working to make
the entire system cohere. In this endeavor he had the most important
help a philosopher can hope for: an opponent of nearly equal brilliance. This was Arcesilaus, whose career as a philosopher falls mostly
during the careers of Zeno and Cleanthes; but Chrysippus will have
been thirty-five or forty before Arcesilaus' death in 241 BC. Arcesilaus
was the head of the Academy, and so the direct successor of Plato, but
instead of propounding a set of doctrines, as the earlier heads had,
Arcesilaus adopted a policy of arguing against the views of all other
schools, probing and criticizing, and always providing arguments on
both sides of a question. With no other school did he carry on as
continual and close-fought a controversy as with the Stoics. By the
time Chrysippus was in a position to revise Stoicism, he will have
benefited from Arcesilaus' acute diagnoses of its shortcomings and
inconsistencies.

We know the names of a few important Stoics over the next
hundred years: a second Zeno (of Tarsus), then Diogenes of Babylon
and Antipater of Tarsus followed Chrysippus as heads of the school,
and left behind views that suggest at least philosophical activity, if not
innovation. By the late second century BC, the Mediterranean world
was coming to center around Rome; thus it is not surprising that the

The Ancient Stoics: People and Sources ~ 13

two most important Stoics of that era have strong ties to Roman aristocrats and intellectuals. Panaetius of Rhodes (*c.* 185–110 BC) and his successor Posidonius of Apamea (*c.* 130? –50? BC) may have introduced real changes in the Stoic program by criticizing Chrysippus, and taking a greater interest in the writings of Plato and Aristotle. Unfortunately, so little of their work remains that it is hard to tell what amounts to real disagreement with Chrysippean Stoicism, and what is merely a difference of emphasis.

Cicero (106–43 BC), the great Roman orator and statesman, was not himself a Stoic, but he studied Stoicism extensively and knew Posidonius personally. Though he declared his allegiance to the Academic school, he was certainly sympathetic to Stoicism, especially Stoic ethics. His writings are one of the most important sources for our knowledge of Stoicism, and he did more than anyone else to translate Stoic terminology from Greek into Latin. During the centuries when Latin was the language of culture in Western Europe, and Greek forgotten or known only to a few, Cicero's discussions of Stoicism were one of the two most important ways that Stoic ideas could reach and influence an educated audience.

The other was the writings of Seneca (4 BC–65 AD), who was himself a professed Stoic. His moralizing, maxim-mongering style has contributed much to the popular image of Stoicism through the centuries; his constant sermons against vanity and vice, and his frequent and histrionic advice to find relief in suicide, all contribute to a curiously wrought-up exponent of tranquility, an over-heated advocate of cool. He was for nearly a decade the chief adviser to the emperor Nero, whose promising early days in power gave way to increasing dementia and savagery. Seneca was in no way the cause of Nero's corruption, and indeed at last became his victim, when the emperor accused him of conspiracy (Seneca sought the relief he had so often advised). Nevertheless, Seneca did assist Nero in some of his enormities, and certainly profited from his position as adviser to the emperor; if he moderated some of Nero's madness, he still is tainted with some of his crimes. It is rather sad that his immense intellectual and practical abilities brought him to the attention of the emperors he served; like Cicero before him, he might have cut a better figure for philosophy if he had never covered himself in political ignominy. On the other hand, the political excesses of those brutal times may have been lessened around the edges now and then by having philosophers near the seats of power: if they did not produce utopias, these philosophers at least did no worse than the non-philosophers around them.

In the capital city of the Roman Empire there were many foreigners, some willing immigrants, some imported slaves, some speaking Latin and some still conversing in their native tongues. Musonius Rufus was a rough contemporary of Seneca's, an Italian native of aristocratic family, and a Stoic. We know of him because some of his speeches were recorded by a student named Pollio and published; excerpts are preserved in a compilation assembled in the 5th-century AD by Johannes Stobaeus. (Musonius lectured in Greek, as was still common among Roman intellectuals—although Cicero wrote in Latin to popularize philosophy, it is clear that he was fluent in Greek, and his private letters are sprinkled with unselfconscious Greek phrases.) From these excerpts we can see that Musonius was a fine and inspiring speaker, with notably attractive views about the importance of educating women.[6]

Another of Musonius' students was Epictetus, whom we met above. He spent his early life as a slave in Rome, working for one of Nero's advisers, and began studying philosophy with Musonius while still a slave. He was banished from Rome along with other philosophers in one of the two purges that occurred in 89 AD and 92 AD; he will have been about 35 or 40 then. He lived the rest of his life in Nicopolis, an active town in Western Greece, where he had the good fortune of having his teachings taken down by one of his pupils, as mentioned above. His life was generally uneventful, but certainly not unremarkable; although he never married, and spent most of his adult years in the quiet life of a provincial teacher, his rise from slavery to freedom to international renown makes a fascinating story in itself. There is also a famous story that dates from his youth, and indicates something of his astounding personality. Before he was freed it happened one day that his master crippled his leg, so that Epictetus was lame for the rest of his life. An early author tells us that the owner began to torture him by twisting his leg, and that Epictetus said to him, with a gentle smile, and no hint of alarm in his voice, 'If you keep that up, you are going to break it.' The owner continued twisting Epictetus' leg, until it broke. 'Didn't I tell you it would break?' was Epictetus' only comment.[7]

Within a year or two of Epictetus' death was born the Stoic who finally carried philosophy into the emperor's seat, Marcus Aurelius (121–180 AD). While actively campaigning to secure the borders of the Roman Empire, Marcus also took time to jot reflections in his journal—and did so in Greek, still the custom for an educated Roman aristocrat. Marcus' 'Meditations', as they are called, are deeply influenced by Epictetus and Musonius, but the humorous touches of the ex-slave are replaced by the nearly stifling gravity of imperial responsibility. Marcus was a good emperor and a good man; if he added nothing to the Stoic philosophy, he at least gives us a fascinating record of the impression it made on his mind, and of how he used its guidance in the bustle of a soldier's and politician's life.

There is only one more name to be mentioned, whose relation to Stoicism shows something of its fate in later years. Simplicius was a leading Platonist of the mid-sixth century, a scholar of all the ancient schools who is now best known for his invaluable commentaries on Aristotle (when Galileo was writing his Dialogues to attack the physical system of the Medieval Aristotelian scientists, he named his fictional Aristotelian opponent 'Simplicio'). He wrote an extensive commentary on a short collection of Epictetus' sayings, in which he tries to show how they can be useful to the early education of the aspiring Platonic philosopher.[8] He is not advocating Stoicism; he is advocating Stoic moral guidance on the road to Platonism. He no longer treats Stoicism as a complete philosophical system; the systematic brilliance of Chrysippus is neither defended nor attacked in his commentary. Instead, Stoic philosophy is treated as a source of inspiring ethical maxims that can be detached from some of the more confused or misguided physical and logical theories that the Stoics also espoused.

16 ~ *The Ancient Stoics: People and Sources*

Our Sources for Stoicism

I have already mentioned the four sources that account for well over half the bulk of our testimony and evidence concerning Stoicism: Cicero, Seneca, Epictetus, and Marcus. But in light of the previous gallery, you will notice that all these authors date from the later, Roman period. For none of the early Stoics do any complete works remain. Our knowledge of them is derived in part from quotations in the four Roman authors, and also from quotations found in other sources. Here too, the bulk of the quotations come from a handful of sources; learning about them can give us a sense of the treacherous fate that Stoic writings suffered.

The most important source for biographical information about the early Stoics, and also an invaluable source for their philosophy, is an author named Diogenes Laertius. He seems to have lived sometime around 250 AD, but we do not know where he lived, or what profession he plied. There is no reason to think he was much of a philosopher, or much of a biographer, for that matter. There is probably not a single fact in his books that he mentions from personal knowledge—he certainly did not know any of the important philosophers he describes, nearly all of whom had died centuries before him. All he did was go through a good library, copying, quoting and summarizing, without making the least improvement on his sources, which include more than 350 books by 250 authors, not including the sources he forgets to cite. He prefers a juicy piece of gossip to a solid piece of thinking any day; his purpose is to write about the lives of the philosophers, and their views are brought in primarily to demonstrate their foibles. He is not careful in his selection of sources, compiling all kinds of unlikely rubbish, and makes no attempt to judge between the competing and contradictory accounts that he assembles side by side. (His accounts of the deaths of the Stoic heads are typical: Zeno, we are told, stubbed his toe and then held his breath until he died; Cleanthes was recovering from a pain in his gums when he decided to starve himself to death; Chrysippus drank some wine unmixed with water—an extravagance among the Greeks—and died from dizziness;

or perhaps he died from laughter, watching a woman feed figs to a donkey.) There is only one reason, in fact, that we read Diogenes: somehow, his third-rate, Reader's Digest Guide to Ancient Philosophy survived, when nearly all of the original documents he based it on perished. Works of real genius now survive only through the odd paragraph pasted into this scrapbook. Nietzsche, who wrote a long essay on Diogenes Laertius, called him the 'clumsy watchman guarding treasures whose value he does not know'.[9]

Of slightly earlier date (150–200 AD?) is a clever and canny skeptical philosopher named Sextus Empiricus. As an avowed enemy of all positive philosophical systems, his sole reason for discussing Stoicism is to demonstrate its uselessness, incoherence, and intellectual nullity. But Sextus has a saving grace: no matter how petty his refutations may be, his reportage is utterly scrupulous. His complete reliability in detailing the views of his opponents makes him a priceless boon to the student of ancient philosophy, and especially to the student of Stoicism.[10] Sextus has a fine feeling for argument, and interesting philosophical views of his own, derived from the revival of skepticism that passed under the name of Pyrrhonism.

Earlier still is an Academic philosopher, and priest of the temple at Delphi, named Plutarch of Chaironea (50–120 AD). Plutarch is more famous for his lengthy series of Lives of illustrious Greeks and Romans, a translation of which provided Shakespeare with most of his knowledge of Julius Caesar, Antony and Cleopatra, and Timon of Athens. But Plutarch also wrote a great many essays on philosophical topics, some of them by way of popular pieces and conversation starters, some containing more serious work. His most serious essays are those in which he attacks his Stoic and Epicurean opponents; his treatises 'On Stoic Contradictions' and 'On the Common Notions' contain many verbatim quotations from Chrysippus' own writings, with which Plutarch seems to have been quite familiar.

Galen (130–210 AD) is most famous as a medical author, but he was thoroughly conversant with the views of all the philosophical schools, and was a good if unoriginal philosopher himself (he wrote a treatise titled 'The Best Doctor Must Also Be a Philosopher'). Hippocrates and Plato are his two gods, and the Stoics are either redundant when they agree with them, or culpable when they dissent—such is the burden of his treatise on 'The Opinions of Hippocrates and Plato', an invaluable source for details about Stoic psychology. Anti-Stoic polemic may be found in many of his treatises, often usefully supported by quotations from Chrysippus.

Johannes Stobaeus assembled a long anthology or collection of philosophical texts of all sorts sometime in the fifth century AD. His method is simply to transcribe whole chunks of earlier texts; he writes out for us extensive passages from some of Plato's dialogues, and if they had not survived independently we should now be very grateful for it. He also wrote out a very long account of Stoic ethics, usually attributed to Arius Didymus, who may have been writing around the turn of the BC/AD divide.

Arius himself was probably a Stoic, but it is notable that none of the other sources—Diogenes, Sextus, Plutarch, or Galen—is a Stoic, and three of those four are bitter enemies of Stoicism (Diogenes is merely a nitwit). Plutarch's standard procedure is to find a statement in one of Chrysippus' books, and claim that it contradicts some other statement in another of his books. Neither statement is given any context; we usually get only a sentence or two, and sometimes less, surrounded by Plutarch's victorious crowing that he has caught Chrysippus in a contradiction. It is usually easy to see why there is no real inconsistency in Chrysippus' maintaining both theses simultaneously; the wonder is rather that Plutarch should have thought this puerile procedure would bother any Stoic, or reassure any non-Stoic. Galen also makes Chrysippus his target, though his method is to claim that Chrysippus was in disagreement with his elder, Zeno, or his successors (especially Posidonius), who all agree (according to Galen) with the wisdom of Plato and Hippocrates. Again, we are given the view of Chrysippus one sentence, sometimes one paragraph, at a time, and must struggle to understand what he was saying through the haze of malicious interpretation that Galen has laid over it. Diogenes is too dim to have any axe of his own to grind, but it is clear that at least one of his sources liked to collect alleged discrepancies between the views of Cleanthes and Chrysippus.[11]

The Ancient Stoics: People and Sources ~ 19

The Stoics, in other words, are the victims of a history that, like most histories, was written by the victors: a nearly uniform hostility towards Stoicism pervades the ancient sources. Our job is to take each of the isolated sentences, free it from its polemical context, and see how they might fit together with what our other sources tell us, so as to reconstruct the system we might have found in Chrysippus' own writings, had they survived.

NOTES

1. The followers of Zeno were originally called 'Zenonians,' or even 'Socratics.' There is no evidence that Stoics after Chrysippus were called 'Chrysippeans' (unlike Aristo, the renegade student of Zeno whose followers were called 'Aristonians', DL 7.161 = SVF 1.333). The label 'Stoics' may have arisen as an attempt to avoid favoring either teacher. An ancient aphorism (DL 7.183 = SVF 2.1 = IG2 II–I) said, 'if there had been no Chrysippus, there would have been no Stoa', and surely part of its point was to attest to his centrality in establishing the school's doctrine. But a slight change of emphasis in translation may bring out the verse's real point, namely 'if there had been no Chrysippus, it would not have been called "The Stoa".'

2. Plutarch de audiendo 47E = SVF 1.464; similarly at DL 7.37.

3. DL 7.171.

4. DL 7.182.

5. DL 7.179 = SVF 2.1 = IG2 II–I.

6. Stobaeus 2.31.123, 2.31.126.

7. Origen Contra Celsum 7.53.

8. I can highly recommend the recent translation of Brittain and Brennan (2002).

9. Nietzsche in a letter to Erwin Rohde, quoted in Kaufmann (1967), 505.

10. I repeat here some material from Brennan (2000c).

11. Cf. e.g. DL 7.127 = IG2 II–94, 7.139, 7.157 = IG2 II–20; see also SE AM 7.227 = IG2 II–8 and 7.372 = IG2 II–9. Antipater, who was the sixth head of the Stoic school (Zeno of Tarsus and Diogenes of Babylon came between him and Chrysippus) is credited with an entire treatise titled 'Concerning the disagreement between Cleanthes and Chrysippus' (Plutarch Sto. Rep. 1034A = SVF 3. Ant.66). This may be the ultimate source for some of these comparisons, even if Antipater's point was to resolve the appearance of disagreement rather than to call attention to it.

3

The Ancient Philosophical Background

Stoic ethics arises as the last of the distinctive ethical outlooks to be developed in ancient Greece. It comes after the astounding period of philosophical creativity that stretched from Socrates (469 BC–399 BC), through Plato (429 BC–347 BC), to Aristotle (384 BC–322 BC), and it both borrows from and presupposes elements in all of their systems. Some ancient critics of the Stoa charged, in fact, that Socrates, Plato, and Aristotle had all been in fundamental agreement about ethics, and that the Stoics had merely repackaged the same view, wrapped up in misleading jargon to give it the appearance of novelty.[1] This charge is doubly false—there was genuine innovation in the Stoic picture, some of it revolutionary, and there was genuine disagreement between Socrates, Plato, and Aristotle, some of it fundamental. But there's something right about the charge as well, particularly when we view the Stoics from the vantage point provided by the millennia: they did owe a great deal to their predecessors, which is why we must start with their predecessors in order to understand them.

The goal of this chapter, then, is to sketch in the philosophical background to Stoic ethics: what stock of shared assumptions and presuppositions about ethics did the Stoics start from in their own investigations? What questions and problems did they inherit, and what conceptual vocabulary did they inherit for solving them? It is this shared background of Greek ethics that the Stoics are least likely to have discussed explicitly in the exposition of their own views, or their criticisms of others, precisely because it was assumed on all sides. That is why it is worth spending some time making ourselves familiar with the climate of ethical investigations, the milieu of theorizing, in which Stoicism took root, before we look at their own system in their own words in the next chapters.

The greatest influence on the Stoics came from Socrates, as he was depicted in the dialogues of Plato, Xenophon, and other of his disciples whose works we have lost. Indeed, one ancient source tells us that the early Stoics were willing to be called 'Socratics'.[2] Socrates had a double impact, both as a theoretician and as a role model.

As a role model, the character of Socrates that emerged from the writings of his disciples impressed the Stoics with his genial imperturbability, his calm indifference to poverty, physical discomfort, and death. He seemed always to be happy, and his happiness seemed to come strictly from inside of him. He had none of the external accoutrements of an enviable or lavish life—no wealth, political power, or good looks—and he seemed to need none of them. He seemed to have everything he needed or wanted, and this self-sufficiency came through in every aspect of his life: his unshakeable confidence in conversation, his courage on the battlefield, his integrity in personal dealings, and his insusceptibility to any temptations of the flesh. The narrator of Plato's *Phaedo* tells us that he was the 'best, wisest, and most just' person of all those whom Phaedo knew—but he also seemed to be the most serene, the most contented, and the happiest. His contentment and his virtue seemed to go hand in hand—it was because he had everything he wanted that he was not beholden to anyone, had no need to flatter, wheedle, or cringe, could not be seduced or intimidated; but it was also because of his moderation, temperance, and courage that he could have so little and want no more. This extraordinary personality made a great impression on the ancient Greeks, just as it makes a great impression on anyone today who reads Plato's *Apology* or *Phaedo*.

But had he been only a personality, he would not have been a philosopher.[3] His other legacy consisted in his continual engagement with a set of philosophical issues, ideas, and controversies. Only a portion of his impact here came from his explicit espousal of positive views. Of equal importance were the assumptions that guided the questions he asked, and the very fact of his method of pursuing philosophy through questions, the so-called Socratic method or method of elenchus, with its emphasis on clarity, consistency, and explanatory power.

Providing a careful, rigorous, and well-defended interpretation of the philosophy of Socrates is a task beyond the purview of this book, but for the purposes at hand even a casual and impressionistic account will be helpful. We can sum up the philosophical content of Socrates' contribution to the Stoic background in the following theses:

(1) There is a certain condition of an individual's life as a whole, called *eudaimonia* in ancient Greek, variously translated as 'happiness', 'well-being', 'success', 'flourishing', and the like (I shall usually use 'happiness').

(2) Things are good for agents, or benefit agents, to the extent that they contribute to their happiness.[4]

(3) People always choose what they take to be good for them (i.e. beneficial or productive of happiness) in preference to things that they take to be bad for them (harmful, destructive of happiness) or less good. All human beings act only for the sake of their own happiness (psychological eudaimonism), and they are rationally justified in doing so (rational eudaimonism). All desire is desire for what agents believe to be good for them.[5]

(4) An individual's happiness is primarily (perhaps exclusively) determined by the condition of their soul, rather than by the condition of their body or their other possessions.[6]

(5) Among the conditions of the soul, it is virtue that is of central importance to an individual's happiness—being virtuous is at least necessary for happiness, probably the greatest single

The Ancient Philosophical Background ~ 23

determinant of happiness, and possibly the only thing needed for it (different dialogues suggest different views).[7]

(6) There are four virtues—courage, justice, temperance, wisdom—but whoever has one has all of them (sometimes piety features as a fifth on this list). They are closely connected, inasmuch as all of them involve knowing how to identify and make proper use of what is really good and bad. So, for instance, courage involves knowing that slavery is worse than physical discomfort; temperance involves knowing that health is a greater good than the pleasures of indulgence, and so on. To the extent that all of them can be analyzed as the knowledge of what is really good and bad, really beneficial and harmful, it seems that there is only one virtue, which goes under four different names (though in most contexts 'wisdom' will be the most illuminating name for it).[8]

(7) The knowledge that virtue consists in is structured like a craft or science, for example, like the craft of carpentry or architecture, or the science of geometry or medicine, with fundamental principles and derivative theorems. If you have this knowledge (that is, if you are virtuous), then you can provide definitions of virtue and all the particular virtues and explain how they are related to one another; you can tell, of any particular action, whether it is virtuous or not; and you know what the human good (happiness or eudaimonia) consists in, and what actions and objects are beneficial or harmful.

We can see how some of the famous dictums of Socrates follow from this set of beliefs. Thus if it is rational to be concerned for one's happiness, and this is centrally a matter of the state of one's soul, and in particular of one's virtue, then it becomes rational to be concerned for the virtue of one's soul. If virtue is necessary for happiness, then it is never rational to act in a way that will destroy one's virtue, since this will preclude the attainment of happiness. If virtue is the greatest single determinant of happiness, or indeed sufficient for happiness, then it follows from this that it is a mistake to commit an injustice for the sake of one's body or for external possessions—it is a mistake in that these things have much less of an effect on one's happiness than it is commonly supposed. The loss of money, the infliction of pain, and even death, are not genuine harms, because they take little or nothing away from one's eudaimonia or happiness. (My repetition of the Greek word is an acknowledgment that these claims will seem utterly implausible on an ordinary modern understanding of 'happiness'.) Thus it follows that no one ever commits an injustice willingly, in the sense that anyone who does commit an injustice must believe, mistakenly, that it will benefit them. If they knew that it would make them wretched, as it will, they would not have the least inclination to do it—and that is not a counsel of saintliness, but merely a fact of psychology.

Part of what makes it difficult and controversial to attribute philosophical positions to Socrates is that our best source for his views is the dialogues of Plato. Since Plato wrote them, we must always wonder how much of their content conveys Plato's own views, rather than Socrates', even when the views are made to come from Socrates' mouth. But there is nothing anachronistic about our attempts to distinguish the views of Plato and Socrates; it is clear that ancient readers did the same. Certain doctrines, even when expressed by Socrates in the dialogues, have been thought to reflect original and innovative contributions by Plato. The Platonic innovations that are most important for understanding Stoicism are the following.

While Socrates repeatedly emphasized the importance of caring for one's soul, Plato went much further in proposing theories about the soul's real nature, inner workings, and status as an entity. In the *Phaedo*, Plato offered a series of arguments for the immortality of the soul, arguing that it is an immaterial, non-physical entity that existed before this present life, and survives the body's dissolution intact, to be punished or rewarded in an afterlife. The soul's pre-existence is made to account for its ability to discover philosophical truths about the real essences of things, truths that it learned by direct experience of the immaterial Platonic Forms during its disembodied life.

In the *Republic*, Plato proposed that a complete understanding of psychology requires us to hypothesize that the soul has parts inside it. One part of the soul is rational, able to follow reason and discern true from false, always desiring wisdom, virtue, truth, and whatever is really good. Another part is irrational, liable to be deceived by images rather than reality, desiring things that look good even when they are not. The irrational part can be subdivided into one part that loves honor and competition, and further parts that love physical pleasures of various sorts. Each of the parts, rational and irrational, has desires of its own; each of them is able to do some thinking and planning on its own, and each of them is capable of moving the human being to action without the help of the others. Indeed, sometimes one part can move the agent to action even when the other parts are resisting it, as when an agent's desire for pleasure leads them to do something which their reason says is wrong and their honor-loving part says is shameful. It is these very cases, in Plato's view, which provide the best evidence for the existence of these invisible parts of an invisible soul; only by positing independent parts with independent agendas can we explain the full range of irrational behavior that we see around us. Failures of will-power, self-deception, self-betrayal and self-destruction, obsessions and addictions are all best explained as the result of the interplay of different intra-psychic factors. We will see that the Stoics did not accept this new doctrine of irrational parts in the soul, but their theories were built at least in part in response to it.

Plato's *Republic* also gives the classic articulation to a philosophical demand and a method of attempting to satisfy that demand. The demand is to show a sort of convergence between justice and happiness, to show that by living justly we will also live happily.[9] The way to show this, in the *Republic*, is by using what I'll call a bridge-argument, which demonstrates the identity of justice and happiness by providing two lines of argument to show that each of them is identical to a third thing, namely psychic health. The health of the soul stands like a sort of central pier in this two-span bridge, providing a way of seeing one and the same thing as both justice, when viewed as the right organization and subordination of desires, and happiness, when viewed as a sort of internal harmony and satisfaction of desires. In one way this is simply an elaboration of the principle, already employed in Socrates' discussions, that virtue should benefit its possessor. Even in Homer we can see the idea that if a king is virtuous and governs righteously, his flocks will increase and his trees will be heavy with fruit.[10] But as Plato shows in the second book of the Republic, this sort of cultural lip-service to the convergence of virtue and happiness is a far cry from a proper demonstration that virtue itself, apart from any accidental advantages it may sometimes bring, is the same thing as happiness itself. Nothing like an adequate demonstration can be attempted without providing new analyses of both terms, analyses that go beyond thinking of virtue as the mere adherence to rules, and happiness as the mere possession of goods.

Finally, there is the fact that Plato set a new standard for the systematicity of philosophy. The Greek philosophers before Socrates were primarily known for their speculative investigations of astronomy, cosmology, and metaphysics. Socrates was said to have brought philosophy down to earth, by turning its attention to human conduct, and shunning the physical and metaphysical speculations of his Presocratic predecessors.[11] Plato showed how all of the parts of philosophy must be woven together and pursued as a whole. It is not enough to know what virtue is; we must then ask how it is possible to come to know such a thing (thereby doing epistemology), and what sort of thing it is that we know when we know it (thereby doing metaphysics). The Republic shows Plato at his most systematic, tackling every kind of philosophical topic in one coordinated, unified way, fitting together and interrelating not only ethics, epistemology and metaphysics, but psychology and politics, aesthetics and the philosophy of mathematics, theology, and the philosophy of education. The ideal of this sort of comprehensive and coherent system made a powerful impact on the Stoics as well.

Plato's student Aristotle had the least visible impact on the Stoics, and there have even been modern critics who denied that the Stoics were familiar with Aristotle's writings.[12] But in at least one respect, Stoic ethics bears a clear mark of Aristotelian influence. This is in their acceptance of the basic structure of an ethical theory as that is laid out in the first book of Aristotle's *Nicomachean Ethics*. There, Aristotle begins with the idea of doing something for the sake of an end, and argues that all of the activities in a human life must be directed towards some end as well. We can define this end structurally by saying that it is that thing that we do everything for the sake of, which is not itself done for the sake of some further thing. This specifies its place in the network of ends and end-related activities—it is the final end and the highest end—but does not give it any particular content. Only a little more content is given by saying, as Aristotle proceeds to say, that this end is also the good for human beings, and is the same thing as happiness. As he notes, the claim that our highest good and final end is happiness will be agreed upon very generally, but with regard to what happiness is, people will still disagree widely. If you ask people what happiness consists in, and what all of our actions in life are aimed at and for the sake of, some will say it is pleasure, some honor, some wealth. Aristotle has his own proposal on this score, but even by posing the question in this way, he bequeaths to later philosophers an outline or schema that becomes the canonical, ubiquitous way of specifying an ethical theory. Each school must say what it takes the final end to be; what is its summum bonum, its specification of the highest good for human beings. After that is spelled out, each school must show, on the one hand, how acting for the sake of that end will amount to acting virtuously, and on the other hand, how acting for the sake of that end will amount to living happily.

Furthermore, there was another school of ethics, contemporaneous with the Stoics though slightly older, the Epicureans. They very consciously rejected many of the ethical views of the Socratic line—in particular, they argued aggressively that only pleasure is good, and that virtue is worth caring about only to the extent that it produces pleasure, or reduces pain. In this, the Stoics did not follow them, as we'll see. But there were points of agreement between the two schools. Perhaps most important was their endorsement of an empiricist account of our acquisition of concepts and our understanding of word-meanings. They thought, that is, that when someone has a full command of the concept of a cow, or understands what the word 'cow' means, this can only have come from experiences that they have had, whether of sensing cows directly (seeing them and so forth) or learning about cows from other speakers. And what goes for 'cow' goes equally for 'Jove', or 'gods' or 'good' or 'justice'. Both schools agreed that these experiential origins place strong constraints on what a philosophical or scientific theory can reasonably and meaningfully claim to discover, without lapsing into meaningless nonsense.

This empiricist strategy forced the Epicureans and the Stoics to stick close to ordinary language and popular opinion, keeping their theories consistent with the dictates of experience and the concepts that arise automatically from experiences common to any upbringing—what they called variously 'preconceptions', 'common conceptions', or 'natural concepts'[13]. Or at any rate, it forced them to make a good show of doing all this—much philosophical ingenuity, as often, was expended in putting forward the most outrageously counter-intuitive conclusions, and trying to show that they follow from the most tame and uncontroversial intuitions. Critics were unimpressed; Plutarch[14] wrote a vehemently anti-Stoic tract entitled 'Against the Stoics, On Common Conceptions' designed to show that Stoic views conflicted with common sense, common usage, and common experience. Galen claimed that the Stoics were engaged in mere linguistic legislation—instead of giving us a philosophical analysis of what we really mean by our words, the Stoics were ordering us to use words their way, capriciously laying down the law to the language like so many Hellenistic Humpty-Dumpties. The Stoics fired back; Chrysippus wrote an entire treatise titled 'On the fact that Zeno Used Terms in their Proper Significations', defending the Stoics' claim to adhere to ordinary usage.[15]

But the attempt to conform to preconceptions was not idle game-playing. It was part of an attempt to provide epistemological underpinnings for the Stoics' continued allegiance to the Socratic method of dialectic. Socrates himself seems never to have noticed, or never to have fully appreciated, the question how his method of testing views for consistency could act as a way of discovering the truth. Why does not the drive for consistency, no matter how rigorously carried out, merely lead to a consistently false or deluded picture? What gives us any reason to hope that the people Socrates speaks with will have a few true beliefs sprinkled in among their false ones, and that they will reliably relinquish the false ones instead of the true when Socrates points out their inconsistency? Plato's introduction of Forms provided one way of ensuring that every person would have the rudiments of a true account somewhere present in their mind, ready to emerge from the obscuring overlay of false belief once that was swept aside by dialectic. But remarkably few people in the two centuries after Plato's death seem to have found this solution at all plausible—when Stoicism was being formulated, recourse to Platonic Forms was simply not a live option. Instead, the rudiments of true belief are guaranteed to exist in every individual because they are acquired naturally, from the environment, by the sensory equipment that every unimpaired child enjoys. By encountering many bodies, cows, and humans; by seeing, feeling, and otherwise sensing them, children develop preconceptions of body, cow, human and so on, preconceptions that really deliver the truth. In the same way, the Stoics held, our fundamental ethical concepts acquire their reliable content as well, and can thus serve as the raw material for philosophical development, as basic principles that can be elaborated, refined, and analyzed into a complete systematic theory of ethics.[16]

From this brief and impressionistic survey, we can see that the Stoics will have set about constructing their ethical theory within fairly clear guidelines, with fairly clear notions of what theoretical work an ethical theory must do. We can also see that the picture of an ethical theory that they worked with is not the same as our picture. It may be helpful here to contrast ancient and contemporary ethics in a fairly abstract way—abstract both in that I will be focusing on large-scale, structural points of similarity and difference, and in that I will abstract from the historical differences between ancient schools, and the equally wide variations in contemporary outlooks.

In many ways, the ancient concept of ethics is the same as our contemporary one—or to put that differently, the ancient Greeks set the broad outlines of ethical theorizing so clearly and definitively that we still work within their framework. But we will also see some differences in expectations, too.

To begin with the similarities, an ancient ethical theory was certainly supposed to provide guidance about which actions are wrong, or impermissible, and which actions are right, or permissible, and which actions are obligatory—those which it is wrong to fail to do. And the theory should not merely give us guidance in the form of a list or catalogue of actions, it should also help us think about what it is that makes right actions right and wrong actions wrong. A mere list, without any rationale to back it up, can never be extended when new cases are met—or at any rate, the extension must either be entirely arbitrary, or it must be based on some attempts, however feeble, at seeing the underlying rationale behind the items on the list. So: all of the ancient ethical theories certainly took it as part of their job to provide us with ways of thinking about which particular actions are right or wrong, and what is the general nature of rightness and wrongness in actions.

Secondly, the ancient theories were just as interested as modern theories—indeed, more interested than some modern theories—in providing ethical judgments of the intentions, motives, and characters of agents. They too could distinguish between the question whether an action, viewed from the outside, is permissible or impermissible, and the question whether the action was done with generous intentions or selfish ones, in a praiseworthy way or in a blameworthy way, from a virtuous character or a vicious one, and so on.

Finally, the ancient theories also pronounced on the values of outcomes, things, and states of affairs, making judgments about what sorts of things bring value, worth, meaning, and goodness to an individual's life, or to a community or the world at large. So here are three areas of clear overlap between what ancient ethical theories try to cover, and what we try to cover when we do ethics today:

The Ancient Philosophical Background ~ 31

theories about permissibility and obligation in actions; theories about moral worth in agents and their motives; and theories about the values of the outcomes and consequences of actions. But there are also some things that will seem odd about how the ancients did ethics, especially if you have studied some contemporary views.

To begin with, ancient ethics tend to orient themselves around the question of what sort of life an individual should live. Nowadays, we tend to think that the first and central job of an ethical theory is to give us principles for judging the rightness and wrongness of actions, or for deciding, when faced with a complicated and ethically fraught situation, what the ethically correct thing to do is. We imagine scenarios in which the rights of one person are put into conflict with the interests of another, or in which the preservation of some people's lives will preclude the preservation of others, and we think of it as the main job of an ethical theory to show us the way out of the dilemma. We want it to act like a computer program in which we can type in the hypothetical situation, specified to any degree of detail, and the program will pop up and tell us the unique answer, the right thing to do in that situation.

I've already said that ancient systems do some of that too, but they do not focus on doing it, and they certainly do not start by doing it. They start, in the main, by arguing about what sort of life an individual should live—what makes for a valuable, worthwhile life—and make that their central concern, with other ethical concerns radiating off from it. The question of Socrates in the *Republic* is often quoted in this regard, when he says 'do you think it a small matter to determine which whole way of life would make living most worthwhile for each of us?'[17] Determining which whole way of life would make living most worthwhile for us—that, and not the assessment of individual actions, or the ability to provide solutions to complicated dilemmas and far-fetched scenarios, is held to be the central concern of ethics.

Related to this is the fact that ancient theories tend to focus less on the question of regulating interpersonal conduct than modern theories do. Instead of evincing a universal interest in all aspects of how we ought to live, ethics by now has a tendency to shrink to the question of how we ought to treat other people, or what obligations we have to others, so that it may seem odd or tendentious to think that an ethical theory can tell you how to live your life in general. The Stoics, for instance, want to say that there is a proper way to hold one's toothbrush. 'Oh', it's natural to ask, 'they thought that even the way you hold your toothbrush could have an effect on others?' No, it's not that they thought that toothbrushing comes into ethics because it has surprising and unobvious consequences for other people—the way environmentalists show us that ostensibly private and apparently innocuous choices about consumption have far-ranging effects on others. The idea was, rather, that there is an ethical way to brush one's teeth, despite the fact that this has no effect on any other person. This may seem less surprising when put as a point about morality—we may find it easier to think that even when we are by ourselves, there are moral choices to be made and moral mistakes to be avoided—that without harming any other person, we can still do something morally wrong. That's a familiar enough thought about morality. Indeed, it is partly because morality tends to pry into our private lives that we feel a certain distaste for it, and a compensating greater comfort with the idea of ethics. Ethics, like the law, seems to restrict its ambitions to a public sphere, or at least a sphere where others are involved; when morality wants to police even the victimless crimes, we may feel it is being too intrusive.

Be that as it may, the ancient view tended to start from a picture of a whole life for an individual, and offer judgments and guidance about how every aspect of that life, public and private, interpersonal and solitary, should be lived, without giving any special emphasis to the question of what we owe to other persons, or how complicated dilemmas should be solved.

With all that by way of prologue, we can now turn to looking at the Stoics themselves.

NOTES

1. This was the view of Antiochus of Ascalon, thoroughly expounded by Cicero in the fourth and fifth books of his treatise *de Finibus*; see Woolf (2001).
2. Sedley (2003), 11 fn.3 cites Philodemus *de Stoicis* XIII. 3.
3. Something of that fate, alas, befalls the Cynic school, whose members did a far better job imitating Socrates' outward flourishes than imitating his interest in dialectic, definition, and doctrine—See Long (1999b).
4. *Euthydemus* 278e
5. *Euthydemus* 278e, *Protagoras* 358d, *Meno* 77–78
6. *Apology* 29d–30a, *Apology* 30d, *Crito* 47e–48a
7. *Crito* 47e, *Gorgias* 507a–c, *Gorgias* 470e.
8. *Protagoras* 329–330 with 349a–d and 361a–c.
9. Kavka (1985).
10. *Odyssey* 19.107–114
11. Cicero, *Disp. Tusc.* 5.10
12. The most thorough denial is that of Sandbach (1985). To be more precise, the question is whether the Stoics were familiar with the in-house treatises that make up our current corpus of Aristotelian works. Aristotle also wrote more popular treatises that were well known in antiquity, though they are lost now.
13. preconception (*prolêpsis*), common conception/ common notion (*koinê ennoia*), natural conception/natural notion (*phusikê ennoia*): DL 7.54 = SVF 2.105 = LS 40A = IG2 II–3; Aëtius 4.11.1–4 = SVF 2.83 = LS 39E = IG2 II–12. Stoic respect for preconceptions guarantees their system's agreement with nature: Plutarch *Comm. Not.* 1060A = LS 40R.
14. For the dates and allegiances of Plutarch and Galen see Chapter 2.
15. Cited at *DL* 7.122 = SVF 3.617 = LS 67M = IG2 II–94.
16. For an attempt at an empiricist account of the acquisition of an ethical concept, see Seneca *Ep.* 120 = LS 60E = IG2 II–109.
17. *Republic* 344e, trans. Grube/Reeve; cf. *Gorgias* 492d

4

An Overview of Stoic Ethics

Now it is time to take an overview of the Stoic system, before we look more deeply into particular parts in later chapters. Our survey of the previous systems has helped us to see what the Stoics would expect an ethical system to contain.

To begin with, the Stoics assume that all human beings wish to be happy, and that happiness is our end, that is, that for the sake of which we do everything we do. They also tell us what happiness is: it consists in following nature. To follow nature means to act in accordance with our own nature as human beings, but also to act in accordance with Nature as a whole, that is, the entire cosmic order governed by Zeus.[1] By following nature, we will be happy. By following nature, we will also be virtuous. In fact, this second point explains the first, since the Stoics tell us that only the virtuous are happy. Furthermore, they say that virtue is the only thing that is good in any way, shape or form. Only what can benefit us, that is, make us happy, is good; and only virtue does that.

In particular, the Stoics insist that we are wrong to think that pleasure is good; wrong to think that money and fame are good; wrong to think that health, freedom, and life are good. We are also wrong to think that their opposites (poverty, dishonor, illness, slavery, and death) are at all bad for us—they do us no harm, and do not make us unhappy. Only vice does that—it alone is bad. Unfortunately, all of us are awash in vice—everyone that was alive in the time of the Stoics, including the Stoics themselves; every historical figure they knew of, including their most revered predecessors such as Socrates and Diogenes the Cynic; and (I am confident they would say) everyone alive in this day and age as well.[2] We are all of us tainted by vice.

Well—none of us is perfect; perhaps that's not such a strange claim to make. But the Stoics made it stranger, by insisting that every one of us is equally vice-ridden or vicious, equally far from virtue, equally sinful and unhappy. Socrates was not more virtuous than his persecutors; Zeno himself, the founder of Stoicism, was just as vicious as the most hardened criminal. And accordingly, all of us are equally far from being happy, equally far from attaining our end, equally far from living in accordance with nature.

The Stoics liked to discuss ethics by describing what a perfectly virtuous person, a Stoic Sage, would be like—they talked about what the Sage does, and how the Sage is, as a way of saying what we ought to do, and how we ought to be. There is also a contrary character, the non-Sage, who is the embodiment of vice.[3] But far from a fictional device or hypothetical illustration, non-Sages are to be seen everywhere, according to the Stoics, since all of us are non-Sages.

The Stoics did allow that virtue was possible for human beings—it is not an unrealizable ideal, merely a very demanding one—and they described what it would be like to make progress towards virtue. They even allowed that some people do make progress. They simply denied that making progress towards virtue was the same thing as becoming more virtuous, or less vicious. The person making progress is not in an intermediate category between virtue and vice. Progressors are wholly vicious—they are full-fledged non-Sages, as vicious as those making no progress at all. The Stoics employed vivid analogies to drive this home; the person who is a foot below the surface of the ocean may be making progress towards fresh air, but he is drowning just as much as the person fifty fathoms under.

Sages, in contrast, are completely virtuous, and their virtue permeates every one of their actions. They are not only virtuous when they do things like rescuing drowning children, abstaining from pleasure, or donating their worldly goods to charity. Every action that Sages perform—shopping for groceries, brushing their teeth, going for a walk—originates from the same virtuous state of their soul, and every one is a virtuous act. Nor are some of their actions more virtuous than others, or some virtuous because they facilitate others. It is not that the buying of the groceries is virtuous because it will allow the Sage to give them away later, or that the brushing of teeth is virtuous because it will keep the Sage healthy enough to rescue drowning children when needed. It is tempting to think that we can tell, in advance, what sorts of actions virtuous actions are—for example, the rescuings, the abstainings, and the donations—and that these are virtuous in some primary, intrinsic, or paradigmatic way, where the shoppings, brushings, and walkings are virtuous only derivatively, instrumentally, or by courtesy. But the Stoics deny this.

They also deny that any one vicious action is more vicious than another. It is a bad thing to murder your parents. It is the sort of thing that non-Sages do—though not many, luckily—and it is a vicious action, which stems from their vice. And if you are a non-Sage, it is also a bad thing to brush your teeth—even if you brush them in the same way that a Sage would, it is still a vicious action, because done by a non-Sage. Indeed, if you are a non-Sage, it is a bad and vicious thing to honor your parents selflessly and from a heart brimming over with love and esteem. It is no less vicious than the murder; it is vicious to the same degree, and for the same reason, that the murder is: because it stems from a vicious state of the soul. Someone who honors their parents selflessly and lovingly may be making progress, but their progress does not make them any more virtuous or happy, and it does not make their action any less an act of vice.

How might we set about living in accordance with nature, and how could we—or at least someone—come to be virtuous? The greatest impediment to our progress is our false beliefs about what is really good and bad. We must come to learn that nothing but virtue is good, nothing but vice is bad. The rest are all said to be indifferent; it makes no difference towards one's happiness or unhappiness whether one has wealth or poverty, health or disease. But it is hard to come to see this—hard to break ourselves of the habit of believing that money and honors are good.

Non-Sages desire money, and desire honors, and when they get them they feel pleasure, believing that they now have something really good. Non-Sages fear poverty, and fear disgrace, and when they encounter them they feel dejection, believing that they now have something really bad. Desire, pleasure, fear, and dejection: these are the four great emotions or passions that characterize the mental life of the vicious and unhappy non-Sage. Sages do not feel these things. That is because they do not have the false beliefs about what is good and bad. Not believing that money is good, they neither desire it when they lack it, nor feel pleasure when they have it. Not believing that poverty is bad—or illness, pain, mutilation, or torture—they neither fear these things in prospect, nor feel dejection when they are present.

Stoic Sages live without these four passions. But they are not thereby reduced to catatonic paralysis; they still have motivations to act. The life of a Sage looks, in most respects, like any other life; they eat food, avoid unnecessary risks to life and limb, and hold jobs that earn them money. What allows them to pursue things like food, and avoid things like injury, both of which they view as indifferent to their happiness, neither good nor bad, is the fact that these indifferents are still open to assessment on a different scale.

The Stoics say that among indifferents, some are 'promoted', and some are 'demoted'—food and health are instances of the promoted indifferents, starvation and disease instances of the demoted indifferents. The fact that an indifferent is promoted gives the Sage some reason to pursue it. But the Sage's motivation to pursue it is not the belief that it is good, and so their motivation is not an instance of desire. The Sage does not desire food, but the Sage does select food—selection and disselection are the Sage's replacement for desire and fear.

One way that the replacement makes a difference is in their reactions to the outcome of the action. When a non-Sage desires money, and succeeds in getting it, he feels pleasure; when he fails to get it, or gets something he had feared, he feels dejection. No matter what Sages get as an outcome of their selections and disselections, they feel the same thing—a sense of the indifference of this particular thing, be it health or illness, to their happiness, and a sense of general contentment that things should have turned out as in fact they did.

Why, then, do Sages pursue the food and the health, if having it does them no more good than not having it? If their happiness is complete in their possession of virtue, then what is there to be gained by going for food? If starvation provides the same resulting sense of contentment, why take the trouble to hunt up dinner?

Here we see part of what it means to follow nature. The Sage has observed the natural course of events over a long period of time, has seen which actions are characteristic of which animals, and on the basis of their observations has concluded that it is natural that humans should try to feed themselves, try to avoid injury, even try to marry and raise families (none of the famous Greek Stoics were married, but none of them were Sages, either; Sages will typically marry and have children).

Indeed, from their observation of the natural course of events, they have concluded that it would be unnatural to select starvation when food is present, or to maim oneself when one could preserve one's limbs whole. So they select food because it is a promoted indifferent, and because this very act of selection, in as much as it is an action that follows nature, is also an action that accords with their virtue. By selecting food, and thus following nature, they are performing a virtuous action, and thus sustaining their virtue, and thus preserving their happiness. So attention to nature has led them to attend to the indifferents around them, noting which are natural and promoted, which contrary to nature and demoted, and selecting and disselecting the things in life on that basis. And they do it all without ever treating any of the indifferents, of either sort, as though it was really good or bad—thus they do it without any of the passions that cloud the reason of the non-Sage. And thus they are able to carry on living.

An Overview of Stoic Ethics ~ 39

Except, of course, when they don't. For it is a familiar fact about Sages—and here the popular image conforms to the truth—that they sometimes choose to end their lives, that is, to commit suicide. But that is only a more dramatic instance of a general fact, that Sages will sometimes choose the demoted indifferent, even when the promoted one is available—they will sometimes select illness over health, poverty over wealth, fasting over eating, and so on.

Here we see another part of what it means to follow nature. For a lifetime of observation has led the Sage to notice that there are many anomalies in the course of events—indeed, the orderly and stable behavior of the world and its inhabitants is always being set off by interruptions and exceptions, whether it be the death of a mouse before its natural term, or the eruption of a volcano that devastates an entire city. Along with the nature of human beings there is also the nature of the cosmos at large—the nature that organizes and coordinates all things, living and nonliving. This, the Stoics claim, is the same as Zeus, and Fate, and Reason, too. Nature in this guise sometimes overrides the nature of individuals, whether mice or human beings. And a wise and virtuous Sage observes this. It is natural for people to be healthy—indeed, a healthy body is simply one that is functioning according to nature—but it is also part of the natural plan, manifestly, that people are ill on occasion.

Chrysippus said that as long as it was unclear to him what the future would bring, he would select health—indeed, Zeus himself had fashioned him to select it. But, he continued, if he knew that it was fated that he should be ill, then he would select illness instead. Both of these selections are ways of following nature; both of them are ways of acting virtuously (or would be if they were done by a Sage, rather than Chrysippus, who is a non-Sage). Both of them involve attending to the value of indifferents, whether promoted ones like health or demoted ones like disease, and selecting them as a way of following nature.

The same applies to suicide. In general, it is natural for human beings to preserve their lives, and the Sage will follow nature by doing so. But on occasion, the Sage may have reason to believe that in this instance following nature will consist in terminating their life.

It may be tempting to think that the special occasions will involve some special moral crisis or dilemma. It may be tempting to think that nothing could give the Sage reason to commit suicide except the desire to perform a virtuous action, or avoid a vicious one. Virtue, after all, is the only thing truly good; someone who knows this will happily choose virtue over life, which is a mere indifferent. It is not death that is bad; it is vice that is bad, so the Sage will easily choose death to avoid vice.

But this tempting picture is not the Stoic view. The decision to commit suicide is made solely from considerations of indifferents and their relative preponderance. It is the presence or absence of food and health and the like that causes the Sage to remain alive or commit suicide.

Critics of the Stoa found this absurd; when a Sage has complete happiness in hand (because they have virtue), and suffers only from hunger, or perhaps an incurable illness, or something else which they profess to treat as indifferent, why should they kill themselves? Doesn't this show that they are treating mere hunger or illness as though they are really bad—bad enough to kill oneself over—and treating virtue as though it is a matter of relative indifference, not sufficiently good to make life worth living?

The Stoics reply that they are not treating hunger as though it is a really bad thing, only treating death as though it is really indifferent. After all, suicide is only a matter of killing yourself—it is only death, not something that is really good or bad, not something that affects one's virtue. So there is nothing inconsistent in saying that the decision should be made on the grounds of indifferents and their availability.

Furthermore, the same grounds for suicide will apply in the case of non-Sages, who cannot preserve their virtue by committing suicide (since they have none), and cannot avoid vice by dying (since any action they commit, whether remaining in life or leaving it, will be a vicious one). That said, non-Sages too will sometimes have reason to commit suicide, and the same reason that Sages do, namely the current and prospective distribution and availability of such indifferents as food, health, disease, and so on.

This is also why the Stoics are not bound to say that every non-Sage should commit suicide straightaway, in order to trade the real evil of vice for the mere indifferent of death. They do not think this is the case, even though they are serious about saying that virtue is the only good there is and the only source of happiness, and that vice is the only bad there is and a source of complete misery. There will be the same reasons for non-Sages to commit suicide as for Sages—the same rare and exceptional events will justify the selection of death in place of life, for either one—because the agent's own virtue does not form part of the grounds of making a decision of this sort.

And here again, the case of suicide only shows us in more dramatic terms what applies to all action. Whatever actions Sages take—whether committing suicide or eating breakfast or feeding the starving or brushing their teeth—whenever Sages do something, they do it from a consideration of where the promoted and demoted indifferents lie, and how their actions will affect the distribution of them. It is by selecting and disselecting in this way that the Sage performs the virtuous actions that make up their day—their virtuous waking and virtuous eating and virtuous walking and virtuous talking.

And here we find another reason why virtue cannot form a basis for suicide. It is tempting to think that we, and the Sage, can recognize what virtuous and vicious actions look like ahead of time, independent of the person performing the action. So, it is tempting to think that defending your country is a virtuous action, and so an action that it might well be worth committing suicide in order to accomplish. It is tempting to think that telling a lie is a vicious action, and so an action that it might well be worth committing suicide in order to avoid.

But this is to forget that all of the Sage's actions are virtuous, and equally virtuous, and that all of the non-Sages actions are vicious, and equally vicious. In considering whether to rush into battle and defend his country or avoid the battle and have an ample dinner, it will not help the Sage to ask which of these actions would be virtuous. For whichever action the Sage performs will be a virtuous action. Nor can the non-Sage make any headway by asking this question, since their defense of their country will be just as vicious as their having dinner.

Instead, the Sage must simply follow nature—their own human nature, and the nature of the cosmos at large—and by doing so the performance of a virtuous action is guaranteed. The conscientious non-Sage or progressor, who is guaranteed to commit a vicious action, can at least ask the following question: which of the vicious actions that I can perform right now is the one that the Sage would perform right now in my position? (Or is most similar to the one the Sage would perform, while differing by not being virtuous)?

Here we have introduced the notion of the befitting (*kathêkon*, sometimes translated 'duty' or 'proper function'). An action is befitting if, once it has been done, it can receive a well-reasoned justification or defense. This definition does not say that the action always will receive such a defense, nor who might be able to construct such a defense—in particular, it does not say that a befitting action can only be performed by someone who has the personal resources to offer a well-reasoned justification. The action simply must be justifiable, in principle.

Nor does the definition say anything about the motives or intentions with which the action was done. Perhaps the agent who performed it had no idea that it was in fact justifiable, and performed it on grounds that would tend, if anything, to make it seem an unjustifiable action. The agent's motives do not affect whether it was a befitting action or not.

All of the Sage's actions are befitting. Some of the non-Sages actions are befitting as well: those which—whether the non-Sage reflected on this fact or not—are exactly the ones that a Sage would have performed in the same circumstances. Of course, the non-Sage cannot perform the action from the same virtuous character that the Sage has, and the non-Sage may not understand what makes it a justifiable action. But as we have seen, none of that impugns the action's right to be called 'befitting'.

As an instance, let us take a case of eating breakfast. It is surely natural that human beings should break their fast some time after rising from sleep, and on most occasions there will be no overriding dictate from Nature or Fate to trump the naturalness of breakfast. On some one of those occasions, a Sage will eat breakfast, virtuously. At the same time, let us imagine, and in closely similar circumstances, a non-Sage will eat breakfast, too. Both of them are performing befitting actions.

There are still many differences between their actions. Of course there is the fact that the Sage is performing a virtuous action, whereas the non-Sage, going through what to all outward appearances is the same sequence of motions and procedures, is performing a vicious action. But we can put that difference in other terms, by saying that the Sage is performing a perfect action; the perfect actions, or perfect befitting actions, are a subspecies within the befitting actions. There is also the fact that the non-Sage may well think that eating breakfast is a good thing, or that the food is a good thing; they may well experience desire at the thought of the food, and pleasure in its possession. This is all as bad as can be—the Sage will have none of it—but it does not change the fact that the non-Sage's having breakfast just then was a befitting action.

If the non-Sage does something other than what a Sage would do in a given circumstance, then their action is said to be unbefitting or contrary to the befitting. One of the ways in which Progressors make progress is that they do more and more befitting things, fewer and fewer unbefitting ones. They also stop thinking of indifferent things as though they were good and bad and start seeing them as merely indifferent. Instead of desiring the food or the pleasure it brings or the health it brings as though any of those was a good thing, the Progressor may come to view the food as a mere promoted indifferent, something it is on the whole more natural to take than not to take, at least provided that no special circumstances intervene.

Thus there is a close connection between the natural, and the promoted, and the befitting. As a general rule—subject, though, to exceptions—one should select promoted things, viewing them as natural, and disselect demoted things, viewing them as unnatural, and through both of these avenues one will perform befitting actions.

If in addition, one is a Sage, one will be performing a perfect action as well. Just as it is common both to Sage and non-Sage to be able to select things as promoted, so too it is common both to Sage and non-Sage to perform befitting actions. And in doing this, the Sage is following nature, and thus living virtuously and happily.

In the next chapters, we will work through this same material again, in greater detail. Some of the points that looked mysterious in a swift overview will become plainer; some of the plain and easy points will look increasingly mysterious. To begin our deeper investigation of ethics, however, there is no better way than by stepping backwards to psychology. That way we can understand how the Stoics classify and categorize different kinds of motives, attitudes, and character-traits. To understand the psychology, however, we will need to take an additional step backwards to the epistemology, to see how the Stoics categorize beliefs of various sorts. That is where the next chapter starts.

NOTES

1. On Zeus' governance of the cosmos, see Chapter 13.
2. On the Stoic admiration for Socrates and the Cynics, see Chapter 2.
3. In Greek he is called the Wretch (*phaulos*), or the Witless (*aphrôn*), but using these terms in English might suggest that the Stoics were referring only to an extreme sub-class of vicious types, instead of referring to all of us, no matter how upstanding and respectable.

The Epilogue of Long (2002) contains good material on later and more popular images of Stoics, including the views of such writers as Pascal, Walt Whitman, and Tom Wolfe.

Oldfather (1925) in his introduction describes the immense popularity of Epictetus with, among others, Frederick the Great of Prussia!

Stockdale (1993) gives a good sense of the Invictus reading of Stoicism; I disagree with the scholarship, but the story of Stockdale's experiences as a POW cannot fail to arouse the reader's interest and admiration.

An up-to-date and authoritative discussion of the history of the school and its leading figures can be found in the two chapters by Sedley (2003) and Gill (2003).

Arnold (1911) is not up to current standards for philosophical scholarship, but still gives a charming overview of many personalities, as well as an easy entrée into the role of Stoicism among the Roman aristocracy.

For a vivid sense of the personalities of individual Stoics, I recommend with the greatest enthusiasm Zanker (1995). His book combines art history with intellectual history, and provides not only pictures of the surviving portrait busts, but wonderful commentaries in which he attempts to discern the souls depicted in the marble.

A careful assessment of the evidence for chronology is found in Dorandi (1999) esp. section IV 'The Stoa'. See also Dorandi's extremely useful tables of chronology at Algra et al. (1999), 48–54 and 798–804.

Further discussion of the sources, and of how the sources for this era are to be treated, can be found in Mansfeld (1999a).

One brief overview of Ancient Ethics may be found in Rowe (1995).

Craig (1999) contains useful material in the articles 'Eudamonia' by C. C. W. Taylor, 'Virtue Ethics' by Roger Crisp, 'Socrates' by John M. Cooper, 'Plato' by Malcolm Schofield.

On the role and image of Socrates in Stoic ethics see Long (1988) and Long (2002) esp. chapter 3, 'The Socratic Paradigm'; also Striker (1996b) on the Stoics' relation to Socrates and Plato.

On the Cynics and their ethics see Long (1999b), esp. section III 'Antisthenes and Diogenes—Cynic Ethics'.

Good brief overviews of Stoic ethics may be found in the following sources:

Sharples (1996) chapter 5 pp. 100–113 and chapter 6 pp. 123–127. A very compact but reliable account.

Sedley (1999a) is an encyclopedia article that provides excellent coverage of the Stoics as a whole; sections 14–17 give a quick survey of the ethical theory.

Inwood and Donini (1999). A longer overview than this chapter, but clear and helpful.

Schofield (2003) is rather less useful for the beginner, though it does contain important criticisms of other recent discussions.

Striker (1991) is nearly as long as a short book, though printed in a journal. It is one of the best things written on Stoic ethics.

PART II

Psychology

5

Impressions and Assent

In the opinion of the Stoics, we should begin with an account of impressions and perception, inasmuch as the criterion for judging the truth of things belongs to the genus of impressions. And the account of assent and katalepsis and thought, which precedes everything else, cannot be assembled without an account of impressions.[1]

The Stoics say that every act of perception is an assent.[2]

Man, your mind cannot be hindered, cannot be compelled—that is its nature. I'll demonstrate this to you, first in the case of assent. Can anyone hinder you from assenting to what is true? Can anyone compel you to accept what is false? No one can.[3]

We all know roughly what it means to assent to something—it means to agree with it, or go along with it, or endorse it. And that is also roughly what the Stoics had in mind when they introduced the term *sunkatathesis*—which is what makes 'assent' a tolerable translation for *sunkatathesis*. But of course there are also some differences between the meanings of the two words, and so for the rest of this book I will be using the word 'assent' as a translation for *sunkatathesis*. If I say things about assent that don't sound right, or don't sound like what we would normally say about assent, keep in mind that I am not discussing the ordinary English word, or the meaning that goes along with it, but rather discussing a technical notion introduced by the Stoics.

Assent is the linchpin of the Stoic system. Assent is the fundamental psychological activity—more fundamental even than believing something, or desiring something. It is also the source of human freedom; in whatever way human beings are free, it is the result of the fact that we have the faculty of assent, something non-human animals do not have. Assent is also the key to the difference between virtuous people and vicious people. In fact, every difference that there can be between one person's psychology and another person's psychology can be accounted for entirely in terms of the patterns of assents that they each make.

What then is an assent? To begin with, every assent is an assent *to* something or another—one cannot simply assent without there being something to assent to. What we assent to, according to the Stoics, are impressions—again, I introduce this term not in its ordinary English sense, but as a translation for a technical Greek term, *phantasiai* (singular *phantasia*). There is no harm in thinking of impressions, to begin with, as like the mental pictures that one can call up at will, for example, when you recall an impression of a familiar face. But impressions do not have to be voluntarily brought to mind: when I look out the window right now, the elm trees and buildings conspire to make a certain impression on me, willy-nilly. Nor are impressions necessarily vague (though in English that is often what we mean by saying, for example, 'I had the impression that he was limping'). Quite the opposite; if one can ever see or hear or think of something in a clear and detailed way, that is because one can have a clear and detailed impression of it.

Most impressions arise from our senses, or from our memories of sensory episodes—seeing out the window, or closing my eyes and remembering what I saw. But there are also non-sensory impressions, like the impression that two is an even number, or the impression that I really should help that elderly gentleman. There is no particular picture that goes along with the impression that I really should help that elderly gentleman—not, for instance a mental cartoon of my coming to his aid. But then presumably even the scene before my eyes when I have the impression that I should help him—that is, the sight of him seated on the curb and unable to rise—even this cannot be the impression that I ought to help him, because someone else might be standing right next to me, or even just where I am now, and see the same arrangement of colors and shapes, and have the impression that it is just what the old reprobate deserves.

Now an impression, the Stoics tell us, is a certain alteration or change in the mind. We learn this from a report in which Sextus Empiricus, up to his usual skeptical tricks, reports some later refinements of Zeno's view as though they constituted a catastrophic incoherence in the Stoics' theory.

> According to the Stoics, an impression is an imprint in the soul—and about this 'imprint' they immediately started quarreling with one another. On one side, Cleanthes understood 'imprint' in the sense of protrusions and depressions, like the imprint made in wax by a signet-ring.[4]

The comparison was not original with Zeno—Aristotle, and before him Plato, had both used it in discussing perception—and although it helps us to get started thinking about impressions, it is also pretty clear that its utility as a model for perception is fairly limited.[5]

> But Chrysippus thought that interpretation of 'imprint' was ridiculous. In the first place, he said, when the mind simultaneously thinks about a triangle and a square, one and the same body will have to have different shapes at the same time (triangular, square, even circular) and this is ridiculous...And each new motion will obliterate the earlier impression, just as the second application of the signet-ring wipes out the earlier print, in which case memory is destroyed...So he interpreted Zeno's use of the word 'imprint' non-literally, in the sense of 'alteration', so that the definition reads 'an imprint is an alteration of the soul.'[6]

Chrysippus, as often, came to the rescue of his elders, by denying that the stamping was a matter of literal depressions and protrusions. The point of the comparison is more general, he argued: what is important about the analogy of the signet ring and the wax is that the thing you get an impression of, for example, the mug on the table, is involved in causing a change in your mind, has an impact on it, in such a way that some information is conveyed to your mind about the object of the impression. Perception is the transmission of data from the object of perception to the agent who perceives, where the object itself plays the leading role in the transmission (assisted, of course, by such auxiliaries as light for vision, or a medium for sound-waves). None of our sources tells us whether Chrysippus gave any more details about how the causal process occurs, or how the information comes to be stored in the mind.

So it seems that impressions are the objects of assent; when we assent, we assent to an impression. But the story is slightly more complicated, both because the evidence pulls in two different directions, and also because, when you think about the philosophy underneath it, you can see why there are two directions to be pulled in. All Stoic authors talk about assenting to impressions, and there is no doubt that this was an acceptable way to describe what happens. But there are two texts that look as though they reflect more careful discussions of the topic, and both tell us that what we assent to, strictly speaking, is not an impression, but rather a proposition—something like a statement or sentence—connected with the impression.[7] So, for example, when I look on the table in front of me and see a coffee mug, I have the impression that there is a coffee mug on my table—my mind is reconfigured in a coffee-mug-ish way. But what I assent to when I come to believe that there is a coffee mug on my table is not that reconfiguration of my mind, but rather a proposition, namely 'there is a coffee mug on my table'. Usually, when we talk about impressions, we mention their propositional content: it is expressed by the sentence that comes after the word 'that'. For example, when I have the impression that I should help that elderly gentleman, the proposition that goes along with the impression is expressed by the sentence 'I should help that elderly gentleman.'

Impressions are very different from propositions. According to the Stoics, an impression is just a piece of matter in a certain configuration; it is my mind, altered in accordance with the thing that makes the impression on it.[8] And since my mind is just the hot breath in and around my heart, this means that my impressions are each located somewhere in my rib-cage.[9] The proposition, by contrast, is immaterial, and has no location—it is not dependent on me for its existence, much less for its place of residence.[10] So it is not a trivial difference that the Stoics are overlooking when they sometimes say we assent to the impression, and sometimes say we assent to the proposition. Which is it?

There is some reason to say that it should really be the impression. After all, I can only assent to something that I have some kind of psychological contact with, something that I can be aware of. And I cannot be aware of a proposition directly; I can only be aware of a proposition indirectly, by being aware of the impression that it is correlated with. If you asked me why I assented to one proposition instead of assenting to another, I might tell you that the other proposition had simply never entered my mind—which would have to mean, that no impression corresponding to it had ever entered my mind, although the proposition that I was unaware of was just as real, and just as available for contemplation, as the proposition I was aware of. So it looks as though the thing that I react to when I give my assent must be the impression. And this all goes hand in hand with the fact that, since the propositions are immaterial, the Stoics must say that they cannot play any direct role in acting on other things or being acted on.[11] Actions can take place in accordance with them, and actions will result in making propositions true or false of particular items, but the propositions float on unmolested. Thus when we think about the psychological give and take of being struck by something and assenting to it, it seems clear that the 'it' should be an impression.

On the other hand, there is also something to be said for propositions. Suppose that I go back to my desk again, and try to think about the impression that I have in looking at my desk, divorced from any extraneous propositional additions. I will try merely to see what I see, without using words or thoughts to itemize or describe the scene. If words arise unbidden—like 'there's a coffee stain on that book

Impressions and Assent ~ 55

jacket', or 'I must tidy up'—then I will dismiss them, and return to focusing just on the wordless impression of my desk—only I must dismiss even the verbal caption, that it's 'my desk' that I'm seeing. Suppose that I succeed in just focusing on how things look to me, setting aside all the chatter, and now ask yourself: what is there in all of this for me to assent to? There's a picture, but no statement that goes along with it—not even the statement that this picture really captures how things are. What is there to agree or disagree with, now that no claims are being made? A completely mute and inarticulate impression, one completely stripped of any propositional content, cannot be the proper object of assent, either.

These two lines of thought should make it seem less surprising that the Stoics talk in both ways, both about assenting to impressions, and about assenting to propositions. But perhaps we can do better than mimicking the vacillation in our sources, if we spell out in more detail what role each factor plays in assent. It should be clear that the impression, in as much as it is a physical agent, is the right one to mention in the physical and physiological description of the causal sequence leading up to the physical motion of assent. The trees produced an impression in me, and this impression either elicited or failed to elicit assent in me—a certain motion of the mind, which in turn may result in my taking some action, or in my mind taking on a new impression as one thought leads to another. On the other hand, to the extent that what we are describing is a *rational* agent and not merely a machine, and to the extent that we want to *explain* the changes that do or do not occur when the impression comes in, we need to focus on what the impression is an impression *of*, that is, what its propositional content is. The reason why the agent's assent to that impression caused him to run off screaming is not because the impression had some black patches and some orange patches in it, but because it was the impression *that there was a tiger right there*. The 'that-' clause marks a proposition.

Thus we can talk about two levels at which we can describe assents, and two corresponding objects of assent. But we can also finesse the question, or at any rate paper over it a bit, by talking about 'assenting to the impression that such and such', where this way of talking sounds fairly natural, and runs together the impression and the proposition without prejudice to either. In fact, this is the way that the Stoics normally do talk about it, and it is harmless enough for us to follow them, since we can always revert to our more nuanced account if need be.

But the Stoic habit of talking about 'the impression that there is a coffee mug on the table' and so on should alert us to one further point of considerable importance. In distinguishing the impression from the proposition above, I talked as though an agent's impression has no intrinsic propositional content—as though a visual impression roughly corresponds to the photograph that an idealized camera might take if positioned at the observer's eye. A photograph of the scene in front of you right now could be titled in countless different ways—'there is some furniture in the living room', or 'why it pays to start saving younger', or 'the butler had disappeared', or 'the chair is to the left of the sofa'. Quite generally, if you take any photo you like, there are countless things you could say about it, and countless things you could use it to say ('that's the color I most detest'). None of them is the *only* thing that it says, or the *privileged* thing it says, or the *real* thing it says, as opposed to comments or interpretations artificially foisted on it.

All that stands in sharp contrast to the Stoic way of thinking about impressions. When an agent has an impression, there is, so to speak, a proposition built right into it; there is a unique claim that that picture is making, which is intrinsic to its being the impression that it is.[12] This is not to take back what was said earlier; the impression and the proposition are still distinct things, and distinct kinds of things, in all the ways mentioned. But the Stoic view is that each impression arrives bundled with one and only one proposition, and no impression—at least no impression in the mind of an adult human being—is a mere unlabeled picture. The impression is individuated both by its purely sensory content—the idealized photograph—and by its propositional content; any change in either makes for a distinct impression. Now on a very still day it might occur that exactly the same visual image should filter through my window, and that my gaze should remain utterly fixed, while my mind wanders from the thought that elm-leaves are darker than oak-leaves, to the thought that both trees must be at least thirty feet tall. Since the visual scene has remained utterly the same during these two thoughts—an idealized camera would have taken two identical pictures—it may seem that here we have one impression which has received, successively, two different captions. This would confirm our non-Stoic sense that there is no unique and privileged statement that a picture makes, merely various comments that we observers may add to it. The Stoics would agree with us on the substance, but describe the case differently: they would say that I received two impressions, not one, and that each impression had as an intrinsic part of itself both a certain visual character (the picture common to both) and a certain relation to a proposition (but a different one for each). The first one was essentially and intrinsically the impression that elm-leaves are shinier than oak-leaves—that is not a mere piece of arbitrary captioning, but a necessary part of that impression's content, that is, part of what makes it the impression that it is.

And this is another reason why the Stoics can afford to be casual about saying that we give our assent to impressions. If impressions were like photos in being open to multiple interpretations, then saying that I had assented to an impression would leave it unclear which of the many propositions I had assented to. But since each impression is correlated with one unique proposition, such a question cannot arise.

Having an impression—for example, having the impression that there is a coffee mug on my table—is not yet having any belief of any kind. That follows only if we assent to the impression. The clearest way to see the difference is by considering persistent illusions—those curious phenomena, especially optical phenomena, that look deceptive, even once we know we're being deceived. For instance, there are the Muller-Lyer lines (see next page).

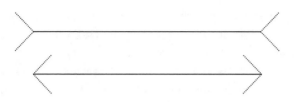

Even after one learns that the two lines are the same length—even after you take a ruler and measure for yourself—it still looks as though the Y-line is longer than the arrow-line. You keep on having the distinct impression that it's longer. But once you have measured them, you no longer believe it's longer. You resist the illusion: you no longer assent to the impression.

On the other hand, we generally tend to assent to most impressions that arise for us, and we generally are not deceived in doing so. I have the impression that there's a coffee-cup on the table; that it is hot outside; that most prime numbers are odd; that not all prime numbers are odd; and so on. I assent to all of these impressions, and as a result I have the beliefs that correspond to them. Indeed, my belief that it is hot outside simply is nothing over and above my assent to the impression that it is hot outside: a belief is a kind of assent. The act of believing, of assenting to the impression, is a kind of endorsement of the impression, saying 'yes!' to it, agreeing that it gets things right, that the world really is as the impression depicts it to be (and as the correlated proposition describes it to be). When we assent to an impression, we swing the whole weight of our actions and beliefs behind it, like jumping to grab a rope that will rescue us from a balcony. From there out, unless we reconsider it, we will act as though that impression is solid and reliable, and will make plans based on it.

Not assenting, or withholding assent, by contrast, means not endorsing, not jumping. Withholding assent from an impression does not always involve branding it deceptive, as we do in the case of persistent illusions. In that case, we go beyond withholding assent to the impression, to the further act of assenting to an impression that is the contradictory of it—I not only do not formulate the belief that the one line is longer, I actually take the positive step of believing that it is *not* longer, which means assenting to a second, contradictory impression. (We usually say, 'I don't believe it'; but that is ambiguous between not believing, and believing the contradictory.) Typically, though, I will suspend judgment or withhold assent from an impression, without taking any stand on its contradictory. Is that Fred I see down in the bakery aisle? For a second it looked like him—but it is quite a distance, and his head was turned, and I didn't get a really good look, so I do not assent to the impression that it was Fred, I just suspend judgment. That's not to say that I come to believe it was *not* Fred, either; I just am neutral on the issue. I had the impression it was Fred, but instead of assenting to it, I suspended assent.

When the impression is a deceptive one, then if I assent to it I have a false belief. A true belief, accordingly, is an assent to a true impression. Or rather, as we saw above, a true belief is an assent, strictly speaking, to a proposition that is true; for the propositional aspect is especially salient and important when we are thinking about assents and impressions not as psychological pushes and pulls but as things that can be true and false, rational and irrational. What if the impression was true, after all, but I didn't assent to it? What if it really was Fred, but I cautiously refused assent? Well, since I didn't formulate any belief, it follows that I did not formulate a false belief. I may have made some other mistake, or have acted culpably in some other way—it may be that my failure to acquire a true belief about Fred resulted partly from a false belief that he never wears yellow trousers like the ones I just saw. Or perhaps on this occasion I ought to have taken a second look, because it is important that I find Fred, or perhaps in general I am too inclined to doubt things, and so miss out on true beliefs that would have been valuable to me. Those questions arise later, when we look at someone's overall habits of belief and doubt. But the simple question gets a simple answer: if you never assent, you will never have a false belief.

An assent, then, is a sort of motion of the mind, that arises in response to a modification of the mind, which in turn was usually brought about by some object outside of the mind, for example, a tree or a coffee-mug. In terms of this schema we can now define not only belief and knowledge, but also desire and fear and any other emotions there are. We can define virtue and vice, and define what happens when one progresses from one to the other. And we can define how one person's mind differs from another's.

NOTES

1. *DL* 7.49 = *SVF* 2.52 = LS 39A = IG2 II–3.
2. Aëtius 4.8.12 = *SVF* 2.72.
3. Epictetus Discourses 1.17.21–22.
4. *SE AM* 7.228 = *SVF* 2.56 = IG2 II–8.
5. Plato, *Theaetetus* 191cd; Aristotle, *de Anima* 424a19.
6. *SE AM* 7.229–230; 7.373 = *SVF* 2.56 = IG2 II–8, II–9.
7. *SE AM* 7.229–230; 7.373 = *SVF* 2.56 = IG2 II–8, II–9.
8. Aëtius 4.12.1 = *SVF* 2.21 = LS 39B = IG2 II–13.
9. *DL* 7.159 = *SVF* 2.837 = IG2 II–20; Aëtius 4.5.6 = *SVF* 2.838; Galen *De Foetuum* 4.698 = *SVF* 2 761 = LS 53D.
10. Propositions immaterial: *SE AM* 11.224 = *SVF* 2.170; *SE AM* 7.38 = *SVF* 2.132 = IG2 II–39; *SE* 10.218 = *SVF* 2.331 = LS 27D = IG2 II–34. The proposition might be dependent on me in the special case in which I am mentioned in it, e.g. 'this one is dead', said with demonstrative reference to me, will apparently cease to exist if I die (Alexander *in A. Pr.* 177–178 = *SVF* 2.202 = LS 38F). But the claim at SE AM 8.70 (= *SVF* 2.187 = LS 33C = IG2 II–41) that 'sayables' (of which propositions are one type) 'subsist in accordance with a rational impression' should not be taken to mean that the typical proposition's existence is dependent on any rational agent having an impression of it. This is ruled out by the fact that every event in the universe is caused, and every causal outcome involves a sayable (*SE AM.* 9.211 = *SVF* 2.341 = LS 55B = IG2 II–44; Clement *Miscellanies* 8.9.26 = *SVF* 3. *Archedemus* 8 = LS 55C), but for the vast majority of causal interactions, no human agent will ever form an impression of the event. (Could these sayables still subsist on the impressions of an omniscient Zeus? Perhaps a story of this kind could be told, but it would still show that propositions do not depend on human thoughts.)
11. Stobaeus 1.138 = *SVF* 2.336 = LS 55A = IG2 II–43; *SE AM* 9.211 = *SVF* 2.341 = LS 55B = IG2 II–44.
12. For more details see Brennan (2003), 261 fn. 8

6

Belief and Knowledge

In examining the Stoics' views on belief and knowledge, we are exploring the area of philosophy now called 'epistemology', from the Greek word for knowledge, episteme. The Stoics were deeply influenced by their predecessors in all aspects of their epistemology, as in other areas; one can find traces of Platonic and Aristotelian influence, as well as traces of Epicurean influence in some of their terminology. As always, Plato made the first, pathbreaking moves, in his dialogues the *Meno* and the *Theaetetus*. But the Stoic treatment of epistemology changed the course of the discipline in a radical way. Much philosophy since Descartes has been consumed with skepticism and the possibility of knowledge, and this entire skeptical turn would not have occurred without the background of Stoic epistemology.

As we saw, the Stoics define belief in terms of assent to impressions. But before we turn to their definition, we should spend a second getting clear on what exactly it is they were defining.

In ordinary English, there are a few senses of the word 'belief' that are narrower than the one that the Stoics are going to define, and one sense that is wider. To begin with, when we speak about someone's 'beliefs', we often have in mind their most firmly-held convictions, or the credo by which they live. Nothing so deep or heavy is involved here. As philosophers ordinarily speak about beliefs, we have a belief anytime we take the world to be a certain way, or anytime we think something is the case. I believe it is sunny outside; I think I left my watch on the night-stand; I bet there are over fifty people in this room: all of those are ways of expressing a belief. The content does not need to be profound, and the conviction does not need to be firm.

There is another sense in which we use the word 'belief' or 'believe' in order to provide a contrast with 'knowledge' or 'know'. 'Do you *know* that you left your watch on the nightstand, or do you merely *believe* that you did?' In philosophical parlance, the term 'belief' does not contrast with knowledge, but rather covers both cases; knowing is a kind of believing, too. Sometimes I believe something but do not know it (for example, that it is raining somewhere in Brazil); sometimes I both believe something and also know it. Saying that I believe it does not exclude my knowing it, too; that is why I can say 'I *believe* my hand is in my pocket, and in fact I *know* it is!' To refer to the beliefs that do not come up to the standard of knowledge, philosophers sometimes use the term 'mere belief'; the Stoics used the term 'opinion'.

There is another sense of 'belief' in which we can say that someone believes things that they are not currently thinking about. For instance, it is unlikely that at breakfast this morning you were thinking about the respective weights of penguins and hippopotamuses. The thought that hippos weigh more than penguins probably never crossed your mind, from the moment you woke until well after breakfast was done. And yet there is a sense in which it would have been true to say of you, even then, that you believe hippos weigh more than penguins. For instance, if someone had interrupted your breakfast and asked you whether you think hippos weigh more than penguins, you would have readily agreed. The same goes for a host of other things you weren't thinking about: that the United States is over 200 years old, but less than 300; that there are just as many odd integers as even integers; that the chair you were sitting on would not dissolve into butter-cream frosting, and so on. All of these form part of the background of what you believe, of how you see the world.

Philosophers nowadays sometimes say that we have two sorts of beliefs: 'occurrent beliefs', that is, ones that are occurring to you, or that you currently are thinking about; and 'dispositional' beliefs, that is, ones that you are disposed to have if the question arises, or ones that are part of your make-up or disposition, even though they are not at work in your thoughts right now.

The Stoics make a slightly different distinction; their term 'belief' applies only to thoughts you are having right then, things that are really on your mind. A belief on the Stoic view is an event, like a sneeze; at 8:05 I was believing I should get out of bed, then a little later I believed I was in the kitchen, then I believed the coffee was done, and so on. If it is not playing an active role in my thoughts, then it is not a belief, on the Stoic view. And instead of talking about 'dispositional beliefs', as though they were another kind of the same thing, they talk about having a 'disposition to believe', that is, a feature of your psychology which is not a belief, but makes you the sort of person who *will* have a belief when the occasion arises. This seems to me a slightly more accurate way of speaking. A disposition to laugh at knock-knock jokes is not itself a laugh, so it would be rather odd to say that there are two kinds of laughs, the occurrent kind I do after you tell me a knock-knock joke, and the dispositional kind I was having this morning at breakfast, while sorrowing over the latest news from sub-Saharan Africa. It would have still been true to say of me, even as I was sighing over the fate of AIDS victims, that I have a disposition to laugh at knock-knock jokes; not every grim reflection cures one of frivolous tendencies. But it would surely be false to say that I was, at that very time, laughing, and the falsehood would not be much mended by saying that I was having a dispositional laugh.

So there is one sense in which the Stoic use of 'belief' is narrower than our use, and two senses in which it is wider: it does not include background, latent, or 'dispositional' beliefs, but it does include those beliefs which amount to knowledge, and it includes all thoughts about how things are, whether the topic is profound or trivial and whether we are firmly convinced or not.

Now we can give the Stoic definition:

Stoic Definition of Belief: a belief is an assent to an impression.

Note first of all that on this definition a belief is an assent, i.e. one kind of assent: that is why a belief is an event, an action, something that occurs at a particular time (perhaps a brief time, like a sneeze, or a longer time, like an extended chortle, but still an event rather than a state). Then note that the definition does NOT say

A belief is an impression that you assent to,

or

A belief is a combination of an assent and an impression,

or

An impression turns into a belief once you assent to it.

It is true that the sequence of events goes something like that: first one gets an impression, and then an assent either follows or does not, and if it does then the assent is a belief. But assents and impressions are completely different kinds of things. An impression is a certain way that your mind is arranged, a certain pattern or image in your mind. In this respect it is like an arrangement of furniture in your living-room. It is essentially a static thing, which in principle could have always been that way, and could last till eternity. It is true that there was probably a time, fairly recently, when a series of events produced the arrangement of furniture in your room, but the event of producing the arrangement is a different thing from the arrangement that it produced. So too, there is an event that produces an impression in your mind—that is, the *getting* of the impression which is, for instance, the event of some visible object in the world interacting with your vision so as to make a visual impression. But the impression that you get is a state, not an event. That is why a belief, which is an event and not a state, cannot be an impression, even one you assent to; or a combination of an impression and something else, even an assent; or an impression that has turned into something. States and events are completely different sorts of things; on the Stoic view an impression is a state, and a belief, because it is an assent, is an event.

There are different kinds of beliefs, on the Stoic view. The most important kinds follow from the fact that there are different kinds of assents, and different kinds of impressions to assent to. To begin with impressions, the most important difference is between those that are true and those that are false. We saw earlier that there is a slight vacillation in the evidence between texts that say that we assent to impressions, and texts that say that we assent to propositions, where the second view seems to be the more precise one. Here too there is some vacillation. Many texts say that impressions are true and false, but the more precise view seems to be that what is primarily true or false are propositions, and that impressions are true or false only in virtue of the truth or falsehood of the proposition they are correlated with. A belief, in turn, is true or false depending on whether the impression (or rather proposition) to which it is an assent is true or false.

Among true impressions, the Stoics claimed that there was a special class whose members have a certain sort of vivid clarity, fidelity, and reliability, and these they called *kataleptic* impressions. The word *kataleptic* was their invention; it may have suggested such connotations as 'gripping', 'grasping', 'graspable', or 'comprehensive', but we can learn less from etymology than from example and analysis. When you see someone at a distance on a foggy evening, you may have the impression that it is your friend Fred. And it may well be Fred, in which case your impression is true. But on the other hand, it may be someone else, of Fred's rough build and size, who looks rather like Fred from that distance in this light. All that you have is the impression that it is Fred; the impression could be coming from Fred, or from something other than Fred. Your impression could be a true one, but there is no guarantee; there is nothing about this vague and indistinct impression that allows you to discriminate between Fred and someone else rather like him.

Such an impression is not a *kataleptic* one—certainly not if it is a false impression, and not even if it is true. The Stoics give the following definition:

A *kataleptic* impression is one that

(1) comes from what is, and

(2) is stamped and sealed and molded in accordance with what is, and

(3) is of such a sort that it could not come from what is not.

The first clause says that the impression must be true; to be a *kataleptic* impression, the impression must really come from what it claims to depict (i.e. if it's the impression of Fred in the distance, then it must really be coming from Fred). The second clause extends the metaphor of the signet ring and wax. It has two parts as well; a correspondence claim, and a causal claim. To be 'stamped in accordance with what is' means that the impression has features that correspond to features that the object has; there is an isomorphism or mapping between the features of the object and features of the impression. If Fred has his head on his shoulders, then the impression of Fred should have an impression of a head on the impression of shoulders. The causal claim goes beyond this to say that the correspondence should be causally produced exactly by the object's possession of those features. If my impression of the tower represents the tower as round, that should be because the round edges of the tower caused something corresponding to round edges in my impression of the tower. It should not be because the square edges of the tower got lost in the mist. The correspondence between impression and object must be caused by the object, just as the correspondence between the impression in the wax and the shape of the signet-ring is caused by the ring. (We'll later see that this account must be modified slightly.) Finally, the third clause tells us that all of this should happen in so complete, detailed, and thorough a way that the resultant impression could not have arisen from anything other than the very thing that did give rise to it (which by the earlier clauses means, the very thing it represents itself as coming from). To have a *kataleptic* impression that

Belief and Knowledge ~ 67

this thing in front of me is a horse means that I must see this horse closely enough, and clearly enough, that my impression could not be an impression coming from two guys in a horse suit, or from a robot shaped like a horse, or from a movie of a horse, or a hologram of a horse. To be *kataleptic*, the impression has to come with a sort of guarantee: if you are having this impression, then things are really as the impression says they are.

We may wonder whether it is ever possible to have such an impression; can't you always be fooled by a good replica? Could you ever be sure that it is Fred, even close up on a sunny day? What if Fred has an identical twin who looks the same? Can there ever be an impression that represents its object so exhaustively that no other object could give off the same impression? If nothing else, can't you have the same detailed impression of Fred in a dream, when Fred is not around?

These are the standard worries of the epistemological skeptic (i.e. the skeptic about belief and knowledge, rather than the skeptic about morality, divinity, other minds, or what have you). It is a fact of the first historical significance that full-blown, systematic epistemological skepticism is not articulated until after Stoic epistemology is being developed. Academic skepticism, the creation of Arcesilaus, is a response to Stoic epistemology, largely carried out in the technical terminology of the Stoic school, and intended to demonstrate to the Stoics, on their own terms, that if they are right about what a *kataleptic* impression would amount to, then no one can ever have one. And Sextus Empiricus, the author whose skepticism made the greatest impression on Early Modern philosophers like Descartes, is quite explicit about the fact that his skepticism consists in his denial that we can ever get a *kataleptic* impression of something. His skepticism is never phrased in terms of the claim that we do not or cannot *know* things; what he denies is that we can '*kataleptize*' them. For everything that Sextus argues, it may be perfectly possible to know plenty of things, provided that knowledge does not require *kataleptic* impressions. It is a tribute to the power and influence of the Stoic analysis of knowledge that later readers understood this fairly local assault on Stoic theory as an all-out, universal assault on human knowledge.

But what is the connection between a *kataleptic* impression and the possession of knowledge? This answer turns on the existence of two kinds or grades of assent, which the Stoics call 'strong assent' and 'weak assent'. At a first approximation, we might think of these as rather like being strongly convinced of something and being weakly convinced of it. But it is clear that the Stoics were not so much interested in how firmly or dogmatically I *do* maintain my belief, as they were in the question of how consistently and rationally I *could* maintain my belief, in the face of various challenges. I might espouse some position with great fervor, but then abandon it immediately when I'm shown it contradicts some other view I hold. In that case, my assent was a weak one, all along, because it crumbled when challenged by cross-questioning. Or, I might declaim at length about how one should always take public transportation instead of taxis, but then start speaking in favor of taxis when my finances improve. Here my assent was challenged not by rational cross-questioning, but by the pressures of ease and temptation, and here too it was found to have been weak all along. Strong assent is assent that cannot be reversed or overturned by any amount of rational questioning, no matter how skillfully conducted, or by any amount of emotional or psychological pressure. (It is rather like witnesses in a law-case; the good witness is not the one who begins with fire and bluster, but the one who can patiently stick with their story under any cross-examination, no matter how thorough or bullying.)

In these terms, it is very simple to give the Stoic definition of knowledge:

Knowledge is strong assent to a *kataleptic* impression.

Here too, as earlier with 'belief', it is worth saying a word about how the Stoic use of the term 'knowledge' differs from our own—and here the difference is more severe. Since knowledge, like all belief, is an assent on the Stoic view, it follows that people only know things when they have them in mind, and are thinking about them—it is an event, not a disposition. In the case of 'belief', we saw that English recognizes both an event-like sense and a state-like, dispositional sense. With 'knowledge', the case is more extreme; the state-like sense predominates in English, and the event-like sense is awkward to the point of non-existence. It is not only correct but perfectly natural to say of someone busily thinking about what to have for dinner that he knows algebra, or knows his children's birthdays, though he is not thinking of either. And it is very odd to say of the same person, when they are recalling those same birthdays, that he 'is knowing' the dates ('is in the middle of knowing them'?). We might say instead something like 'he knows the dates, and right now he is *thinking* about them, too'. The Stoics would describe the same case by saying 'at dinner he had a disposition to know the dates, and right now he *is* knowing them, too', which sounds peculiar in English. Unfortunately, no other word will better convey the Stoic doctrine, and so I will use the term 'knowledge' while at times drawing attention to the difference by such unnatural constructions as 'doing a bit of knowing' or 'having an episode of knowledge'. It is true that they also used the term 'knowledge' (or rather 'episteme') on occasion to describe the disposition-like state that we more naturally call knowledge.[1] But it was the episodes of knowing something, that is, attending in a knowledgeable way to something one knows, that the Stoics thought were the fundamental unit in the analysis of knowledge, just as the episode of believing something is fundamental in the analysis of belief.

Thus an episode of knowing something, for example, knowing that my hand is in my pocket, involves having a strong, irreversible assent, to a *kataleptic* impression. There are two criteria here; the assent must be strong, and the impression must be *kataleptic*. If either fails, then the assent does not constitute (a bit of) knowledge, but rather what the Stoics called 'opinion' (*doxa* in Greek). How often are both criteria met? The first one is met quite often; it seems to be the Stoic view that *kataleptic* impressions are fairly common. We receive clear and accurate impressions of many things in our daily life, and on the basis of this we are able to form a whole host of true beliefs, and we form reliable dispositions to form further true beliefs and avoid false beliefs. Whenever we assent to a *kataleptic* impression, we not only have a belief (inasmuch as it is an assent to an impression), we also have a true belief (since all *kataleptic* impressions are true). We furthermore have what the Stoics call a *katalepsis*, that is, an assent to a *kataleptic* impression. But a *katalepsis* is still an opinion, not a (bit of) knowledge, if the assent is weak instead of strong—that was the second criterion.[2] And strong assent turns out to be very rare indeed—only the perfectly wise Sages ever have it. For only Sages have such a consistent, virtuous, error-free view of the world that they can never be caught out in a contradiction, or never tempted to go back on an earlier position. No non-Sage can ever really know anything.

But it is also part of the Stoics' view that, in order to maintain their firm, unassailable position of epistemic invincibility, the Sages must never have any opinions at all. Naturally they should never have any weak or reversible assents, and naturally they should never assent to any false impressions; but in order to ensure that no instability or inconsistency has a chance to creep in, the Sage must never assent to anything that is not *kataleptic*, and must never assent except strongly. Every one of the Sage's beliefs is an episode of knowledge. It may seem perverse for the Sage to decline to assent to true beliefs, merely because they are not *kataleptic*—doesn't that mean he is passing up many opportunities to increase his stock of usable information about the world? And why is it any better to *fail* to believe something that is true, than to believe something that is false?

The answer to the first question is that it is phrased in a misleading way: it makes it look as though the Sage considers an incoming impression and sees that it is true, but refuses to assent to it because it is not *kataleptic*. But the truth of the impression is exactly what the individual, even the Sage, *cannot* see; all that he can tell is whether it is *kataleptic* or not. Judging from the outside, as it were, we may be able to tell that the impression is a true one, but from the inside all the Sage sees is an impression that is so vague or indistinct that it could just as well be false as true. If he lowers the bar on clarity and reliability far enough to let this one in, then he will inevitably let

Belief and Knowledge ~ 71

some false ones in, too. And believing something false is much worse than merely neglecting to believe something true, because it means that your total stock of beliefs now contains at least the germ of an incoherence, a contradiction between this false belief and true beliefs you may have or be committed to. And that means that none of your assents can have the kind of stability and irreversibility that strong assent must have.

This position has a number of interesting consequences. For our current project of reconstructing the Stoic position, it shows us that there is no such thing as strong assent to what is false or non-*kataleptic*; for only Sages have strong assents, and they only assent to what is *kataleptic*. Any assent in a non-Sage is a weak one, whether given to a false, true, or even *kataleptic* impression. Thus some of the squares in the chart below turn out to be empty, even though it might seem at first that they are theoretical possibilities:

	false	true non-K	true and *kataleptic*
strong:	(empty)	(empty)	knowledge and *katalepsis*
weak:	false opinion	true opinion	true opinion and *katalepsis*

For our understanding of the origins of modern skepticism, it shows us part of why the burden of proof has tended to favor the Skeptic. It was not the Skeptics themselves, but the anti-Skeptical Stoics who first raised the bar for knowledge to such high, perhaps unattainable heights. The Stoics themselves thought that their Stoic Sage should be, in the loose sense, very skeptical, that is, very circumspect and reluctant to give assent.[3] The Sage must never opine, that is, must never give his assent to anything that is not fully *kataleptic*. That means that the Sage must withhold assent on many occasions when the rest of us would probably take a chance on it (for example, when it looks like Fred in the distance). Furthermore, the Sage will never assent to anything if there is the chance that their assent would need to be reversed in the face of any questioning or examination, no matter how lengthy. All of these provisos and cautions led the Stoics to a position in which they said that no ordinary person, and not even the heads of their own Stoic school, ever knows anything; only an ethical and epistemic super-being, the Stoic Sage, is capable of genuine knowledge. Given this position, it is clear that the Skeptics had to give them only the barest nudge in order to push them off the Skeptical cliff. The Stoics have already conceded that all of our ordinary claims to know things are false (since only Sages have knowledge, and none of us are Sages); but in that case they agree with the Skeptics that no one currently knows anything. The difference between Stoics and Skeptics is merely over whether there is the theoretical possibility that someone could know something; and this in turn comes down to the question whether there is such a thing as the *kataleptic* impression. For even the perfect Sage must suspend judgment until a *kataleptic* impression comes along; if none ever comes, the Sage himself is effectively a skeptic, always withholding assent no matter what impression occurs to him. Thus the entire debate between Stoics and Skeptics came to turn on the existence of the *kataleptic* impression.

One of the ways that Stoic epistemology left its mark on Skepticism and later debates is through the focus on episodes of knowledge. In Plato and Aristotle, discussions of knowledge tend to focus on an agent's possession of a complex, comprehensive, and systematic understanding of some area of science. Examples of knowledge tend to be things like one's knowledge of geometry, where hundreds of separate propositions, theorems, and axioms are connected together in a systematic way. Having scientific knowledge of a derivative theorem is in large part a matter of understanding how it can be derived from and explained by other theorems and axioms it depends on—you don't really *know* Euclid's proposition 34 unless you understand its relation to all the other important propositions in that area of geometry—and that may well entail knowing geometry as a whole. This model was applied equally to such areas as ethics; following the lead of Socrates, philosophers like Plato and Aristotle tend to think that you do not really *know* that murder is wrong unless you also know exactly when it would and would not be virtuous or just to kill someone, and that this knowledge in turn cannot be divorced from knowledge of what virtue as a whole is, and when it is better to live or die oneself. This picture is most clear in Plato's *Republic*, where all of the sciences are said to be connected to one another, and none of them can be fully understood unless one understands the Form of the Good itself, which unifies and systematizes all of the local areas of knowledge underneath it in something of the way that the axioms of geometry unify and generate the whole science of geometry.

Something of this same emphasis on systematicity and consistency is still to be found in Stoicism, in the claim that knowledge requires strong assent, which in turn requires the impossibility of being led into contradiction by any chain of argumentation, no matter how wide-ranging it may be. The Stoic Sage, whose stock of beliefs is free of any contradiction, and who cannot be misled or inveigled by either contentious reasoning or the press of temptation, is a very close cousin of Plato's philosopher-king, secure in the vision of the Form of the Good. But when the debate with the Skeptics narrowed to the debate over the existence of the *kataleptic* impression, the emphasis turned from systematic science to local perceptual episodes.[4] The question turned from whether one can know the entire science of political management, embedded as it is in the science of ethics and the science of psychology, to whether one can know that the snake that is now sticking its head out of a hole is the same snake that looked out a minute ago. I said above that it is more natural in English to speak of knowledge as a disposition—my knowledge of Greek, your knowledge of the neighborhood you grew up in. Thus it is worth remembering that when we open recent discussions of skepticism we will probably find fewer of those systematic, Platonic-looking issues at stake, and more of the episodic, Stoic ones: do I know—that is, am I doing a bit of knowing, right now—that this is my hand in front of me?

This emphasis on local perceptual episodes has led some critics to think that all *kataleptic* impressions are perceptual—that is, derived from one of the five senses—but I believe this is false. The Stoics thought that I could know that this is my hand—at least if I'm a

74 ~ *Belief and Knowledge*

Sage—but they also thought that I could know that two is an even number, that virtue is beneficial, that God exists, and that valid arguments can have false conclusions. None of these objects of knowledge looks like a plausible object of perception. If the Stoics nonetheless thought that the Sage could know them, then they must either have thought that one could have non-perceptual *kataleptic* impressions, or that one could have knowledge without *kataleptic* impressions. For several reasons, I think the first is clearly the right conclusion.

To begin with, the debate with the Skeptics would have gone very differently if the Stoic position had been that knowledge can sometimes be had without *kataleptic* impressions. But all of the evidence from that debate points to the conclusion that the Skeptics attacked *kataleptic* impressions, because they could thereby make it impossible for the Stoics to know anything.

Furthermore, one of the central matters for dispute in the debate was the question of practical impressions—that is, the impression that one should undertake some course of action, or do something (we will spend the next chapter considering these impressions in greater detail, but a brief reference here will suffice). The Skeptics claimed that *kataleptic* impressions do not exist. Then they insisted that the Stoic refusal to assent to what is not *kataleptic* would mean that one must never assent to anything at all. The Stoics replied that if one never assented to any impression, one could never perform any action, and thus they claimed that if there are no *kataleptic* impressions the Skeptics would be doomed to live a life of complete inactivity, suspending judgment even about whether to move a muscle or not.[5] Both Stoics and Skeptics agreed that if the Sage never had any *kataleptic* impressions to assent to, he would not have any practical impressions he could assent to, either; thus both must have thought that the Sage only assents to practical impressions that are *kataleptic*. But as we shall see later on, practical impressions are crucially non-perceptual in their character. It is true that part of their content is local and perceptual, for example, it involves my picking up this piece of food that I see in front of me. But the

Belief and Knowledge ~ 75

proposition that makes my impression a practical one must be a non-perceptual assessment of this perceptual item—for example, I must think that it is *good* that I should pick up this food, or *right*, or *reasonable* or *fitting* for me to pick up this food, where none of those predicates expresses a perceptible property. Thus when the Sage performs an action, for example, eating some food, he must be assenting to an impression that is both non-perceptual (in as much as it is practical) and also *kataleptic* (inasmuch as he is a Sage).

The existence of such an impression is also directly attested in an anecdote about one of the early Stoics, a student of Cleanthes named Sphaerus. He was speaking with a king, one of the Ptolemies of Egypt, about the Stoic claim that the wise man never assents to any impression that is not *kataleptic*. The king wanted to refute Sphaerus, and so had some cunningly crafted wax pomegranates brought out. When Sphaerus reached for one of them, the king cried out that Sphaerus had assented to a false impression. It is easy to see his point; because they were such exact replicas, the pomegranates produced an impression in Sphaerus that was indistinguishable from the impression that real pomegranates would have produced; thus Sphaerus' impression that they were pomegranates was not a *kataleptic* one. Or at least that's how the king thought it would go, but Sphaerus had an answer ready: he said that he had not assented to the impression 'that they were pomegranates', but to the impression 'that it was reasonable that they were pomegranates'. He continued by saying that the reasonable is a different thing from the *kataleptic*; the *kataleptic* is unfalsifiable, but the reasonable can come out otherwise, that is, false.[6]

Now since he was claiming not to be refuted, Sphaerus must have been claiming to have assented to a *kataleptic* impression, that is, the impression 'that it was reasonable that they were pomegranates'. And his point was that the reasonable impression, that is, 'that they were pomegranates', could come out false (and indeed had) but that he had not assented to that impression in any case. He had assented to the impression 'that it was reasonable that they were pomegranates', and this one was not falsified—it was still reasonable that they should be pomegranates, even if in fact they were not. Thus the impression he assented to was not falsified, and could retain its title to being *kataleptic*. But that means that he was claiming to have a *kataleptic* impression whose content was the distinctly non-perceptual claim 'that it was reasonable that they were pomegranates'. And this passage is not merely evidence of a one-off face-saving maneuver on the part of a hard-pressed dinner-guest; as we shall see, judgments that something is reasonable are crucial to the Sage's ability to act in the world.

It is worth pausing for a second over the notion of the reasonable, since the story of Sphaerus leaves it rather confusing. One might suppose that a reasonable impression is one that depicts something as being reasonable, or an impression whose corresponding proposition has the word 'reasonable' in it somewhere. Thus one might think that the reasonable impression in Sphaerus' case is the impression 'that it is reasonable that they are pomegranates'. But the Stoic use of the term 'reasonable' is rather like our use of the term 'witty'. A witty remark is not the same thing as a remark that has the word 'witty' somewhere in it—indeed, very few if any witty remarks feature the word 'witty' (as opposed, for example, to the words 'Prime Minister', 'cow', and 'New Jersey'). And conversely, sentences like 'that was a witty remark' or 'she is very witty' are seldom if ever terribly witty themselves—they may be true or false, complimentary, generous, or what have you, but they are not themselves likely to be witty remarks, and certainly not in virtue of containing the word 'witty'. That is how it goes with the reasonable: when the Stoics give us an example of a reasonable proposition, they offer 'I will be alive tomorrow', which may be reasonable enough, but makes no use of the word 'reasonable' or any explicit reference to the notion. So Sphaerus' impression 'that it was reasonable that they were pomegranates', which does explicitly use the word 'reasonable', is unlikely to be the reasonable proposition that he distinguishes from the *kataleptic* one. Instead, the reasonable impression is the one that does not *say* the word 'reasonable' in it, that is, the impression 'that they are pomegranates'. And this is also the one that came out false (since they were not pomegranates). Sphaerus tells us that reasonable impressions can come out false, and the Stoic example of one, that is, 'I shall be alive tomorrow' is also a good example of a proposition that may turn out false. So the picture coheres, as long as we can keep in mind that reasonable impressions are not the same as impressions that use the word 'reasonable', just as witty remarks are not the same as remarks that contain the word 'witty'.

Resistance to the idea that there can be non-perceptual *kataleptic* impressions has generally come from a feature of the definition of the *kataleptic* impression that we examined above. The Stoics claimed that only bodies could do any real causing in the world. Anything that does not have a body—such as propositions, or time, or empty space—cannot really be a cause of anything. That means that it is hard to see how anything but a perceptible body can produce a kataleptic impression, if the content of a *kataleptic* impression must also cause the impression to have the features it does. It is easy to see how the signet-ring molds the wax, or how it molds an impression in me when I look at it; the ring is a body, which directly causes my impression to have the shape and features that it does. Lacking bodies, and therefore lacking causal efficacy, can such things as propositions produce *kataleptic* impressions? Some critics have argued that they cannot, and concluded that all kataleptic impressions must be the perceptual impressions of bodies.

Here we are fortunate in having a passage that tells us that the Stoics did countenance non-perceptual kataleptic impressions, and gives us a start on resolving the puzzle. They did not loosen the restriction that only bodies can be genuine causes; instead, they crafted the definition of the *kataleptic* in such a way as to allow for indirect causal influence from non-bodies:

The Stoics say that sometimes a gym-teacher or drill sergeant teaches the student to make certain movements by taking the student's hands and moving them rhythmically, whereas sometimes he stands off at a distance and makes the rhythmical motion himself so as to offer himself to the student as a model for imitation. In the same way, some objects of impressions as it were get into direct contact and lay hold of the mind and make the imprint in it that way (e.g. white, black, and bodies in general), whereas others are of such a nature that the mind takes an impression *after* them, but is not impressed *by* them; these are the non-bodily propositions.[7]

Here the claim is made that the proposition is not the direct cause of the impression, but that the impression comes to have the features it has at least in part because the proposition has the features that it has. Even though there is no signet-ring doing the forming, the mind forms itself into a signet-ring shape, rather as a skillful mime can arrange his body as though he were slouching against a wall, even though there is no wall to slouch against. That is how the proposition is an indirect part of the causal story: the impression is modeled *after* the proposition, that is, has features that correspond to it, and has those features in some sense *because* the proposition has the features it does. This is sufficient to satisfy the causal component of the second clause in the definition of the *kataleptic* impression, that the impression should be *stamped and sealed and molded* in accordance with *what is*. It is natural to read that clause as requiring the stronger causal relation, that the object must cause the impression, but from this passage in Sextus it is clear that being modeled *after* the object counted as being molded *in accordance with* the object.[8] The quotation does not give us everything we would like to know; in particular, we are not told what exactly does cause the impression to have the shape that it does.[9] But this text does at least tell us that the Stoics had faced the question whether there could be kataleptic impressions of incorporeal items, and clearly decided to admit them.

At the end of this chapter, then, we know how to take the notions of assent and impression and produce definitions of belief, knowledge, and opinion. We know what a *kataleptic* impression is, and how there can be *kataleptic* impressions with both perceptual and non-perceptual content.

1. *SE PH* 2.81 = IG2 III–39; Stobaeus 2.74 = *SVF* 3.112 = LS 41H = IG2 II–95.5l; *DL* 7.47 = *SVF* 1.68 = LS 31B = IG2 II–3.

2. There is a passage from Arcesilaus (*SE AM* 7.153–154 = *SVF* I.69, 2.90 = LS 41C = IG2 III–18) which has caused some confusion about the status of *katalepsis*, but once we keep in mind a point about Stoic metaphysics we can see that Arcesilaus is just being mischievous. As nominalists, the Stoics denied the real existence of species and genera, e.g. 'animal'. There are human beings, of course, and bluebirds and shrews and so on, but once you have enumerated all the particular animals there is no further thing, 'animal', like a Platonic Form of Animal or the genus of animals, over and above the particular animals— 'animal' is a mere name. Using this Stoic doctrine against the Stoics, Arcesilaus argued that there was no such thing as *katalepsis*, because the Stoics themselves agreed that every instance was either an instance of knowledge, if it occurred in a wise man, or an instance of opinion, if in a Fool, 'and beyond those there is nothing else other than that they share a mere name'. (Long and Sedley do not seem to capture the point of the nominalist tu quoque when they translate 'and there is no further variation except a purely verbal one'.) This is a typically charming and clever move on Arcesilaus' part—especially the high Platonic fillip of using *metalambanô*, a word for sharing/participating in a Form—but it neither makes deep problems for the Stoics, nor shows us anything deep about their epistemology.

3. Frede (1983), 170 notes that Stoics will sound skeptical for another reason: in light of their claim that there are no Sages among us, they must also conclude that there is no knowledge among us. It is part of the Stoic picture that none of us—and none of the school's teachers, either—really knows anything. They insist that knowledge is possible—to that extent they are not skeptics—but they deny that any of us know the things that we commonly claim to know.

4. This raises a question: why is there no record of a Skeptical attack on the possibility of strong assent? After all, the existence of strong assent is just as necessary for knowledge as the existence of a *kataleptic* impression—indeed, the possibility of strong assent is exactly equivalent to the possibility of the Sage (since all and only Sages have strong assents). I suspect that this is the right way to understand Carneades' line of attack in his introduction of the impression that is 'undiverted and thoroughly explored' (SE *AM* 7.166–184 = LS 69D, 69E = IG2 III–18). The features that he is packing into these descriptions of impressions are more properly thought as features of the agent's assent or disposition to assent.

5. On the 'inactivity' argument see Plutarch *Adv. Coll.* 1122A–F = LS 69A = IG2 III–12.

6. *DL* 7.177 and Athenaeus 354E = *SVF* I.624, I.625 = LS 40F = IG2 II–1.

7. *SE AM* 8.409–410 = *SVF* 2.85 = LS 27E.

8. That the passage about the drill-sergeant in Sextus applies to *kataleptic* impressions is made clear a few sections earlier in *SE AM* 8. 405–406.

9. About my scale model of the Eiffel Tower we can certainly say that it has some of its features 'because' the Eiffel Tower has the corresponding features, and that it is shaped 'in accordance with' the Eiffel Tower. But after we have said all of that, we can also say something more about the model, namely who or what actually gave it that shape (e.g. the human model-maker). In the case of impressions that are modeled after propositions, what causal agent does the modeling? It is hard to see what the Stoics can say here. The problem is somewhat analogous to Aristotle's complaint about Plato's incorporeal forms, that they do a tolerable job as paradigms for individuals, but cannot do the job of being moving causes (e.g. *Metaphysics* 1. 991a8). Thanks to Brad Inwood for reminding me that the Stoics—or our sources—come up short here.

7

Impulses and Emotions

There is an old tradition—clearly articulated already in Aristotle—of describing human rationality as a two-fold thing.[1] On the one hand, there is the kind of rationality involved in how we acquire and manage our beliefs and knowledge. Here, we consider such questions as whether we reason soundly or jump to a false conclusion; whether we proportion our beliefs to our evidence, or instead cling passionately to hypotheses for which we have little or no evidence.

The second kind of rationality involves action, and here the questions involve whether we employ effective means of accomplishing the goals we set for ourselves, whether we say one thing but do another, whether we give up things that we truly value for the easy attainment of trivialities, and so on. This second kind of rationality is called 'practical rationality'—that is, the rationality that we manifest in our practices, in how we act and behave; the first is called 'theoretical rationality', that is, the rationality of our theorizing, of our beliefs and knowledge, independently of any practical application they may have. The delusional patient who thinks that chocolate bars are really time bombs planted by space aliens manifests an extreme theoretical irrationality; the more common neurotic who thinks that chocolate bars are unhealthy but cannot stop eating them manifests a typical practical irrationality.

In these terms, we have so far only been discussing the psychology that corresponds to theoretical rationality, that is, the psychology of belief and knowledge, without regard to action. But we are now in a position to be able to consider the psychological sources of action. What is going on in someone's mind when they undertake an intentional action, whether something grave like pulling a trigger, or something nearly unconscious like walking across the room? For it to be an intentional action, it must be possible to give some account of what was in the agent's mind when they were doing it, what they meant to achieve by doing it, and so on. Before turning to the Stoics' own view, I want to offer a brief sketch of an alternative view that has strong roots in the history of philosophy (it looks somewhat like Aristotle, as well as somewhat like Hume), and which also appeals to many people, philosophers and non-philosophers alike, as a plausible and common-sense view.

This is the idea that intentional action is to be explained as the outcome of two things, combined in a certain way: a desire, and a belief. For instance, if we ask why Fred lifted his mug, then the answer comes in three parts: (a) Fred had a desire, in this case a desire for a sip of coffee; (b) Fred had a belief, in this case the belief that there was a mug in front of him that contained coffee; (c) Fred's belief and desire were simultaneously present to Fred, and combined with one another in such a way as to lead Fred to lift the mug. Given his desire for a sip of coffee, and given his belief about the contents of the mug, it seemed to him that the most salient and efficient means of satisfying his desire was to lift his mug to his lips.

Note that we are not only offering an explanation of Fred's behavior—that is, a story that helps us to understand why Fred is in charge of his actions and not acting mechanically or in a crazy way. We are also making a claim about what actually caused him to do what he did, that is, what was happening in his mind, prior to his lifting the mug, that played some kind of causal role in the lifting of the mug. He lifted it to his lips *because* he wanted a sip of coffee, and believed

Impulses and Emotions ~ 83

there was some in the mug. On the other hand, we are not making a claim about some sort of explicit or conscious sequence of thoughts that he had. There may be some cases in which agents consciously reflect on their desires, consciously survey the environment and catalogue the available means to satisfying them, and then work through a sort of internal argument, with sub-vocalized premisses and conclusions echoing in their heads. But that is surely the less common case, and the lack of explicit thought in the more common case is no bar to the correctness of the analysis, even as an account of psychology. Fred may never register the thought 'I believe there is coffee in this mug' before he lifts it, but if he accidentally sips some chicken bullion and then spits it out, he will explain his action by saying (amid the splutters) 'I thought there was *coffee* in that mug!' This analysis depends so little on the antecedent presence of conscious thought that it seems equally applicable to animal behavior, over a broad range of cases. The squirrel wants nuts, and thinks there are some in the lunch-bag on the park-bench; that is why it is foraging in the bag. In giving this analysis of the squirrel's behavior, we are not supposing that it has any ability whatsoever to think thoughts 'out loud' as it were. But we nevertheless think that something like desires, and something like beliefs, are active in the animal; at the very least, it acts on internal drives that it satisfies in accordance with the information it acquires about its environment.

In Aristotle's discussion of practical rationality, he rightly notes that desire and belief must be synthesized and integrated with one another in the proper way—if the two never join hands, as it were, no action will emerge. In addition to an itchy flank, and the perceptual awareness of a rough-hewn fence-post, the cow must so to speak see the post *as* a handy flank-scratcher, or feel the itch as a yearning towards *that* rough surface. If the desire remains entirely general—a sense of unease that has no idea of its satisfaction—or the belief remains entirely particular—such-and-such object at such-and-such location, but with no conception of the uses to which it might be put—then the action will not ensue. Aristotle compares this situation to what is needed in the case of theoretical reason to convert two beliefs into an argument whose conclusion is a third belief. As detective stories like to point out, it is not sufficient merely to have all of the necessary facts; in order to draw the right conclusion, you must also see that two of them go together in a certain way. You can see the outline of the puzzle-piece, and see the gap in the puzzle, and still not see that they fit together; you need the further experience of having the picture snap into focus, of seeing this piece *as* the filler for that gap, of seeing this fact *as* the key to that mystery. Only then do you get the conclusion, when you have synthesized (=put together) the premises in the right way. On the other hand, Aristotle does not introduce a third mental entity to stand for the synthesis of belief and desire. According to his discussion, when belief and desire interact in the right way, what arises is not another thought, but the action itself.

There is something to be said for his approach; if one introduces a third item, it may seem that we will need to introduce a fourth, and then a fifth, and on and on without ever reaching the action itself.[2] Fred's desire for coffee by itself does not lead to action, that much seems clear. But then suppose that Fred sees the mug, and by synthesizing his desire for the coffee with his belief about the mug's contents he comes up with a third, synthetic judgment that combines the belief and the desire, something like 'here is some of the very thing I've been desiring'. Aristotle may have been concerned that even then a gap might yawn between thought and action; what is to stop Fred from having that synthetic thought and still not acting? That third thought might need to be synthesized with a further thought, like 'if this in front of me is the very thing that I've been desiring, then I should reach for it'. But then even the product of those two thoughts might reveal a gap: once one thinks, 'so, I should reach for it,' what guarantee is there that one *does* reach for it? Thoughts might lead to more thoughts, without ever leading to the action itself.

To avoid this sort of never-ending regress, we must assume that there is some last mental event that immediately precedes, and is the sufficient cause of, the ensuing action. This is Aristotle's way, and it is also the Stoics' way. However, the Stoics give this last event the form of a belief, where Aristotle felt it important to deny that it looks like a further belief. The Stoic name for the immediate mental antecedent of a voluntary action is 'impulse' or *hormê*; their doctrine of practical rationality and the psychology of action is all a matter of providing details about the nature of impulses.

Here again I should say a word about what I do and don't mean by 'impulse', prior to giving the Stoic definition. The major cautionary note to be entered is that the English word frequently conveys either a sense of groundlessness and whimsicality in one's action, or on the other hand a suggestion of vehemence and psychological compulsion. The first is common in talking of an 'impulse purchase', or in saying that one did something on a mere impulse; the second is featured when we discuss someone's violent or anti-social impulses, i.e. powerful and dominating drives that exercise a nearly irresistible force in the agent's mind. None of this should be read into the Stoic discussion of impulse; although they will agree that some impulses are whimsical and others compulsive, they will be equally willing to speak of impulses that are non-whimsical (well-reasoned, steady and deliberate, say) and impulses that are non-compelling. Of course, every impulse is compelling in one sense; if you have it, then you act (thus in Stoic terms impulses are not the sort of thing that one can suppress; where we might say that you suppressed an impulse, they would say instead that your mental state never amounted to an impulse). But if it is ever possible to act calmly, diffidently, and with a roughly equal readiness to act on the opposite course, then this action too stems from an impulse. Indeed, every intentional action stems from an impulse; once again, 'impulse' is just the Stoic name for the event that takes place in the mind and gives rise to (and at least partly constitutes) an intentional action—it is, as it were, the psychological side of intentional action.

Now we can give the definition:

> An impulse is a belief that attributes a certain kind of
> value to the agent's own potential action.

An example will help: the impulse behind Fred's reaching for the mug is the belief 'it would be a good thing for me to have a sip of this coffee right now'. The resemblance to the desire/belief model should be clear; the belief-content is captured by locating the action in the agent's own immediate environment (me, this, now), and the desire-content is captured by the evaluative judgment that the action would be a *good* one (though as we will see, this is not the only evaluative judgment that can produce action). To this extent, the Stoic impulse looks a great deal like the synthetic conclusion that Aristotle envisions but does not name. The Stoic impulse is not like an Aristotelian desire; it is not a mere inclination or drive, waiting around for information about the environment to provide it with effective satisfaction. The impulse is completely sufficient, by itself, to produce immediate action.

Now previous chapters have shown us that beliefs themselves are amenable to analysis on the Stoic doctrine; every belief is an assent to an impression. So we can also offer this definition of an impulse:

An impulse is an assent to an impression of a certain kind,
i.e. an impression that attributes a certain kind of value to
the agent's own potential action.

For convenience we can abbreviate the description of the impression and say:

An impulse is an assent to an evaluative impression.

The Stoics also had a special term for the impressions involved in impulses; they called them, naturally enough, 'impulsive impressions'. Since impulses are assents, impulses are events; mental events. And another Stoic characterization of impulse brings out that aspect, by saying that an impulse is a movement of the mind towards something. The thing that it is a movement *towards*, however, is not quite the object of the assent. What I assent to is an impression (or proposition) as a whole, for example, 'it would be a good thing for me to have a sip of this coffee right now'. What my mind moves towards, in making that assent, is the potential action mentioned inside the proposition, which in this case is something like 'to have a sip of this coffee right now'.[3] It is mentioned in the form of a predicate-clause, or *katêgorêma*, represented as a verbal-phrase in the infinitive, that is, 'to do such and such'; several texts tell us that all impulses are directed towards such predicates.[4]

To learn more about impulses, we should examine the varieties and kinds of impulses there are. To begin with, the Stoics will countenance both true and false impulses. In one sense, this is not surprising, inasmuch as impulses are beliefs, that is, assents to impressions, and beliefs and impressions are the sorts of things that can be true or false.[5] But in another way it seems very odd. Fred's impulse to pick up the mug caused him to pick up the mug; but what could be true or false about that impulse? It might be inconsiderate, or well timed, or graceful, but in what way could it be false? We might suppose that the possibility of falsehood enters with the belief-like portion of the impulse: a false impulse would be, for example, one in which Fred identifies this thing here as a mug of coffee, when it is actually beef consommé. But this does not seem to be the Stoics' main point in saying that impulses can be true or false. I do not deny that the Stoics might have classified a case like the coffee/consommé mistake as a false impulse; that is consistent with the evidence. However, the emphasis in the evidence shows that when the Stoics think of impulses as true or false, it is the desire-like portion that they are referring to. What is true or false about Fred's impulse to pick up the coffee is his evaluative judgment, that his picking up the mug right now is a *good* thing to do.

Here we must cross an intellectual divide in order to appreciate the Stoic view. Because of the influence of Hume's views on psychology, it is very natural among both philosophers and non-philosophers to suppose that to the extent that impulses are like desires, they cannot be the kinds of things that are true or false. One either has a desire or one does not; in neither case can it be said that what one has or lacks is either true or false. Hume argued this by claiming that desires, unlike beliefs, do not represent the world as being a certain way, do not make the kind of claim that could be correct or incorrect. Instead desires are, in his terms 'original existences'; they are not copies or images derived from the world that could be assessed as accurate or inaccurate by comparison to it. Hume argued further that there was really no way for reason to offer any sort of assessment of the desire itself. Given that the agent already has the desire, reason might assess the appropriateness of a plan for satisfying it; it might estimate the likelihood of success or the efficiency of the means. But as to whether one should have this desire or not have it, or have this one or a different one in its stead, reason was incapable of judging; any desire is just as reasonable as any other.

I doubt that anyone in antiquity held this view; it is, at the very least, clear that the Stoics did not.[6] Their whole understanding of impulses is built around the idea that every impulse *does* embody a representation, in the heart of the desire-like portion of the impulse, which makes a claim about how things are, and thus can be assessed as true or false. Like most ancient philosophers, the Stoics assume that there are facts about which things are good or bad; thus when Fred believes that a sip of coffee would be good, his belief is fully amenable to rational assessment (it turns out to be false). As noted earlier, the Stoics thought that there is nothing really good except virtue, and nothing really bad except vice. Thus all of the things we normally desire and fear—health and sickness, chocolates and spiders, fame and humiliation, life and death—all of these things are really indifferent, neither good nor bad. Thus our desires for them, or fears of them, insofar as they attribute goodness or badness to the objects we desire or fear, are all uniformly false. And ditto for the pleasure that we feel after winning the lottery, or the pain that we feel on being dismissed from our job.

From the fact that impulses can be true and false, we may be led to inquire whether they can be *kataleptic*; as I suggested in an earlier chapter, the answer is surely 'yes'. Indeed, just as all impulses are beliefs, so some of these impulses will constitute (bits of or episodes of) knowledge. These are the Sage's impulses; they are each true, *kataleptic*, and knowledgeable assessments of the value of a course of action.

Considered merely as beliefs, then, impulses fall into the groups that we observed earlier in relation to belief; there are the false and

Impulses and Emotions ~ 89

the true, with *katalepsis* as a subset of true belief, and knowledge as a subset of *katalepsis*. Every impulse, like every belief, is either an episode of knowledge (in the Sage), or an episode of opinion (in the non-Sage). The Sage, we might say, *knows* what he is doing, and especially the *value* of what he is doing, while the non-Sage knows neither.

But we can also divide up impulses less along the lines of epistemology, and more along the lines of evaluation, by looking at the content of impulses. There is practically no limit to the contents that a belief can have—one can believe, as it were, anything about anything. But most of those beliefs would not be the sort that could ever constitute an impulse. I believe that four is an even number—but what action could this belief impel me to undertake? I think Kansas is further west than Maryland—but by itself, this thought does not move me. On the other hand, there are other thoughts that seem more likely to lead to some action. These are the ones that depict an action that I could perform, for example, taking a hot shower, and claim that, for one reason or another, that is the thing for me to do, or that is what I should do.

The 'should' here is not meant to mark anything specially moral or preachy; it merely represents the practical analogue of assent in the theoretical case. In theoretical beliefs, I have an impression that represents things in a certain way, and my assent is something like my saying to myself, 'yeah, that's the way things are'. In the practical case, I have an image of myself taking a hot shower, and I think, 'yeah, that's what I should do'. Maybe it strikes me as something pleasurable, or something healthful, or something required by social etiquette, but for one reason or another, it seems like the thing to do. That is the core content that makes an impulsive impression what it is; it represents a course of action as the thing for me to do. Assenting to that impression means having the impulse, and acting.

When the Stoics set about detailing particular classes of impulses, the class that they tell us most about is the one that they also tell us we should not have: the class of passions, or emotions, as they are usually called. There are four main emotions on the Stoic account, usually given the names pleasure, pain, desire, and fear. These in turn have sub-species, and the Stoics seem to have delighted in detailing, for example, the kinds of fear one can suffer (hesitation, superstition, bashfulness, panic, and a dozen or so more).

The names are potentially misleading; in English 'fear' is the name of an emotion, but 'pleasure' and 'pain' are usually the names of physical sensations, and 'desire' seems more like a kind of motivation than like an emotion per se (some sorts of desires may carry an emotional coloration, for example, yearning, but others seem more businesslike). Part of the job of making sense of the Stoic picture can be done by choosing translations that make the Stoic 'emotions' sound more like emotions: while 'pain' and 'pleasure' are traditional translations, it might be more useful to speak of 'dejection' and 'joy', since these correctly emphasize the mental over the physical. Another part of the job should be done by agreeing that what the Stoics are discussing is something more like motivations than emotions; their treatment of fear puts it in parallel to desire, by focusing less on how it feels, and more on the fact that it makes you avoid or flee from something, just as desire makes you pursue or go towards something. It is worth saying again that all of the items we are now calling 'emotions' are, on the Stoic view, a subset of impulses: thus they are mental events that immediately eventuate in an intentional action. This puts the topic at some distance from our normal talk of emotions, since some of those have no intrinsic propensity to produce actions of any kind. Thus Stoic 'emotions' do not include things like what it feels like to stub your toe—neither we nor they would call that an 'emotion'—but they do include such things as drives and aversions, which we might not usually call 'emotions'. And while we might include certain feeling-tones like sunniness or gloominess as emotions, even if they do not produce any action, the Stoics will exclude them as ineffectual. What does not lead to action is not an impulse, and so not an emotion.

But at some point this line of thought should provoke a question about why the Stoics employed the vocabulary of emotions at all, if they had so little interest in the phenomenology of emotions—why

Impulses and Emotions ~ 91

use the word 'emotion' to begin with, and why use dozens of other words that can only be translated 'jealousy', 'longing', 'cheerfulness', 'rage', and so on, if the qualitative phenomena are of no interest?[7] After all, the inclination to associate emotions with characteristic patterns of introspectible qualia is not merely a modern preoccupation; it is already a thought in Homer that wrath is sweeter than dripping honey.[8] What justifies the Stoics in identifying wrath with a characteristic belief, rather than with a characteristic drippy sweetness?

Here it may help to keep in mind a general Stoic view that identifies reality with causal efficacy.[9] Only things that can act or be acted upon can be truly said to be or exist; and although the primary consequence of this view is a restriction of 'being' to bodies, I am inclined to think that the view plays a role in this context as well. Alongside the causal criterion for existence, which states that only causal agents really exist, we may posit a predicative version of the principle, that only the causally-F agent is really F, that is, that what is really F is whatever plays the role that F plays when F is invoked in causal contexts. On the Stoic view, the proper signification of the term 'winter', for instance, turns out to be not a period or length of time, but a causal agent: winter is the air above the earth, cooled because of the distancing of the sun.[10] This is to award proper ownership of the term to the entity that explains the causal claims we make in using the term. When we say 'it's winter now', no causal claim is made, but when we say, 'the winter has killed my fruit-trees' it is very plausible to claim that it is the chilled air to which we are referring.

In the case of the emotions, then, the Stoics would have felt justified in saying that 'wrath' properly denominates a certain belief, rather than a certain feeling-tone, because it is the belief that provides the explanation in claims like 'his wrath led him to strike his friend'. By contrast, the sweet or drippy kind of wrath, and the way that emotions feel in general, would be seen as causal dead-ends, and so not deserving of the names. This view can also be seen in the Stoic view that the proper signification of 'pleasure' is a certain belief; it is the belief that motivates and causes. The Stoics need not deny that pleasure typically feels like something; they simply claim that the feeling-tone doesn't do any work, and so does not deserve the name. Of course, the feeling-tone might be made the object of a further belief, and that further belief might lead to action—my awareness that I feel a sort of agreeable buoyancy in my chest might lead me to think (falsely) that I am in a good condition, and this might eventuate in the belief that the Stoics call 'pleasure'. But the Stoics will still claim that the buoyant feeling by itself is causally impotent; no action will ensue unless some belief is formed. It is easy to see how this view that physical feelings are essentially inert, having no tendency to produce action when considered apart from beliefs they might figure in, could lead to the view that even physical torture has no particular power to produce action in its victims, provided that they can regulate their beliefs.

Even after we are done adjusting different portions of the picture to try to get translations to fit preconceptions, we will find that there is still room for puzzlement about how exactly the Stoics conceived of what they called emotions, and also how they might have conceived of what *we* call emotions. We will turn to that after getting a better picture of the Stoic theory—but for the sake of convenience, and of conformity with other literature on the topic, I will continue referring to them as the four 'emotions', and continue giving them the conventional names 'pleasure', 'pain', 'desire', and 'fear'.

Here the best way to proceed is to present the Stoics' definitions of the four emotions:

Desire is the opinion that some future thing is a good of such a sort that we should reach out for it.
Fear is the opinion that some future thing is an evil of such a sort that we should avoid it.
Pleasure is the opinion that some present thing is a good of such a sort that we should be elated about it.
Pain is the opinion that some present thing is an evil of such a sort that we should be depressed about it.

Note, to begin with, that all four are said to be opinions—either weak assents, or assents to non-*kataleptic* impressions (whether false or true). Note also that two of the emotions deal with opinions about the future (desire and fear), and two deal with opinions about the present (pleasure and pain); two are opinions about goods (desire and pleasure), and two are opinions about evils or bad things (fear and pain). Obviously, these four emotions are the result of combining two dichotomies, of time (present/future) and value (good/bad). Thus they can be represented graphically as the four quadrants of a square, as shown in the graph below.

		Emotions	
		Good	Bad
Times	Present	Pleasure	Pain
	Future	Desire	Fear

Each of the definitions also falls into two halves; one that gives us more of the evaluative content, and one that specifies the action. Insofar as it is a belief, the object of my assent is the whole impression, with emphasis on the evaluative content (is my taking a sip a *good* thing? yeah, that's what it is); insofar as it is an impulse, it also specifies an action that the impulse is directed *towards* (sip the coffee—yeah, that's the thing for me to do). Thus alongside of the full definitions, we also find the Stoics offering two kinds of abbreviated definitions, which emphasize respectively the opinion-like side of the emotion, or the action-like side of the emotion:

Opinion–Definitions:	Action–Definitions:
Desire is the opinion of a future good	Desire is an irrational reaching-out
Fear is the opinion of a future evil	Fear is irrational avoidance
Pleasure is the opinion of a present good	Pleasure is irrational elation
Pain is the opinion of a present evil	Pain is irrational depression

The action–definitions may seem to introduce something new: the notion of irrationality. But this was already contained in the full definitions, and it is also contained in the opinion–definitions, by the very specification that the emotions are all a form of *opinion*. The Sage never opines, and having an opinion is always a form of irrationality in one way or another. Either one is assenting to the wrong sort of impression (a false or potentially misleading one), or one is assenting from a weak and unstable disposition. In other words, you assent, but you are also disposed to assent to things that are actually in contradiction with what you are assenting to now. Your total stock of belief-dispositions is inconsistent and chaotic, just waiting for the right event to come along and shove it into open incoherence. That is why all emotions are irrational, according to the Stoics. This is well illustrated by a passage from Epictetus, in which he contrasts the Sage's non-emotional affection with the non-Sage's irrational emotion:

Only the Sage can love anyone. 'How's that?' you say, 'for I'm no Sage, but I love my son all the same!' . . . But did you never see puppies fawning over one another, playing and tumbling together so that you say 'what could be more affectionate?' Do you want to get a good sense of their affection? Just throw a hunk of meat in the middle and you'll find out. You and your son—just throw a chunk of property between you, or a pretty girl you both love, and you'll find out how quickly he is willing to see you in your grave, and you're praying for him to die.

(*Epictetus* 2.22.3–11)

The father says that he wants to help his son; he even believes (opines) that it would be good for him to help his son, and thus he has an emotion. But because he also believes that money and sex are good things, he cannot keep a firm grasp on his benevolent attitude towards his son; at any moment, the right temptation will make him assent to the thought that it would really be a good thing if he were to get rid of his son once and for all. The father's desire to help his son is an emotion, an irrational striving towards something that appears good to him; but so is the father's desire for this piece of property, for this pretty girl. The thought that money or sex is a good thing is surely false, on the Stoic view; the thought that it would be a good

Impulses and Emotions ~ 95

thing to help his son is not clearly a false one on their view (we'll need to look more closely later) but it is still an irrational one to the extent that the assent which constitutes this belief arises from a tumultuous mind, full of conflicting pulls and pushes, beset by unclarities about the real nature of what is good.

When the agent has an impulse that labels something 'good', it is quite clear that the Stoics mean that he thinks of it as something good for himself. Likewise, when he thinks of something as an evil, or as bad, he thinks that it is bad *for himself*. And both of these thoughts can be put more generally by saying that the agent is thinking that the object in question will make a difference for the agent's own happiness. When I want a new car, when I think it would be a good thing for me to get a new car, I do so because I think it will make me happier. I think it will make a difference to my happiness. But the Stoics deny that anything other than virtue and vice can make a difference to your happiness in this way. Only virtue and vice are truly good or bad; the rest are completely indifferent.

The most common sense in which emotions are irrational, then, is that they are false. Most of the desires that animate people most of the time—the desires for money, sex, reputation, property, and so on—are all false, inasmuch as they claim that these things are really good when in fact they are completely indifferent. But even if an emotion involved a true evaluative judgment, that is, attributing goodness to something that is really good, it would still be irrational, given that it involved weak and vacillating assent.[11]

When we looked at a completely general sketch of a non-Stoic psychology above, we saw that we could explain all intentional action in terms of two elements, belief and desire. If desire now turns out to be necessarily irrational, is *all* human action irrational? No, because the 'desire' that we are now defining as a Stoic emotion is not the same as the 'desire' that we invoked earlier in offering a non-Stoic general account of human action. Or, to put it differently, the Stoics think that 'desire' in the sense of an irrational opinion is only one species of the general motivating force that we earlier referred to as 'desire' in sketching out the desire/belief model. One can be motivated to go for something, in the Stoic view, without having an irrational opinion of the sort that the Stoics condemn.

This is good news for Sages, of course—it means that they can perform intentional actions in the world without becoming irrational. It is also good news for non-Sages, because it means that we can set about avoiding emotions, without thereby being reduced to inactivity. There is a way for us to view our activities, and to conceive of the world around us, that will allow us to be motivated to continue with our daily lives, while not drawing us further into the trap of emotions.

The key point is that the emotions form only one class of impulses; there are two other classes that are not emotions. Since emotions are opinions about what is good or bad—that is, typically false, and invariably irrational—it is not surprising that there is another class of impulses that consists in episodes of knowledge about what is good and bad. The non-Sage has the thought that some money, for instance, is a good thing and that he should go towards it. But money is not a good thing; virtue is the only thing that is truly good. When the Sage has the thought that virtue is a good thing, and that he should go towards it, his impulse has almost the same structure as the emotion of desire, but it has none of the objectionable features of the emotion. It does not make a mistaken evaluation—it does not attribute genuine goodness to something that is actually indifferent. And it does not involve a weak assent; the Sage's stock of belief-dispositions is so coherent that no new evidence or argument could ever cause the Sage to withdraw his assent to the claim that virtue is a good. Thus, the Sage can go for virtue, can be motivated to pursue virtue, without having an emotion.

Impulses of this kind—true, knowledgeable, attributions of goodness and badness to the only things that are truly good and bad—were given a special name in the Stoic theory: *eupatheiai* (*eupatheia* in the singular). There are three of them, volition, caution, and joy, and we frequently see them defined as follows:

> Volition is rational reaching-out
> Caution is rational avoiding
> Joy is rational elation

These are clearly reminiscent of the shorter, action-definitions of desire, fear, and pleasure, except that the *eupatheiai* are all rational, where the emotions were all irrational: those emotions are, as it were, the evil twin brothers of these three *eupatheiai*. Because of that parallelism, we can feel some confidence in supposing that the Stoics will have accepted parallel full definitions as follows:

Volition is the knowledge that some future thing is a good of such a sort that we should reach out for it.
Caution is the knowledge that some future thing is a bad thing of such a sort that we should avoid it
Joy is the knowledge that some present thing is a good of such a sort that we should be elated at it.

The fact that there is no *eupatheia* that is analogous to pain follows from the fact that vice is the only thing that is truly bad, and that the Sage has no vice. Thus a Sage could never think (much less know) that there was something bad present to him. The Sage may be confronted with starvation, humiliation, torture, and so on, but the Sage will never feel that anything actually *bad* is happening to him, since those things are not really bad. Something bad really *would* be present to him if he acquired some vice, but as a Sage he is free from vice. Thus there is never a reason for the Sage to feel depressed or downcast, and so there is no way to feel 'rational depression'. But Sages are aware of their own virtue, and feel joy at it; they can direct their efforts towards maintaining their virtue in the future, and thus exercise volitions; and they can take steps to avoid becoming vicious in the future, which means being cautious.

Some of the Sage's actions are motivated by *eupatheiai*—the ones in which they are interacting with virtue and vice themselves. But if that were the only alternative to emotions, then it would leave the rest of us non-Sages in the lurch. Only Sages can have *eupatheiai*, since only they can have knowledge of anything; the rest of us cannot have them.

Thus it is important to recognize that the Stoics admitted a third kind of impulse, separate from emotions and *eupatheiai*, which I will call 'selections'. (In fact that name is properly applied only to half of the category, namely those that are like desires in making us go for things. The other half, which are like fears in making us avoid things, are more precisely called 'disselections', but no harm is done by referring to both selections and disselections under the common name 'selections'.) Selections differ from either emotions or *eupatheiai*, because they do not involve our attributing goodness or badness to the objects or actions in question. Instead, they involve looking at an indifferent thing in the future, and judging accurately that it is indifferent, but judging also that given the nature of the object and our situation there is still some reason to go for it or avoid it. For instance, Sages do not think that food is a good thing; it is merely indifferent. Still, on the whole there is some reason to eat it, connected to the fact that there is some reason to keep up one's health, and in general to behave in the way that we seemed designed by nature to behave. If there were some special circumstance at work in this case, then the Sage might not go for the food—in some special cases, after all, the Sage not only does not attempt to preserve his health, he even takes active steps to kill himself. But absent any special circumstances, the thing to do is to maintain one's health, to go for food, to avoid getting hit by cars, and so on. So the Sage can have impulses whose contents are represented in the following definitions:

Selection is the belief that some future thing is an indifferent of such a sort that we should reach out for it.
Disselection is the belief that some future thing is an indifferent of such a sort that we should avoid it.

Note that I have used the term 'belief' in these definitions; I do so in order to make the definitions apply both to knowledge and to opinion, both to Sages and to non-Sages. Now the Sage's beliefs are not opinions; they are all episodes of knowing something. So definitions of the Sages' selections would be more precise about the kind of belief they have:

The Sage's selection is the knowledge that some future thing is an indifferent of such a sort that he should reach out for it.

The Sage's disselection is the knowledge that some future thing is an indifferent of such a sort that he should avoid it.

But non-Sages can also have beliefs that constitute selections, although theirs fall short of knowledge and so are opinions:

The non-Sage's selection is the opinion that some future thing is an indifferent of such a sort that he should reach out for it.
The non-Sage's disselection is the opinion that some future thing is an indifferent of such a sort that he should avoid it.

The non-Sage can have, and act on, selections and disselections of this sort. When he does, he is not having an emotion. But he is still experiencing an impulse, a motivation, which can lead him to act in the world. Thus the non-Sage can avoid emotions, but still perform actions, because of the possibility of selection.

If we look at the impulses of a Sage, then, we will find two kinds: *eupatheiai*, that orient the Sage towards true goods and bads, and selections and disselections, that allow the Sage to navigate unemotionally through the world of indifferents, doing on every occasion what it is reasonable to do. If we look at the impulses of a non-Sage, we will find that they, too, come in two kinds: emotions, which are mistaken beliefs about what is really good and bad, and selections which differ from the Sage's selections only in failing to be real instances of knowledge.

Ethical progress comes largely through the replacement of emotions by selections. Prior to studying Stoicism, we are emotionally driven towards many things. We imagine a sumptuous dinner, and think it would be a really good thing to have; then if an accident prevents us from enjoying it, we think we have really missed out on something good. We think it would be terrible if we lost our job, and we live in fear of getting cancer, because it strikes us as a pretty bad thing. All of these thoughts need to be replaced. We must approach the dinner without any thought that it is really a good thing. True, there is some reason still to take steps to eat some food—we will see later why it is a rational thing to do—but we should pursue it with the full awareness that it is indifferent to our real happiness and well-being. We should also take steps to avoid getting cancer, if we can, but not because it would be a bad thing if we got it. We replace desire with selection, and replace fear with disselection, always keeping in mind that the things that we are most inclined to fear or want are really only indifferents, really have no effect whatsoever on our happiness or misery.

If we rid ourselves of desire and fear, does that rid us of emotions? Not yet, since there are two other emotions, pleasure and pain. These two have no correlative selections; there are no impulses that one should have in place of pleasure and pain, as one should have selections and disselections in place of desire and fear. We should rid ourselves of pleasure and pain, and replace them with genuine indifference—no impulse at all. When we win the lottery, we should not believe that a good thing is present to us, and have the impulse to feel elated; on learning that we have cancer, we should not believe that a bad or terrible thing is present to us, and have the impulse to feel downcast or depressed. Instead, we should simply note that, whatever is present to us, it is a matter of indifference. If it is not virtue or vice, then it makes no contribution to our happiness or unhappiness. Thus there is really no impulse to have; there is nothing to feel about them, except mere indifference.

The Stoics make this clear by saying that the kind of value that indifferent things have is a value that matters only for choosing them or avoiding them, selecting them or disselecting them.[12] That means it is a value that they have only in prospect, only when considered as items in the future. Health has some of this value, and more of it than disease does; that's why, other things being equal, it is reasonable for me to select health. But the value it has might be called a sort of 'planning-value' only; it matters when we are making plans for the future, and disappears when the future becomes the present. It is reasonable for me to take steps today to maintain my health tomorrow, because my health tomorrow has more planning-value today than does my being sick tomorrow. But when it gets to be tomorrow, the 'pay-off' value of my health and sickness are the same: they are both completely indifferent. That is why I should feel exactly the same indifference tomorrow whether I wake up healthy or sick; there is nothing good or bad present to me that would justify elation or depression, and so no impulse of any kind is called for.

Progress in replacing emotions with selections is exactly the same thing as progress towards knowing the true value of things. I hear Epictetus saying that only virtue is good, and I believe him. But do I now know it? By no means; not as long as I keep on desiring money, desiring sex, desiring dozens of other things as though they were truly good. My desires show that my assent to the true Stoic view is still weak and unstable, that I don't really know the value of things. Starting from the first day I hear Epictetus, I begin strengthening and stabilizing my assent to what he says, by replacing my emotions with selections. The process of changing my individual impulses and the process of changing my disposition to have various impulses is one and the same process—as most ancient philosophers agreed, we learn to be virtuous by acting virtuously. Every time I refuse to assent to the impression that this promotion would be good for me, or that losing my sight would be bad for me, I am getting closer to knowing what I only weakly believe right now. Even after I have made so much progress that I have not had an emotion in weeks or months—so that I have greeted every indifferent thing with the indifference it deserves, and selected it or disselected it only as reason dictates—even then I do not yet *know* that only virtue is good. For it may be that my assent is still weak, and that if a great enough temptation were to befall me tomorrow I would succumb to it.

And what is a temptation? It is a persuasive appearance that something indifferent is really good or bad. When I am being tortured to tell where my friends are hiding, the temptation is the appearance that what is happening to me is really bad, that I am suffering horribly, that my life is being ruined. It is very persuasive; the thumbscrews and rack put pressure on my beliefs, and make me doubt what I heard from Epictetus. Pain is not bad, he told me, but it certainly *feels* bad right now. The impression that something horribly bad is being done to me, and that a halt to the torture would be incredibly good for me, is nearly overpowering in its persuasiveness.

If I assent to these impressions and formulate a belief, then my belief will probably result in my taking the action of betraying my friends. Resisting this temptation means reminding myself that having all of my limbs in working order is not a good thing, that losing my fingers is not a bad thing, that only virtuous behavior will really make me happy, here or anywhere. Or temptation comes in the overpowering impression of pleasure, in the impression that having sex with this stranger would be incredibly good for me, would make my life better and happier. The prospect of pleasure is persuasive, too, and it seems impossible to hang on to one's belief that pleasure is not really a good thing, when in the grips of desire.

But someone who really *knows* what is valuable has no trouble with any of these temptations. It doesn't take an 'effort of will'; if you are still making efforts to believe, then you clearly don't know it yet. Nor does it take 'strength of character', or 'strong moral fiber'—unless you mean by those things exactly what the Stoics mean, that is, a completely consistent and coherent set of beliefs, such that you have no latent beliefs that run contrary to what you firmly know. If you know that only virtue is good, and only vice is bad, then no torture or seduction can cause you to doubt it in the least. That's not a claim about a moral superman, that is just a claim about what knowledge is like. After all, if you consider something that you really know, you should find this a fairly plausible claim. I know that four is an even number; put me on the rack and see if you can get me to say something different. Or rather, see if you can get me to *believe* something different, for as to getting me to say things, that is an easy matter: threaten me with torture and I'll tell you it's odd, or purple, or anything else you want me to tell you—you can easily get me to believe that torture is bad. But can you as easily change my belief that four is even? Regardless of what I *say,* will I really stop believing that four is an even number, that I can take any four things and divide them into two groups of two, without anything left over? Torture or not, I don't see how I could ever think of four, think of dividing it into two even groups, and think that there will still be one left over. It's not that I am brave or heroic, it's just that this is

Impulses and Emotions ~ 103

something I *know*. And if I knew in the same way that only virtue is good—if it was just dead obvious to me, as four's evenness is—then no torture could make that fact look different, either. That is how it is for the Sage, who really knows the facts about value. But for me—well, as to what is really valuable in life, as to whether pain is bad or merely indifferent, on these matters I am far from knowledge.

Thus the person who is making progress towards virtue must practice and practice, until it is not only true that they *have* not had any emotions for some time, it is also true that they *would* not have any emotion, no matter what temptations they might encounter. Only then do they *know* what is valuable, when their assent is unshakably strong.

We can also define virtue and vice in these terms now:

Virtue is an unshakable and consistent disposition to assent only to kataleptic impulsive impressions
Vice is an incoherent and vacillating disposition to assent to impulsive impressions some of which are not kataleptic.[13]

Not only can we characterize virtue and vice in terms of the dispositions to assent, we can also see how to reduce the characterization of someone's mind to a matter of assent. When we are not thinking of Stoicism, it is natural to suppose that two people's minds can differ in any number of ways—in what they like, in whom they recognize, in how they learn, and so on. One person likes chocolate ice cream, another dislikes it; one knows the Gettysburg address by heart, the other does not. Within the Stoic theory, these all really amount to one sort of difference: a difference in one's disposition to give assents to impressions.

Imagine a class of machines that are distinguished by how they cause a tennis-ball to rebound when it is projected at them. The simplest machine of this class might be a single flat wall, like a practice wall; when the ball is thrown at it, it bounces back, in a relatively limited number of ways, according to relatively simple calculations of trajectory.[14] The next most complicated machine in this class might be a hand-ball court with one of four walls removed; when a tennis-ball is thrown into the court at different speeds, in different directions, it will exit out the back in ways that are predictable from the shape of the court, the number of surfaces it hits before leaving, and so on. And it is not only true that, if we know the configuration of the court, and the entry-conditions of the ball, then we can predict how it will exit. It's also the case that if we had an exhaustive list of entry-conditions and the resulting exit conditions, then we could determine that the simplest machine that could produce these results would be a machine of exactly this configuration, that is, a handball court.

Now we could imagine a two-player game in which one person secretly alters the inside of the hand-ball court by changing the angles of the walls, or installing partitions and baffles, and the other player has to guess the new configuration merely by bombarding the darkened court with tennis-balls and seeing how they rebound. This sort of game is played in reality by scientists of many kinds— those who attempt to understand the surface of a crystalline lattice by bombarding it with sub-atomic particles, for instance, or those who attempt to understand the metabolism of a cell by exposing it to a variety of nutrients and seeing what waste-products emerge. All of them are attempting to characterize a complex structure in terms of its characteristic responses to an array of external inputs or stimuli.

Stoic psychology conceives of the human mind as an assent-machine. In the handball court, both inputs and outputs are in terms of directions, trajectories, and velocities. In the mind, the inputs are impressions, and the outputs are only two: assent, or suspension. The difference between the greedy person and the one who cares little for money can be captured by providing a complete list of the kinds of impressions to which their assents would differ. The difference between someone who knows Cayley's Theorem in the algebra of permutations and someone who does not can be captured by the impressions to which they would assent. Here it is worth keeping in mind that the Stoic view is not that any difference in the contents of two people's minds *will* emerge during their lifetimes in a difference in their assents, or that mere coincidence of one or two assents proves similarity of contents between two minds, even over a small range of topics. For instance, you may have the impression that Cayley's theorem is true, and assent to that, whether or not you know what it says; thus the mere fact that your assent on that matter agrees with the assent of someone who knows Group Theory is no proof that you yourself know Group Theory. Two handball courts with very different arrangements may give equivalent returns for one or two lucky shots. But if you were to keep up the bombardment long enough, the differences would emerge. When the Stoics model the individual's entire mental contents in terms of differential dispositions to assent, they are imagining the results of an exhaustive process of testing, a hypothetical bombardment from all angles. Who you are, what you amount to, is a matter of how you would respond.

This Stoic habit of focusing on the disposition, and measuring it not by someone's actual responses to easy cases, but by their counter-factual responses to hard cases, led them to express their views in ways that were extreme and counter-intuitive. Some of these views came to be known quite early on as the 'Stoic Paradoxes',[15] and they appear frequently in the more popular treatments like those of Cicero and Epictetus.

When the Stoics say that all who are not Sages are insane, it is as though they were saying that all mud stinks. 'But it doesn't *always* stink', you say. Stir it with a stick; you'll smell it. So the hot-tempered person isn't always angry, but just stir him up and you'll see him in a rage.[16]

In some cases, it seems that the Stoics were needlessly courting misunderstanding; any appearance of paradox in saying that all non-Sages are raving lunatics could have been cleared up by saying that they are all prone to rave in the right circumstances. But in other cases, their insistence that we gauge the person by what they *would* do seems less paradoxical and more insightful—in choosing friends or employees, or in judging people's character, much of our interest in their past behavior stems from a larger interest in predicting how they will react to the whole range of possible future circumstances.

One's mind, then, is simply one's total disposition to assent. Epictetus refers to our mind in this sense as our *prohairesis*; this term applies equally to a virtuous mind or to a vicious one. One's *prohairesis* is one's total disposition to assent; when one becomes a Sage, one's *prohairesis* can be called one's virtue; prior to that, one's *prohairesis* may also be called one's vice (e.g., 'it was part of his vice that he was prone to anger').

There is another aspect to desire and fear that is relevant to the learner, according to Epictetus. This is the fact that these emotions make a sort of implicit promise in the mind of the person having them; they promise you success in getting what you want or in avoiding what you fear.[17] Desiring involves contemplating a future action you could take, and thinking of it as a good thing. It also involves some imaginative dwelling on what it will be like to possess what you want, some wishful thinking about how your life will be when you get it. You want a new car; you imagine what it will be like to drive it, what your friends will say when they see it, the vacation you will take with it that you couldn't take without it. Your view of the future more and more often includes the car as a component of your future life. This is what it is for a desire to promise you what you desire, and it is part of how emotions become entrenched in your thinking. It is also part of how intense desires and intense fears lead to intense pains when things do not turn out as you wish.

Thus part of your work as a student of Epictetus is actively to counter these promises, by reminding yourself that the future is uncertain. You must first replace your desire with a selection; and even as you set about pursuing the food that it is reasonable for you to eat, you must remind yourself that something may arise to prevent you from eating it. Epictetus refers to this as having your impulse 'with reservation'; when you select something, you should not promise yourself that you will get it, but only think 'I will get it, if nothing prevents my getting it', keeping in mind that you may get it, but that you also may not get it. The reservation is this 'if'-clause, through which you free yourself from the dangerous expectation set up by promising yourself success.

Sages also employ reservations, as a matter of course, because of their overall refusal to assent to anything that they cannot know, that is any impression that is not *kataleptic*.[18] The belief involved in a reservation is not a practical one—it is not an impulse of any kind, but a mere prediction about the future, and a highly cautious one at that. Since Sages never assent to anything that is not absolutely guaranteed to be true, they would never promise themselves the future attainment of something like food or health. They will pursue these things, when it is reasonable to do so, but with a full awareness that they may not get what they pursue.[19]

The future is uncertain; reservation is one of the devices that keep the Sage from having uncertain opinions about it. We should also keep in mind that Sages can have *kataleptic* impressions of non-perceptual propositions—for instance, they can have the completely secure and reliable impression that it is reasonable to pursue some action, or that it would be good to do it, or that the action has some planning-value. On the one hand, these are certainly not perceptual impressions, like seeing the mug in front of me; I cannot *see* or otherwise perceive the outcome of my actions, or even whether I shall be alive in a few minutes to continue with my endeavors. On the other hand, the truth of a belief like 'it would be reasonable for me to eat dinner tonight' does not depend on whether I actually succeed in eating the dinner, or even whether I remain alive tonight. The Sage has acquired a great deal of experience about the world and his place in it; he knows what sort of a creature he is, and what actions are reasonable for such a creature to take, in light of the various and shifting circumstances he may find himself in. From all of this knowledge of nature, he can actually *know* that it is reasonable to eat dinner tonight, and thus take steps to do so. If some new and unanticipated events occur that prevent him from eating his dinner, then this will not change the fact that it was reasonable, earlier, to pursue dinner. However, events may make it clear later on, say around dinner time, that it is no longer reasonable to pursue it, in which case the Sage will simply stop having the impulse to have dinner. Depending on what happens, he may even replace it with an impulse to fast, instead. This sort of reaction is illustrated in a passage from Chrysippus that Epictetus quotes:

So long as the future is uncertain to me, I always cling to the things that are more natural for attaining what is according to nature. For God himself fashioned me to select them. But if I knew now that it were fated for me to be ill, then I would even have an impulse towards being ill. For the foot, too, if it had any sense, would have an impulse towards getting muddy.[20]

The Sage can have a *kataleptic* impression that his health has more planning-value than his illness, and on that basis select future health. But, of course, he may still wake up ill. In that case, having learned that Zeus has some special instructions for him, he will no longer keep striving to be healthy just then. Nor will he have any other impulse towards the illness he finds himself with—he will treat it with indifference, as he would have treated his health, too. Someone who keeps wanting to be healthy when they learn that they are fated to be ill is only courting frustration, and also showing that they think they know better than Zeus does, what should happen in the world. But that is part of what desire does; by promising you that you will get what you want, it makes it hard for you to respond to reality when it doesn't go your way.

Thus Sages use reservation and attention to what is reasonable in order to remain in a state of knowledge about the world and their actions in it, which can also flexibly accommodate new events as they occur, including those new events that preclude the Sage's attaining the object of their earlier impulse. The Sage may not get dinner, but he will still retain his virtue, for he is constantly changing his impulses, updating them in response to new information about the plan of Zeus, trying to conform his will to the will of Zeus.

At the end of this chapter, we know what an impulse is, and what the three main kinds of impulse are: emotions, *eupatheiai*, and selections. We know what it means to say that emotions are irrational, and how we can continue acting and living effectively without emotions, whether or not we are Sages. We have seen how to characterize virtue and vice in terms of the agent's disposition to assent to impulses. To sum up this chapter, it may help to see three charts that show the relation between the four emotions, the three *eupatheiai*, and the two selections:

		Emotions		Eupatheiai		Selection	
		Good	Bad	Good	Bad	Preferred	Dispreferred
Times	Present	Pleasure	Pain	Joy	[none]	[none]	[none]
	Future	Desire	Fear	Volition	Caution	Selection	Disselection

NOTES

1. E.g. *Nicomachean Ethics* VI. 1–2.
2. Aristotle shows an interest in related problems of regress in theoretical argumentation in the Posterior Analytics, especially *PA* 1.3, but he does not explicitly address the concern about practical rationality that I mention here. If this is not a concern that Aristotle had, it is at least one that Simon Blackburn writes about in *Mind*, vol. 104, no. 416, October 1995, pp. 695–711. He is offering a practical paradox that is explicitly a variation on the theoretical paradox offered by Lewis Carrol in his classic paper 'What the Tortoise said to Achilles', *Mind* 1895, reprinted in *Mind* 1995.
3. Impulse = motion of soul towards something (*epi ti*) from Stobaeus 2.86 = *SVF* 3.169 = IG2 II–95.9, which also specifies that for humans it is a motion of the mind (*dianoia*) towards some action (*epi ti tôn en tôi prattein*). Stobaeus 2.88 = *SVF* 3.171 = LS 33I = IG2 II–95.9b tells us that every impulse is an assent, but that assents have one sort of thing as their object (propositions), whereas impulses are directed *towards* a different thing (predicates). I thank Brad Inwood and Jacques Brunschwig for discussions of this passage.

4. Stobaeus 2.97 = *SVF* 3.91 = LS 33J = IG2 II–95.11f; Stobaeus 2.88 = *SVF* 3.171 = LS 33I = IG2 II–95.9b.

5. 'Not surprising' but not entailed by the mere fact that impulses are beliefs and beliefs can be true or false. Ostriches are birds, and birds can weigh more or less than an ounce; it does not follow that ostriches can weigh more or less than an ounce. For all that has been said so far, the Stoics *might* have claimed that although impressions in general can be true or false, impulsive impressions are all uniformly true (or false).

6. Michael Frede has been arguing for some time that the Humean conception of reason and desire is completely out of place in antiquity. I think he is right to reject it as an anachronism, perhaps the most misleading one afoot among current critics of ancient philosophy. See Frede (1996) and (1999a).

7. For lists of such terms, see Andronicus *peri Pathôn* 2–5, excerpted at *SVF* 3.397, 3.401, 3.409, and 3.414. These paragraphs quote material from my Brennan (2003).

8. *Iliad*, 18.108–109.

9. E.g., *DL* 7.134 = *SVF* 2.300 = LS 44B = IG2 II–20.

10. *DL* 7.151 = *SVF* 2.693 = IG2 II–20. I borrow the translation, and the general line of thought (though not the application to emotions), from LS vol. 1.177 (they do not give it as a numbered fragment).

11. In Brennan (1998a) and (2003) I proposed that there may be a sub-class of emotions that involve true beliefs—'veridical emotions'—such as believing that my vice is a bad thing that I should flee. This could still count as a case of fear, and still be subject to the normal Stoic prohibition on emotions. Kamtekar (1998) considers the curious case of *aidôs*—the sense of shame or propriety—which looks like an emotional disposition, but which Epictetus urges his students to cultivate. How can he be urging his students to have an emotion? I do not find an answer in her excellent discussion, but I wonder whether some progress could be made by introducing a further sub-class, namely *kataleptic* emotions. They would still be emotions, inasmuch as the non-virtuous agent's assent was weak. But they might escape the general prohibition, inasmuch as they involved assent to the kataleptic. If emotion is the evaluative analogue of opinion, then it was always a mistake to attribute to the Stoics a sweeping ban on all emotions. In the purely epistemic case, there is no general ban on assenting to *kataleptic* impressions; it is false impressions, and true but non-*kataleptic* impressions that we must avoid. If the evaluative case runs parallel to this, then it should be possible to have a permissible emotional analogue of *katalepsis*, which is an emotion and an opinion when had by a non-Sage, but a *eupatheia* and knowledge when had by a Sage. And this in turn would show both why Epictetus can still encourage his followers to have it, and also why *aidôs* is listed both as a species of the emotion of fear (Nemesius *de nat. hom.* §20 = *SVF* 3.416) and as a species of the *eupatheia* of caution (Andronicus *peri Pathôn* 6 = *SVF* 3.432). The veridical emotions

mentioned above would be prohibited only when the evaluative impression was true but not *kataleptic*.

12. *Axia eklektikê*, see Stobaeus 2.83–84 = SVF 3.124 = LS 58D = IG2 II–95.7f.

13. Emphasize 'disposition'; this definition does not say that the vicious person actually does assent to any non-*kataleptic* impressions, only that their disposition still has this character. A vicious person might assent to nothing but *kataleptic* ones, either because of a lucky run of accidents or because this vicious person is a progressor on the verge of Sagehood (see Chapter 10 for the case of the progressor, who does everything the Sage does but is still not virtuous). Still, their vice would always consist in the fact that their disposition to assent was imperfect, in such a way that were they presented with certain non-*kataleptic* impressions (e.g. of temptations appearing good or tortures appearing bad), they would assent in the wrong way. They still have the disposition to assent, even if they never face a circumstance in which it is triggered.

14. Perhaps a black hole would be even simpler, to the point of degeneracy. As with the zero-function $f(x) = 0$ no matter how the tennis ball is thrown at it, what comes back is nothing.

15. Comments attributed to both Zeno (*Gnomologion Monac.* 196 = SVF 1.281) and Cleanthes (*Epictetus* 4.1.173 = SVF 1.619) seem to record their reactions to the charge that they were propounding paradoxes. The comment attributed to Cleanthes is both more apposite and also better sourced (on Epictetus' date and reliability see the Appendix; the *Gnomologion* is a late Byzantine compendium of uncertain reliability), but the issue may go all the way back to Zeno.

16. Cicero *Disp. Tusc.* 4.54 = SVF 3.665.

17. *Encheiridion* 2.

18. Stobaeus 2.115 = SVF 3.564 = LS 65W = IG2 II–95.11s.

19. See my (2000a) for an argument that reservations are separate, belief-like elements that form no part of the impulse itself. Since I put that article in its final form, discussions with Jacques Brunschwig have persuaded me that the content of the belief is not what I made it out to be in that article. There, I followed the evidence of the Stoics, esp. Seneca, in claiming that the belief that constitutes the reservation is a conditional one, and namely 'I shall get the thing, unless something intervenes.' Brunschwig pointed out that my article already contains an argument that such a content would be too tautologous to play any interesting role in the agent's psychology; I had made the argument against a different analysis, but he has convinced me that a version of it applies to my own as well. It now seems to me that the Stoics were using a conditional sentence when what they really meant was something slightly different: that one should grant some positive subjective probability to both possibilities. Their point is to contrast reservation with the implicit promises made by emotions; where I usually want *p* to happen and believe that it will happen, I should now select *p* and believe that there is some chance that *p* will happen,

and also some chance that p will not happen. That they phrased this position, misleadingly, in terms of conditionals can partly be explained by the fact that no one until quite recently had a very clear or even very natural grasp of thinking in terms of probabilities, and partly by reference to their focus on the question 'what should you do if p does not happen?' See further below on Chrysippus' foot.

20. Epictetus 2.6.9 = *SVF* 3.191 = LS 58J = IG2 II–98.

Stoic texts on epistemology are collected in LS 34 and 39–42, as well as IG2 II–3 to II–19. The texts on impulses and emotions are in LS 57 and 65, and IG2 II–94 and II–95 (see their index under 'passions' for more precise references).

My interpretation generally follows Frede (1983) and Frede (1999b). For different views see Annas (1990) and Hankinson (2003). The commentary in LS is always good.

Inwood (1985) is an excellent book-length discussion of the psychology of action, useful for many points on epistemology, and indispensable for the theory of impulse and its sub-types. A shorter treatment of the same material—with enough disagreement and innovation to save it from slavishness—can be found in Brennan (2003). Inwood provides an even briefer summary of his earlier work in Inwood and Donini (1999), 699–705

The theory of the emotions has attracted a great deal of attention, especially following Nussbaum (1994). Sorabji (2000) is a fascinating survey of every stage of the Stoic interest in emotions, as well as its aftermath in the Christian era. Both of these books err, to my mind, by assuming that the Stoic concern about emotions was like that of the modern psychologist, i.e. that they cared about how emotions feel. I have protested this mistake of emphasis in Brennan (1998a) and Brennan (2003), but no one seems to care how I feel.

I am more attracted to the treatments of emotions that situate them in the ethical and epistemological theory, as for instance Lloyd (1978), Frede (1986), and Striker (1991). I tried to advance this line in Brennan (1998a). Long (1999b) fits into this more sober-sided model, and provides useful material on the physical nature of the soul.

PART III

Ethics

INTRODUCTION TO CHAPTERS 8–10

The core of any ancient school's ethical theory was its account of the *telos*, or final end. In his treatise on the subject, Cicero goes so far as to say that one's position on the final end determines the philosophical school to which one belongs, and that the doctrine of the final end contains the whole of philosophy.[1] On this latter point Cicero is surely overstating the case, but it would not be much of an exaggeration to say that a school's specification of the final end determined the whole of its ethical philosophy, and contained the central tenets that made it distinct from the other schools of the era. This is partly the result of the fact that the final end stands at the center of a wide-ranging conceptual nexus that links together many other key areas in ethics. It is also partly the result of the fact that the ethical theories of all the schools of that era—Stoics, Epicureans, Peripatetics, Academics, and so on—shared a great number of abstract structural features with each other. Because of this uniformity of structure and underlying assumptions, it does sometimes seem as though all of the Hellenistic ethical theories are variations on a theme, with the element of variation provided by the specification of the end. Once we learn the school's answer to the question of the final end, our knowledge of the shared assumptions can make it seem a predictable or even mechanical matter to derive the rest of the ethical outlook by tracing the consequences of that answer throughout the web of concepts joined to it.

We have already seen some of these shared structural assumptions and some of these conceptual connections when we surveyed the ancient philosophical background to Stoicism in Chapter 3. So, for instance, the final end can also be described as the good for human beings, the highest good or summum bonum. It is the same thing as happiness. It sets the standard of reference for rational behavior, since a rational agent ought to be able to specify, for anything they do, how that action contributes to and subserves their final end.[2] And it provides the point of convergence where a virtuous life can be shown to be the same thing as a happy life by means of a 'bridge-argument'.

In constructing a bridge-argument of this kind, different schools accept different trade-offs of ease and difficulty. The Epicureans, who proclaim that pleasure is the end, have an easier time persuading people that a life oriented towards the end of pleasure will be a happy life, but a correspondingly harder time showing that it will be a life of virtue. The Stoics, by contrast, advocate an end that makes that second argument trivial; they claim that the end simply is a life in accordance with virtue. They have their work cut out, however, in showing that the life according to virtue is the same thing as the happy life. Part of that work must be done by their account of what is valuable to human beings (the topic of Chapter 8); another part by their account of why human beings have the sort of end that they do (the topic of Chapter 9, 'Final Ends'); and a third by their account of how individuals strive to distribute value not only to themselves but to the other individuals around them (the topic of Chapter 10, 'Oikeiôsis and Others').

NOTES

1. *de Finibus* 4.14, and see 5.14 where he says that two philosophers generally labeled Peripatetics really ought not to be considered members of the school at all, since they have dissident views about the end, and 'whoever disagrees about this point is dissenting from the entire philosophical system'.
2. This requirement does not prevent the agent from acting in whimsical or apparently pointless ways, since it may well contribute to their end to do so, e.g. by offering relaxation and refreshment. There is nothing irrational about relaxation per se, since it is easy to see how a rational agent could explain its role in contributing to their end. (Nor, for the same reason, is there anything irrational about an occasional refusal to produce such explanations on demand). If the Stoics were sober-sides or killjoys, it is not the consequence of this criterion of rationality, which was the common property of other schools (cf. Aristotle's *Nic. Ethics* X.6 1176b30).

8

Goods and Indifferents

The Stoics distinguished two kinds of values: goods and bads (or evils, but in the non-moral sense), on the one hand, and indifferents of various sorts on the other.[1] Here is a typical text:

The Stoics say that some of the things that exist are good, some are bad, and some are neither good nor bad. The good things, then, include the virtues (wisdom, justice, courage, temperance, and the rest). The bad things include their opposites (folly, injustice, and the rest). Neither good nor bad are all those things that neither benefit nor harm (for instance life, health, pleasure, beauty, physical strength, wealth, fame, and good birth), as well as their opposites (death, disease, pain, ugliness, weakness, poverty, disgrace, low birth, and the like) ... These [life, health, etc.] are not goods, but indifferents in the subclass of 'promoteds'. For as it is characteristic of fire that it warms things and does not cool them, so it is characteristic of the good that it benefits and does not harm. But wealth and health do not benefit, any more than they harm. Furthermore, they say that whatever can be used both well and badly is not a good. But wealth and health can be used both well and badly: therefore, wealth and health are not goods.[2]

It has often been noted that in claiming that only the virtues are good, and that such things as health, wealth, and beauty are indifferent, the Stoics are echoing lines of thought that Socrates expresses in some of Plato's dialogues. In the *Meno, Gorgias*, and *Euthydemus*, as we shall see, there are passages in which Socrates argues that only wisdom is good, because only it is uniformly beneficial to its possessor, whereas the things commonly thought of as good (like money) often make their possessors miserable if they do not have the wisdom to use them well.

There is surely a historical connection between Socrates' views here and the Stoic claim that everything besides vice and virtue is indifferent. But it would be misleading to equate the two views. In the *Gorgias* (468), Socrates explicitly says of the things which are neither good nor bad that they 'sometimes participate in what is good, and sometimes in what is bad, and sometimes in neither'.[3] In the *Euthydemus* (281de), he says that 'the things we called good earlier [e.g. wealth, health, and beauty at 279a] are not good by nature; if ignorance leads them, they are greater evils than their opposites [for example, ignorantly used wealth is a greater evil than poverty], but if prudence and wisdom lead them, they are greater goods'. In the *Meno* (87e–88a), Socrates says 'we say that health, strength, beauty and wealth are sometimes beneficial, but also sometimes harm us'.

All of these views are importantly at odds with the Stoic theory. First, the Stoics would never say that wealth is sometimes good, or that it sometimes participates in the good, or that it is good if it is used correctly. Wealth is never, in any sort of case, a good; it is always and in every case an indifferent.[4] For, among other things, if this portion of wealth on this occasion really were a good, that is, really benefited its possessor, then an agent would have reason to feel that the loss of that wealth on that occasion, or the failure to attain that wealth on that occasion, really was a loss of something genuinely good; and this is not a conclusion the Stoics would support.

Some of the fault for this misinterpretation rests with the Stoics themselves. Their comparison between benefiting and heating in the quotation above suggests that promoted indifferents will be like inconstant heaters. Inconstant heaters sometimes heat and sometimes cool, so by analogy it might seem that promoted indifferents sometimes benefit and sometimes harm. And this misinterpretation may seem to draw support from the next line, which is sometimes translated 'wealth and health no more benefit than harm'. This seems to suggest that wealth and health do sometimes benefit, but cannot be called genuine goods because they also sometimes harm, whereas the genuine good should only benefit without ever harming. But the 'no more' statement does not say that wealth and health ever benefit or harm, only that they no more do the one than the other; and this 'no more' formula can also be used to jointly deny two claims. For example, to say 'the number three is no more blue than it is red' is not to say that the number three is partly blue and partly red, or sometimes blue and sometimes red.[5] It is simply neither blue nor red. So too, when the indifferents are first introduced in the quote above, the text simply says of them that they neither benefit nor harm. That description of them is less misleading than the ones that suggest that they sometimes benefit and sometimes harm. The Stoics clearly reject that variable view, and thus they also reject the view of Socrates in the *Meno*, *Gorgias* and *Euthydemus*.

Second, it is very different to say, as Socrates does, that wealth is a good thing, when it is used rightly, and to say, as the Stoics do, that the correct use of wealth is a good thing. A lump of gold is an object, a thing with a mass and a location; a use or a putting to use is an action, an event located in time. What is good, on the Stoic account, is a certain action, that is, the making use of gold (or poverty or anything in between). It does not follow from this that the gold itself is transmuted into a good thing or object when it is used in a certain way, which is what Socrates says.[6] If it were the Stoic view that the virtuous use of wealth makes wealth a good thing (as Socrates says in the *Euthydemus* that it becomes a great good when wisdom controls it), then it would follow that a Sage with wealth has two good things, namely virtue and this transformed wealth, whereas a Sage without wealth would be lacking this good thing. That is emphatically not what the Stoics say.

Only virtue is good, only vice is bad; the rest are all indifferents of various sorts. How do the Stoics argue for this claim, and why should we believe it? The Stoics employed many strategies. For instance,

Goods and Indifferents ~ 121

they offered brief arguments like the following, quoted by Cicero: 'Every good is a praiseworthy thing; every praiseworthy thing is morally fine; so every good is morally fine.'[7] It is hard to avoid Cicero's verdict that this argument is a 'dagger of lead'; if, for instance, I think that being wealthy is not especially praiseworthy, but still think it is clearly a good thing, I will not grant the first premiss that every good is praiseworthy. Arguments of this kind are unlikely to have provided a solid basis for deeply controversial views about value.

The same, I think, applies to arguments that take as their premiss the claim that virtue must be sufficient for happiness, or that the happiness of the Sage must be completely immune from the vicissitudes of fortune, and go on to say that if wealth or health or the other indifferents were goods, then the Sage's virtue would not guarantee him happiness.[8] The argument's validity is not in question, but its ability to persuade anyone is. Those of us who think that a modicum of health is an important part of complete happiness have long reconciled ourselves to the fact that virtue is not sufficient for happiness, and that no one's happiness is immune from trauma and disease. To say that we must purge anything vulnerable from happiness lest the fear of vulnerability should undermine our happiness is to follow the route of a chef who begins by seeking only the freshest fruits, but from an increasing concern to avoid over-ripeness decides to purchase only plastic fruit instead. Some goods are perishable, and cannot be replaced with imperishable simulacra—that is a common enough view. Perhaps the Stoics can change our minds about that claim, but not merely by threatening us with loss or the fear of loss.

Nor is an agent likely to arrive at the Stoic conception of the good for human beings by reflecting on the desires, preferences, and inclinations that they happen to have, and attempting to construct a life that will allow them to satisfy as many of those desires as possible. Deliberation of this sort might make the agent more efficient and methodical in pursuing the values they already had, but it could hardly produce the sort of fundamental conversion in values that Stoicism requires.

In order to make a really convincing case for changing our ordinary views about which things are good and bad, the Stoics are going to need to start from a more fundamental set of considerations. We can see an example of how they did this by examining Cicero's discussion in the fourth book of his treatise *de Finibus* (On Ends).

In this book, Cicero criticizes Stoic ethics by adopting the stance of one of his older contemporaries named Antiochus of Ascalon, with whom he had studied as a young man. Antiochus was officially a member of the Academy, who proposed the view that the schools of Plato and Aristotle had been in virtual agreement on ethics, and that the Stoic view amounted to pretty much the same as theirs if one discounted the Stoic penchant for mystifying terminology. The view that Antiochus attributed so confidently to the Academics and Peripatetics, and at least polemically to the Stoics, is that the good for human beings is a combination of virtue along with moderate physical advantages, that is, some minimum of health, wealth, and the other things the Stoics classify as 'promoted' but not good. Virtue is by far the most important of the goods in the view of Antiochus' 'Old Academy',[9] and it is necessary for happiness—no one can lead a good and satisfying life who is not virtuous. This fact alone, Antiochus thinks, will ensure that a rational agent will always have reason to do what is virtuous, instead of pursuing some physical advantage in a way contrary to virtue. But he denied that virtue is sufficient for happiness; crushing pain or grinding poverty really are bad things that prevent their victims from being happy, no matter how virtuous they may be. The Stoic claim that health and wealth are literally indifferents, that is, that they make no difference to the agent's happiness, is at first blush an impressive one, if implausible; it degenerates into a laughable evasion when the Stoics proceed to say that agents should pursue health because it is 'promoted' and avoid poverty because it is 'demoted'. Antiochus complains that this re-labeling will not change the agent's outlook. 'Let Zeno show me how I will be better prepared to despise money if I classify it among the "promoteds" than if I call it a good, or more courageous in enduring pain if I label it "contrary to nature" than if I call it "bad".'[10]

Goods and Indifferents ~ 123

In the course of presenting Antiochus' view, Cicero refers to one of Chrysippus' treatises and describes Antiochus' reaction to it; the book in question was probably Chrysippus' own treatise 'On Ends'. It would be immensely valuable for our current concerns if we had a copy of this treatise, but as often we have only an opponent's report of the Stoic view, and must make of it what we can.

Before introducing Antiochus' criticism of the Stoics, Cicero starts by laying out some areas of agreement:

Let it first be granted, then, that we are well-disposed towards ourselves, and by nature have the desire to preserve ourselves. So far we [sc. Antiochus and the Stoics] agree. What follows is that we must give heed to who we are, to ensure that we preserve ourselves in the condition that is proper to us. We are, then, human beings. We are made of mind and body of a certain kind. It is proper for us, as demanded by our primary natural desire, to love these elements and to derive from them our end, the supreme and ultimate good.[11]

Thus Antiochus argued that, since our nature includes both body and soul, so too our *telos* must include goods of the body as well as goods of the soul; and since he takes it that the Stoics agree with him that human nature is compounded of body as well as soul, he then asks them how they can consistently reject goods of the body:

By what means, or at what point did you suddenly discard the body, and all those things which are in accordance with nature but out of our control, and lastly duty itself?[12] My question then is, how comes it that so many things that Nature strongly recommends have been suddenly abandoned by Wisdom? Even if we were not seeking the *telos* of human beings, but of some living creature that consisted solely of a mind (let us allow ourselves to imagine such a creature, in order to facilitate our discovery of the truth), even so that mind would not accept this *telos* of yours. For such a being would ask for health, and freedom from pain, and would also desire its own preservation, and security for the goods just specified; and it would set up as its *telos* to live according to nature, which means, as I said, to possess [sc. not merely pursue] either all or most and the most important of the things which are in accordance with nature. In fact, you may construct a living creature of any sort you like, but even if it be devoid of a body, as is our imaginary being, nevertheless its mind will be bound to possess certain attributes analogous to those of the body, and consequently it will be impossible to set up for it a *telos* on any other line than those which I have laid down. Now Chrysippus, in his survey of the differences between living things, says that some of them excel by the body, and others excel by the soul, while still others are equally endowed in respect of both; and then he proceeds to discuss what constitutes the ultimate good proper to each species. However, while he placed human beings in the genus that excel in the soul, he then went on to define their summum bonum in such a way that they seem not merely to excel by their souls, but actually to be nothing beyond their souls. But the only case in which it would be correct to place the summum bonum in virtue alone is if there existed a creature consisting solely of pure intellect, with the further proviso that this intellect possessed nothing of its own that was in accordance with nature, as bodily health is. But it is impossible even to imagine a self-consistent picture of what such a creature would look like.[13]

The first point I want to draw from this passage is that Chrysippus wrote a book in which he first talked about the nature of various species of living things, and then for each species derived from the account of its nature an account of its *telos*.[14] That this was the direction and order of argumentation in Chrysippus' book is secured, not only by the comment 'then he proceeds to discuss', but also by the whole structure of Antiochus' criticism here.

If this was all that we learned from the passage, it would be significant; it already shows us how Chrysippus drew central ethical theses from considerations of the natures of things. And note that the appeal to nature here is double. For Chrysippus not only derives the *telos* for human beings from a specification of their nature as living things, that is, human nature; he also applies this method to the case of human beings exactly because he takes it to be the right way of operating in the case of any living thing; that is, in the case of anything that can be said to have a *telos*, that thing will have that *telos* in virtue of its nature. Now the first reference to nature already goes beyond anything available to deliberative introspection, or anything we might learn about human nature merely by ruminating on our own desires, preferences and the like. And the second reference to nature, the general claim that anything's *telos* is derived from its nature, clearly involves a very general notion of natures both human and non-human, and entails the claim that at least some general features of human nature are best understood in the light of a more general theory of nature. What comes first here is a view about the relation between natures and ends—any and all natures, not merely human nature. And it is in light of that very general view about all natures that we know how to proceed in the case of human nature. And then, the way that we do in fact proceed in the case of human nature is by specifying it first, as one biological kind on a level with though distinct from others, and then deriving its *telos* from that specification. That is the first thing to notice, and it seems to me a methodological point of some importance.[15]

Cicero does not represent Antiochus as objecting to that method, but he does object to the results that Chrysippus obtained. He argues that Chrysippus gave human beings an end that would be too impoverished even for a hypothetical creature composed only of a soul, much less for the actual composite creatures that human beings are.

Even if we were to imagine a purely psychic creature, the argument goes, one that had no body, then it still would not follow that its *telos* excluded the things that the Stoics exclude from the human *telos*, for example, health and freedom from pain. So, since even the *telos* of a purely psychic creature would still include health, freedom from pain, self-preservation, and the possession of the things according to nature, it is all the more ridiculous for the Stoics to claim that the *telos* of a composite creature like a human being will exclude health and painlessness, and exclude the possession of things according to nature. If even a disembodied soul needs health, then *a fortiori* an embodied human being will.

But this objection is clearly confused. Grant to Antiochus that the *telos* of a purely psychic thing will include the health of that purely psychic thing—it surely does not follow that the *telos* of a purely psychic thing includes the health that the Stoics claim to be indifferent, namely the health of the body. The kind of health that might feature in the *telos* of a disembodied soul would be psychic health, not physical health; and so too for its painlessness (which might be, for instance, mental tranquility), its self-preservation, and its possession of things according to its nature.[16] Antiochus is surely right to say that each of these could feature quite legitimately in the *telos* of a pure soul; but he is wrong to think that Chrysippus has said anything inconsistent with this. Chrysippus only excludes the health of the body from the human end, not the health of the soul. So Antiochus' a fortiori argument falls prey to confusion between the psychic and bodily senses of 'health', 'painlessness', and so on.

The second allegation then picks up on this very reply to the first objection, by granting that what would feature in the *telos* of a pure soul are not bodily health and painlessness and so on, but 'certain attributes analogous to those of the body', that is, the psychic analogues of health, painlessness, and so on. Still, Antiochus insists, these things really must be included in the telos, and so even the *telos* of a pure soul would not be exhausted by virtue alone, that is, even for a pure soul, it would not be true to say that only virtue is the good; and so a fortiori it cannot be true for composite humans. Antiochus phrases this argument in the contrapositive, saying 'the only case in which virtue would be the only good would be if there were an animal that consisted only of a mind, and a mind, furthermore, that had nothing in it that was according to nature, analogous to health [sc. in the body].' And this, he concludes, is incoherent; it makes no sense to imagine a living creature which has a determinate nature and yet has nothing even analogous to health or a state of being according to nature.

But this argument too is clearly inadequate. For Antiochus has overlooked the possibility that virtue might exactly be the same thing as psychic health and tranquility and a condition according to nature, in which case the *telos* could include all of these other things, while nevertheless not containing anything but virtue. And indeed, as we know, this is exactly how the Stoics will have viewed the case; they will say that virtue is the health of the soul, and that it is equivalent to tranquility, the natural condition of the soul, and so on. So there is nothing incoherent in imagining a pure soul whose end contains only

Goods and Indifferents ~ 127

virtue, provided that virtue is in fact the same thing as psychic health, psychic painlessness, and so on.

To sum up these last thoughts: Antiochus has presented two arguments which purport to show that, even if we were to imagine creatures that by nature were purely souls, still the Stoic account of the human end would fail to do justice to their nature, that is, that the Stoic *telos* is too austere even for pure souls, much less for human beings. Both arguments fail, and in such obvious ways that I do not think we can even learn much about Stoicism from their failures. But that leaves untouched the underlying complaint that Antiochus makes, that the official Stoic account of the human *telos* seems more suited to a purely psychic creature, whereas their account of human nature apparently never denies that they are composites of soul and body. What did Chrysippus really say here, and what led to Antiochus' confusion?

Antiochus was clearly perplexed and puzzled by what he found in the discussions of human nature and the human *telos* in Chrysippus' treatise. From his allegation of inconsistency, it seems that what Chrysippus said in his book left Antiochus with the following three impressions:

(1) In discussing the nature of human beings, Chrysippus nowhere in so many words said that human beings were merely souls, or that human beings were not also bodies as well as souls, and may even have affirmed on the contrary that human beings were in some sense composite beings.

(2) But, on the other hand, in discussing the *telos* for human beings, Chrysippus spoke as though human beings were merely souls and were in no way composed of bodies, or at any rate gave humans a *telos* that, to Antiochus' mind, would be appropriate only to creatures that were purely souls and were in no way composed of bodies.

(3) This discrepancy notwithstanding, however, Antiochus found nothing to challenge his conviction that Chrysippus intended to derive each species' *telos*, and in particular the human *telos*,

from a specification of its nature; indeed, it was exactly because Antiochus was convinced that this remained Chrysippus' strategy that he continued to feel that Chrysippus was guilty of an inconsistency.

Unfortunately, we are not in a position to tell exactly what Chrysippus said about the relation of soul and body; Cicero's reference to animals 'that excel in the soul' is too cryptic, and the other evidence is surprisingly taciturn about whether the Stoics said a human being is composed of a soul and a body.[17] Without being able to reconstruct the details of what Chrysippus said, I think we can still attribute to him one very important thesis, provided only that we are willing to dissent from Antiochus' charge of inconsistency. Chrysippus clearly held that, however the metaphysical details should be spelled out, the truth about the nature of human beings is as follows: human beings are of such a nature that only the good of their souls is good for them, and what is good for their bodies is not, in fact, good for them. Or to put this in another way, Chrysippus clearly held that human beings were of such a nature that, for the purposes of understanding their good, they might as well be purely psychic entities.

And here it is worth recalling that it is nothing like an unusual view in Ancient Philosophy to identify the human being with the soul to the exclusion of the body. We hear it in Plato's *Phaedo*, when in answer to Crito's thick-headed question about how Socrates wishes to be buried, Socrates replies 'I am not convincing Crito that I am the one who is talking here; he rather thinks that I am that corpse which he will see'.[18] We hear it again in the pseudo-Platonic *First Alcibiades*, when Socrates persuades Alcibiades that a human being is a soul, not a combination of a soul and body.[19] And we hear it again in Epictetus, who encourages his students to think of the body as a donkey that they have been put in charge of, and says in one fragment 'you are a soul, lugging around a corpse'.[20]

Chrysippus thus argued that the indifferents are not good by starting from an account of human nature that is very radical—very radical, and yet far from uncommon in antiquity, either in

Plato's writings, or the imitations of them, or even in later Stoics. But of course the fact that indifferents are not goods does not exhaust what we need to know about indifferents. We must also come to see why it is rational to pursue them. Here, too, I think, the radical account of human nature does a better job of explaining the Stoic position than an account which begins with our ordinary beliefs and desires about food, health, and the like. On the one hand, we are related to our body in such a way that its welfare is no part of our own good. On the other hand, we have special relation to it that requires us to direct some of our attention towards its maintenance. Here again, the image of taking care of a donkey or some other livestock is suggestive, as is the following passage from Epictetus:

Nature is an extraordinary thing, and 'a lover of animals', as Xenophon said. At any rate, we cherish and take care of our bodies, the most disgusting and filthy things of all—for we couldn't bear to take care of our neighbor's body, even for a mere five days. Just think what it's like—getting up at dawn to wash someone else's teeth, and after he has done his business you have to give him a wipe down there. What is really extraordinary is the fact that we love such a thing, given how much upkeep it requires each day. I stuff my paunch. Then I empty it. What could be more tedious? But I must serve God. That's why I wait, and put up with washing this wretched little body, and giving it fodder, and sheltering it.[21]

If our body is bestowed upon us like a donkey or horse or what have you, then it is part of our job to be diligent grooms, keeping the thing in good shape, in so far as we can. A good groom should see that his charges are fed properly; but of course there would be something deeply confused about a groom or trainer who came to feel pleasure in the horse's eating, who began to confuse the horse's welfare with their own good. All the more so for the horse's breeding; it might well be appropriate to breed the horse that was in your charge, and to make arrangements so that this was done in a diligent and healthful way. But it would be deeply confused—indeed, it would be classically pathological and depraved—to come to feel pleasure in your horse's breeding activity, or somehow to feel a strong sense of identification with whatever pleasure the horse felt.

The model of animal husbandry thus tells us both why the welfare of our body is not part of our good, and also why, and to what extent, we are called upon nevertheless to take pains to see to the needs of our bodies, as well as everything consequent on those needs.

Critics sometimes suggest that the Stoic view of human nature alienates us from ourselves, but to say this is simply to beg the question against the Stoics. If our bodies really are nothing to us—if, for the purposes of ascertaining our good, they do not even count as part of ourselves—then the 'alienated' view is simply the accurate view of human nature, and the normal assumption that our body's welfare is part of our own good is a deep and destructive confusion.[22] To become attached to our body and its travails is to be confused about a central fact of our own identity; it is a failure of self-knowledge. I say this not to endorse the Stoic account of human nature, but only to say that it cannot be effectively criticized merely by appealing to our pre-theoretical intuitions about what we desire, prefer, or dislike; the anti-Stoic charge of 'alienation' is just another leaden dagger. The Stoic account of the human good has to be met on the grounds of physics and metaphysics, with a competing account of human nature.

NOTES

1. My point about the sense of 'evils' is that the Stoic distinction between goods and evils (or bads or ills) on the one hand, and indifferents on the other hand, is a distinction about what things are actually beneficial for individuals in the sense of being productive of their happiness. So far, the Stoics are using the terms 'good' and 'evil' in exactly the same sense as anyone else, e.g. the Epicureans; evils are things that are harmful to my own welfare and happiness, no more. It is only at the next stage that anything like a 'moral' sense of good or evil comes in—when the Stoics offer a positive account of which things are in fact goods and evils, and claim that only moral virtue benefits me and only moral vice harms me. The sense of the words 'good' and 'bad' is constant and unchanged between the Stoic claim that only virtue is good and only vice is bad, and the Epicurean claim that pleasure is good and pain is bad. I think Long and Sedley are not guilty of misunderstanding but only of misleading expression when they write (LS vol. 1 p. 374) 'The most distinctive characteristic of Stoic ethics is its restriction of the ordinary Greek terms for 'good' and 'bad' to what we would

call the moral sense of these words.' This is right if parsed carefully: the Stoics restrict the *referents* of the terms 'good' and 'bad' to the referents that would normally be picked out by the moral senses of those terms (roughly virtue and vice). But they do that without restricting or otherwise altering the *senses* of the terms 'good' and 'bad'; that is why their claim that only vice is bad is a controversial position, rather than a tautology.

2. *DL* 7.101–103 = *SVF* 3.117 = LS 58A = IG2 II–94.

3. The Gorgias passage is thus not a good parallel for the Stoic theory of indifferents; on the Stoic view, items like health and disease are not capable of participating, even sporadically, in goodness. This passage is, however, a better model for the Stoic theory of actions, since the Stoics too will say that some instances of walking are genuine goods, i.e. when the Sage walks wisely, and some are instances of genuine evils, i.e. when any non-Sage walks at all, and so walks viciously (see the chapter on befitting actions). Even here, the Stoics will not say that any token act of walking could be neither good nor bad; it must be performed either by a Sage or a non-Sage, and so be the product either of virtue or vice, and characterized by that causal origin.

4. Here I think that Long and Sedley suggest the wrong view in their commentary (LS vol. 1 p. 358) when they write that promoted indifferents 'lack this necessary relation to benefiting' and that a demoted indifferent like poverty 'does not necessarily harm a person'. The repeated emphasis on the lack of a necessary connection suggests that the problem with wealth is that it is only contingently or sporadically or irregularly good. This is clearly false. What debars wealth from being a good is not simply that it fails to be necessarily beneficial, i.e. beneficial in all possible circumstances. Its failure is much more systematic than that; it fails to benefit in any possible circumstance, just as poverty fails to be harmful in any possible circumstance.

5. This negative use of 'no more' is explicitly noted in the doxography of Skepticism in *DL* 9.75 = IG2 III–22.

6. Though after Socrates says the un-Stoic thing in 281d, that the indifferents are goods or bads when used rightly or wrongly, he then goes on to sound very Stoic indeed in 282a when he says that 'we become happy out of the correct use of things', where the emphasis falls on the use rather than the things. It might well be that a careful and sympathetic interpretation of Socrates' view would conclude on balance that it is more like the Stoic view than I am allowing; my main point is that Stoic view should not be confused with what Socrates at least sometimes says, namely that the indifferents become goods or evils on different occasions.

7. *de Finibus* 4.48, echoing 3.27 = *SVF* 3.37 = LS 60N = IG2 II–102. For the Greek source of the argument, see Plutarch *Sto. Rep* 1039C = *SVF* 3.29.

8. E.g. Cicero, *Tusculan Disputations* 5.40 = LS 63L.

9. Cicero uses this term at *de Finibus* 5.7–8; Antiochus included in it Plato's disciples Xenocrates, Speusippus, Polemo and Crantor, as well as Aristotle and his successor Theophrastus (see 4.3, 5.7).

10. *de Finibus* 4.72.

11. *de Finibus* 4.25, trans. Raphael Woolf.
12. This last reference to duty (see below on befitting actions) is extremely compressed. Of course the Stoics did not 'discard duty' in the sense of denying that certain actions are befitting, but Cicero is claiming that their rejection of goods of the body will implicitly commit them to that denial. Antiochus is here attacking the Stoics with one of their own arguments, developed later at *de Finibus* 4.46 (and cf. *de Officiis* 1.6) which says that a theory that makes health and the like indifferent will be unable to provide a coherent account of befitting actions. This style of argument was crafted by Chrysippus to combat Aristo; see *de Finibus* 3.50 (though this contains no explicit reference to the befitting).
13. *de Finibus* 4.26–29.
14. The introduction of the purely psychic creature is not obviously Antiochus' innovation; Chrysippus may have introduced hypothetical creatures of this sort for his own purposes in developing his survey.
15. This is also why I suspect that the treatise in question was Chrysippus' 'On Ends', that is, a general survey of organisms and their ends, showing how each thing's end is derived from its nature.
16. DL 7.96 = *SVF* 3.107 = IG2 II–94, and Stobaeus 2.74 = *SVF* 3.112 = IG2 II–95.5l mention 'painlessness' (*alupia*) as one of the good psychic states that supervene on the possession of virtue, where this clearly cannot mean the lack of physical pain.
17. The claim that the human being is composed of soul and body is found explicitly in *SE AM* 11.46 = *SVF* 3.96. But the comparison with the parallel reports at Stobaeus 2.70 = *SVF* 3.97 = IG2 II–95.5e and DL 7.95 = *SVF* 3.97 = IG2 II–94, which make no mention of the body, raises the possibility that this claim is added by Sextus. On the other side, one text attributes to Cleanthes the view that only the soul is the human being (Epiphanius *ad Haeres.* 3.2.9 = *SVF* 1.538); unfortunately, this text also attributes to Cleanthes the view that the good and the honorable consist in pleasures, a piece of such flagrant nonsense that it calls into question the evidential value of the text as a whole.
18. *Phaedo* 115cd.
19. *First Alcibiades* 129–130. This dialogue has come down to us among Plato's writings, and was widely thought in antiquity to have been written by Plato. But current critical consensus is split on whether it was written by Plato or by a later author (who must have been a well-informed and sympathetic student of Plato's work in any case).
20. *Discourses* 4.1.79; *fr.* 26.
21. Epictetus fragment 23.
22. *SE AM* 11.194 = *SVF* 3.752 has a verbatim quote from Chrysippus' 'On the Befitting' in which he says, 'the body is nothing to us, just like fingernails or hair.'

9

Final Ends

The Stoic theory of the final end or summum bonum can be rather difficult to come to terms with, for four reasons.

First, because different Stoic authorities gave different answers to the question 'what is the final end?', and sometimes one and the same Stoic gave several answers. But ancient sources also indicate that all of these various answers were supposed to be in some sort of fundamental agreement. So we need to come to terms both with the plurality of different verbal formulae for the Stoic end, and also come to see in what sense they all amount to the same thing.

Second, because some modern critics have seized on one formulation of the final end as though it was authoritative, and tried to make other formulations conform to it, despite the fact that even among the ancient Stoics this formulation—that is, 'living in agreement'—was generally agreed to be the least useful and least informative of the various versions. The resulting distortion has been increased by a pervasive mistranslation of this formula as 'living consistently'.

Third, because much of our evidence for the Stoic view comes (here as elsewhere) from passages in which their opponents attack the coherence, cogency, or plausibility of their views. Opponents claimed that the Stoic theory faced a fundamental dilemma: either it was incoherent, or it turned out to be a copy of the Aristotelian account dressed up in misleading jargon. In order to extract an account of what the Stoics said, we also have to come to terms with this debate, and assess its influence on the transmission of evidence.

Fourth, because the Stoic account of their end and its relation to action simply was complex. After we have done our best to sweep away the malicious misunderstandings of ancient non-Stoics and the well-meaning mistakes of our contemporaries, after we have taken into consideration the scarcity of the evidence that remains to us and the distortions that may have come along with it, what emerges from the evidence is still a theory of considerable complexity.

Our plan of attack will follow those four points in order: first, we will look at a selection of the various formulations of the Stoic end, trying to impose at least some initial order on the multiplicity. Next, we will turn to the problem of 'living consistently', to see why this is a bad translation of an uninformative formulation. Then, we will review the ancient anti-Stoic allegations of incoherence, unoriginality, and other problems with the Stoic end. Finally, we will consider some Stoics' responses to these charges, as well as other texts in which they offer fuller discussions of their end and how they came to formulate it.

Different Stoic Accounts

The following texts contain our two most important catalogues of Stoic formulations of the end:

Zeno was the first to say (in his treatise 'On the Nature of Human Beings') that the final end is 'to live in agreement with nature'. This is the same as 'to live according to virtue;' for nature draws us towards virtue.
(And Cleanthes said the same thing in his treatise 'On Pleasure', as did Posidonius, and Hecato in his treatise 'On Final Ends'.)

Conversely, 'to live according to virtue' is the same as 'to live according to the experience of what happens by nature', as Chrysippus says in the first book of his treatise 'On Final Ends'; for our natures are parts of the whole.[1]

Which is why the final end comes to be 'to live in following nature', where this means 'to live according to one's own nature and the nature of the universe', doing none of the things that are forbidden by the common law, which is the same as the right reason that pervades all things, i.e. Zeus, who is the leader of the entire organization of things. And this itself is both the virtue of the happy person, and the happy flow of life, whenever everything is done according to the harmonization of each person's inner spirit [daemon] with the will of the organizer of the whole. Whereas Diogenes says that the final end is 'to reason well in the selection of things according to nature . . . ' By the word 'nature' in the formula 'to live in following nature' Chrysippus understood both the common nature and more specifically human nature. But Cleanthes acknowledged only the common nature, and did not accept the particular nature.[2]

Zeno defined the final end as follows: 'to live in agreement', i.e. to live according to a reason that is one and harmonizes. For those who live in conflict are miserable. But his successors, adding additional clarifications, expressed it as follows: 'to live in agreement with nature'. For in their judgment, what Zeno had said was something less than a predicate. For Cleanthes, who was his first successor as head of the school, added on the complement 'with nature', and defined it as follows: 'the final end is to live in agreement with nature'. Chrysippus wanted to make this still clearer, so he expressed it as 'to live according to the experience of what happens by nature'. And Diogenes said the final end is 'to reason well in the selection and disselection of things according to nature' . . . And Antipater said it is 'to live in the continual selection of things according to nature and disselection of things contrary to nature'. And he would often put it this way, too: 'to do everything that is up to you, continually and without deviation, in order to acquire the things that are promoted by nature'.[3]

One thing that is immediately clear is that the final end is always expressed as a long predicate-clause in the infinitive, 'to do such-and-such'. To say that it is a predicate (or *katêgorêma*) in the context of Stoic linguistic theory is to say that it is the sort of thing that, when subordinated to a subject case, will produce a complete proposition.[4] That is, 'to run' is a predicate, because when we subordinate it to a subject case, like 'Lassie', we get a complete proposition, namely 'Lassie runs'. So too, we can imagine taking each of the formulae above and subordinating it to a subject case in order to produce a complete proposition, for example, 'Socrates lives according to virtue', 'Socrates reasons well in the selection and disselection of things according to nature', and so on.

The fact that the final end is expressed as a predicate also ties in well with what we learned about the impulses, namely that every impulse is directed towards a predicate; my desire to run is directed at the predicate 'to run'. It thus makes sense that all of the end-formulae should be in predicate-form, since the final end is an object of impulses, indeed in some sense the object of all impulses, or the object of impulse par excellence.

Another thing that is clear is that the various end-formulae fall into a few clusters of related types. First there are the 'nature-' formulae, attributed to the three earliest and most famous Stoics, Zeno, Cleanthes, and Chrysippus:

to live in agreement with nature
to live in following nature
to live according to the experience of what happens by nature
to live according to one's own nature and the nature of the wholes.

Then there are the 'selection-' formulae, attributed to Diogenes of Babylon and Antipater of Tarsus, respectively the fifth and sixth heads of the school:

to reason well in the selection of things according to nature
to reason well in the selection and disselection of things according to nature
to live in the continual selection of things according to nature and disselection of things contrary to nature

Outside of these clusters there are a few other formulae that stand apart. There is the final formulation attributed to Antipater ('to do everything that is up to you, continually and without deviation, in order to acquire the things that are promoted by nature'), which is supposed to be equivalent to the selection-formula, presumably because 'acquiring the things that are promoted by nature' is an indirect way of referring to selection. There is the formula 'to live according to virtue'; we are told that it is equivalent to 'to live in agreement with nature', and much of the hard work in Stoic ethics involves seeing why these should be equivalent. And there is the shortest formula, namely 'to live in agreement'. It is this formula that has caused trouble for interpreters.

To Live in Agreement with

Now, on my view, and on the view of Cleanthes and Chrysippus, this formula is really simply a short-hand that Zeno sometimes used for the formula that he spelled out in full in his treatise 'On the Nature of Human Beings', that is, 'to live in agreement with nature'. Indeed, his successors thought the shorter form was not only conceptually incomplete, they thought it was grammatically ill-formed. That is what they meant by calling it 'something short of a predicate'; it means that they thought it would not make a full proposition when joined with a subject case, because it needs a complement in order to make sense. The term 'something less than a predicate' is the official name of a category in Stoic linguistic theory, just like 'article', 'adverb', 'predicate' and so on, and the example that the Stoics sometimes use for this grammatical category is 'to be in love with'. This is not a predicate, but something less than a predicate, because if you combine it with a subject case you do not get a proposition, only a proposition-fragment, like 'Plato is in love with', which does not yet make sense. If you add in a complement, for instance, 'Dion', then the 'something short of a predicate' is turned into a proper predicate 'to be in love with Dion', and the addition of a subject case produces a proposition, that is, 'Plato is in love with Dion.'

Since 'to live in agreement' is something short of a predicate, on the view of Zeno's successors—indeed, to emphasize their view of the essential incompleteness of this formula, we should probably translate it 'to live in agreement with—'—it also cannot be the object of an impulse. This debars it from being a comprehensible account of the end. So they are making two claims here: first, at the level of syntax, that the formula 'to live in agreement with—' is simply incoherent as it stands; it does not specify a predicate, and cannot be an object of an impulse. Second, they are pointing out that the obvious complement in this context—the one Zeno is twice quoted as endorsing, and the one that Cleanthes and Chrysippus in turn endorsed—is the complement 'with nature'; that is, the standard of reference, the thing that one strives to agree with, is nature. We need to specify a standard of agreement, and that standard happens to be something external to the agent, nature. At this point, the first quotation tells us that Cleanthes and Chrysippus diverge in their interpretations of 'nature'—both agree that we must live in agreement with the common, universal nature; in addition, Chrysippus emphasizes that we must live in agreement with human nature. This sort of divergence is just what one expects when Zeno's followers attempt to interpret Zeno's words; he said 'agree with nature', but nature can be many things.

However, some modern critics come at this from a different angle. They take the second text to be evidence that Zeno never did use the full form 'to live in agreement with nature', but only said 'to live in agreement'. And they prefer a different translation of that Greek phrase, namely 'to live consistently'.[5] Now this gets Stoicism off to a very different start indeed. For Zeno was the founder of Stoicism, and his views on ethics were always authoritative, so it is a significant fact if he wanted to construct his ethical system around a concern with consistency.

This sets a particular interpretive agenda: it suggests that we must view Stoicism as a precursor of more recent interests in rational consistency. What matters for ethics, on this view, is the agent's own consistent application of universal rules of practical reason. And the agent's own reason will be the standard; the agent does not need to look outside of their own reason to find the foundations of ethics. If we follow this interpretive lead, then soon we must ask whether Cleanthes and Chrysippus fundamentally misunderstood their founder and 'imported' a new interest in nature which had not been there, or whether they thought that a concern with rational consistency and a concern with following nature and Zeus would amount to the same thing, perhaps because nature and Zeus are rationally consistent and work by general principles, too.

In my opinion, this whole direction of interpretation is a mistake and a red herring. It is based, first, on a bad translation: the Greek word at issue always means 'to agree' or 'be in agreement', even when, as sometimes happens, the author spells out or implies that the kind of agreement at stake is agreement between different parts of one thing, which will entail consistency. For instance, when Plato has the title character of the *Timaeus* warn that some of his speculations may not be consistent, he says that 'the accounts themselves will not agree with themselves' (29cd). But the fact that 'agree' is used here along with an expressed internal or reflexive standard of agreement so as to convey the notion of consistency does not show that the word 'to agree' should be *translated* as 'to be consistent'; the word itself still means 'to agree', and the notion of consistency emerges from other elements in the context.[6]

In the case of Zeno's short-hand formula, we have no other elements in the context that encourage us to suppose that the kind of agreement at issue is internal or reflexive, and we have the word of his loyal (and by all accounts, unimaginative) student Cleanthes that he meant to specify an external standard, nature. Furthermore, I think that the preponderance of evidence shows that Zeno himself used the 'with nature' complement, so there is no need even to conjecture about a stage in Stoic ethics at which Zeno was fascinated by mere rational consistency.[7]

Accordingly, I also think it is a mistake to say that the Stoics defined virtue as 'a consistent character'.[8] Here too, the Greek simply says 'an agreeing character', or 'a disposition to agree'.[9] And this makes sense given that the possession of virtue is equivalent to having attained one's end. When one possesses virtue, and lives according to virtue, then one lives in agreement with nature, exactly because living according to virtue means living according to a disposition to agree with nature. But having a disposition to agree with nature is a very different thing from having a consistent disposition. For nature itself zigs and zags, and when it does, the virtuous person must zig and zag

140 ~ *Final Ends*

with it—that was one of the lessons of reservation. What matters for virtue is not that my impulse now should be consistent with my impulse then, but that my impulses on every occasion should conform to and agree with the impulses of Zeus, or nature.

Consistency of a minimal sort is important for the Sage's soul, and is guaranteed by the fact that they do not assent to any falsehoods—so none of their beliefs will be in contradiction to their other beliefs. But to say that their souls are consistent in this sense is different from saying that their beliefs will exhibit any large-scale orderliness, systematicity, or pattern—that may also be true for some other reasons, but it does not follow merely from the Sage's immunity to refutation, that is, their minimal epistemic consistency. And it is a still further step to suppose that what makes their beliefs or actions virtuous is that they are characterized by the rigorous and exceptionless application of general principles to particular cases. There have been philosophers, of course, who think that the essence of virtue consists in a respect for universal laws as such, and that such universal laws can be derived from considerations of rational consistency. This is the sort of picture that sometimes motivates interpreters to find references to 'consistency' in the Stoic accounts of the end and of virtue. But I think it is a mistake.[10]

The Charges of Incoherence

From what we have seen so far, it looks as though the Stoics said that the end is to live in agreement with nature or to live in accordance with virtue, and then linked these two formulae by saying that virtue consists in a disposition to agree with nature. Making virtue the end also fits with what we saw in the section on goods, namely the fact that virtue and things that partake of it are the only genuine goods. We will want there to be a clear connection between a school's account of the final end and its account of the highest good, and by saying that virtue is the only good and a life according to virtue is the end we certainly get a clear connection.

But this account has so far not made any reference to the pursuit of indifferents, or to the *telos*-formulae that discuss the selection of indifferents. Ancient opponents of the Stoics were quick to find problems with the way that the Stoics integrated indifferents into their account of the end.[11]

The first sort of dilemma that faces the Stoics might be thought of as 'either Aristo or Aristotle'. Aristo was a student of Zeno, but his views on Stoicism came to be considered unorthodox or even heretical. He rejected the division of indifferents into 'promoteds' and 'demoteds', arguing that there is no ground for any sort of distinction among the indifferents. Accordingly, there is no rationale for pursuing one indifferent rather than another; no reason of any kind to pursue health instead of disease, since everything other than virtue and vice is completely indifferent. As we will see further in the chapters on befitting actions, Chrysippus argued against this view that, far from giving virtue a greater predominance, Aristo's advocacy of complete indifference made virtue completely incomprehensible. What job would virtue have to do, if it were not instructing us in how to make wise choices between indifferents? How would one person be wiser, more courageous, or more prudent than another, if it were all a matter of indifference whether they ate a lot or a little, fought in battle or ran away, lived frugally or spent their way into ruin? Mainline Stoics insisted that Aristo's view was fundamentally wrong; indifferents are indifferent so far as happiness and misery goes, but not so far as rational action goes. In deciding what to select and what to disselect, what it is rational to pursue and what one should avoid, the distinction between promoted and demoted indifferents is of the first importance, and abandoning it as Aristo did will lead to incoherence.

Now Aristotle, or the members of Antiochus' notional 'Old Academy', incorporated such things as food or health into their account of the end in a relatively straightforward way. The final end and summum bonum contains all of the goods, all of the things whose presence in a life goes to make it happier, or whose absence detracts from that happiness. Among these goods, Aristotle said, the leading place is taken by virtue, but food and health and strength and moderate wealth and so on are goods as well, and a happy life should also include adequate provisions of them. They are goods, even if lesser goods than virtue, and there is no point pretending that one can lead a happy and satisfying life without them. Their place in the structure of the final end is dictated both by their intrinsic desirability—we want to be healthy just for its own sake—and by their ability to further our pursuit of other ends, as when our good health allows us to act courageously, or our moderate wealth enables us to exercise the virtue of liberality.

A critic like Antiochus—represented, as above, in Cicero's *de Finibus*—will argue that the Stoics are caught between Aristo and Aristotle, and that they cannot find a stable position in between.[12] Either they agree that we have reason to pursue health, in which case they are agreeing with Aristotle that it is a good—and their use of made-up terms like 'promoted' does nothing to change the substance of their view. Or if they insist that it is neither good or bad, they wind up agreeing with Aristo on its complete indifference, and they are no more able than he was to provide rationales for the ordinary choices that we make in life, and that wisdom requires us to make.

If the Stoics try to claim, in response to this first dilemma, that it is possible to have reason to pursue something without that reason consisting in the fact that it is a good thing, then the critics charge that the Stoics are undermining the very point of saying that the rational choices in a life are structured toward the final end of that life. The final end should be a coherent, unified system—whether it contains only one good, or a large, inclusive set of goods as in the 'Old Academic' picture, they all ought to cohere into a unified goal, and all of the agent's actions ought to derive their rationality from their relation to that goal.

It is contrary to the common conception to posit two ends or goals for life so that all the things we do in life fail to be related to one single thing as their reference-point. But it is still more contrary to the common conception to have one thing be the final end, but relate each of our actions to something else as the reference-point.[13]

This is a plausible objection against the Stoic picture, in which only virtue is said to be the good, but our actions are directed towards the selection of promoted indifferents (or the disselection of demoted indifferents, of course). It seems that the following three theses simply cannot be held consistently:

Our actions in life are rational only to the extent that they are related to the final end;
Only virtue is good; it alone is the final end and reference-point;
It is rational to pursue things other than virtue, like food and health.

Clearly the Stoics must give us a more sophisticated account of how the pursuit of a non-good can be rationally related to the reference point of virtue. Somehow, it must be rational to pursue indifferents, even though they form no part of the good, and cannot be instrumentally useful to the good. Furthermore, it must be rational to pursue them even though it is also a matter of indifference whether they are actually attained or not. (The Stoics are committed to this last by their insistence that virtue, and so the attainment of the end, is not vulnerable to the vagaries of chance outcomes like whether or not a patient lives or dies, whether or not the crops flourish or fail, and so on.)

The selection-formulae represent different attempts to give us this more sophisticated account. The proposal is that we can relate the pursuit of indifferents to the agent's end of a life of virtue by saying that a life of virtue exactly consists in a life in which agents exercise their rationality in the pursuit of indifferents. It is exactly by choosing wisely and avoiding bravely, by selecting temperately and distributing justly, that a life which in some sense is taken up with and given over to indifferents can nevertheless at the same time be a life directed towards the end of virtue.

This is also how the end of 'reasoning well in the selection of things according to nature' can be argued to be equivalent to 'living in agreement with nature', as well as to 'living according to virtue'. The expert reasoning that directs the selection is derived from the agent's experience of nature; virtue is exercised in every act of selection. (It is also worth pointing out here that the references to 'reasoning well' in the formulae of Diogenes must involve an extremely high standard of reason, namely the Sage's own perfected reason.)

Thus what makes it rational for Sages to pursue food is the fact that by this very pursuit they exercise and manifest their perfected rationality and virtue. In choosing when and how much food to pursue—or when not to pursue it at all—they use their experience of the course of nature, and conform their own actions to the course of nature, and thereby attain their own end of living virtuously. This account relates the pursuit of indifferents to the pursuit of the end in a coherent way. It also provides the necessary looseness of fit between the attainment of the indifferents and the attainment of the end; since all of the good of the exercise comes from the choosing and selecting and rationally pursuing, there is no danger that the Sage will lose anything good if chance or accident brings it about that they fail to attain the indifferent they pursue.

But even this attempt at explanation provoked a further round of criticism:

You make the selection of medicines (and their synthesis and use) more choiceworthy than health—and indeed claim that the health itself is not the least bit choiceworthy, but locate the end in your occupation with the medicines. And you say that the striving is the final end of the attaining rather than making the attaining the final end of the striving. How is this any different from saying that health has come about for the sake of medicine instead of medicine for the sake of health?[14]

'Well', says the Stoic, 'it is in the striving that the "acting in a well-reasoned manner" and the "acting wisely" resides.'

Indeed it does, we reply, provided that the striving keeps in view the attainment and possession of what it pursues, and makes that the final end. But otherwise it loses its 'well-reasoned manner' if it does everything for the sake of attaining things whose attainment is neither of any consequence nor contributes to happiness.

This seems to me a powerful objection. What is so wise or reasonable about pursuing things that don't matter? Even if one pursues them in a clever or far-seeing way, why is this any more admirable than the elaborate obsession of a string-collector or hoarder of tin foil? How can worthless things ground the worth of activities directed towards their acquisition? And if it is hard to see why it is worth expending the resources of wisdom and virtue on the attainment of worthless things, why would it help to say that you didn't really care whether you successfully attained them in any case? It would make the string-collector's machinations only more perverse, not less, if he claimed that he himself considered string a worthless possession, and in fact never bothered about whether his plots yielded him another length to add to his collection. If he said that he judged the success of his string-collecting not by whether he got another piece of string, but by how complicated, ingenious, and laborious his efforts had been, I think most of us would judge this a classic case of misplaced labors and a misspent life.

The Model of the Game

Here the Stoics offer a competing model of strenuous efforts directed consciously at an indifferent end: the model of the game.

The materials are indifferent, but the use of them is not indifferent. How then can we preserve our contentment and tranquility, but at the same time act diligently and methodically and avoid negligence? If we imitate dice-players. The chips are indifferent and the dice are indifferent—how do I know which way they'll fall? But to use the throw diligently and skillfully: that is my function . . . You will see the same thing with skillful ball-players. None of them thinks that the ball makes a difference to their good or bad, but the catching and throwing do make a difference. It's in the catching and throwing that the gracefulness resides, that's where the skill resides, the speed, the sensitivity . . . We too ought to display the diligence of the best ball-handler, combined with the indifference due to a ball.[15]

This is a powerful rebuttal. It shows us how it can be perfectly coherent, after all, to expend efforts on an object one takes to be indifferent. And, as recent critics have noted, it functions in part by relying on a distinction between a system of justification that is internal to the game, and a system that is external to the game.[16] Internal to the game are such rationales as 'I dived for the ball in order to prevent the other team from getting it', or 'never risk losing the ball unless you are sure you can score by doing so'. These attribute value to the possession of the ball, a value that can be explained by its role in controlling the pacing and strategy of the game, in scoring points, and ultimately, in winning the game. Internal to the game, we have adequately justified any action when we show how it is related to winning the game, as winning is defined by the game's own rules. Outside of the game, the story is different; the ball itself is likely to have little or no value, and the value of the game as a whole must be established by showing how playing a game of that sort, with those activities and those rules, subserves more general ends that agents have. Perhaps it provides exercise; perhaps it develops a healthy competitive spirit or an ability to cooperate on joint projects; we might say it builds character. These larger, external ends are likely to bear a fairly loose relation to the ends internal to the game. A losing season can build character just as effectively as a heedless stream of wins, and heaven knows one can get just as much exercise on the losing team as on the winning one. Internal to the game's rules and objectives, an afternoon spent racking up fewer points than the opposition must be judged a failure; external to the game it may have accomplished everything that could be desired from participation in such an activity.

This gives the Stoics a way of explaining how it can be rational— despite Plutarch's claims to the contrary—to direct one's wisdom and diligence towards the pursuit of things that one consciously judges to be indifferent. A full consideration of the success of this strategy should wait until we have been able to see more of its connections to the theory of befitting actions. But here we can at least point to a few limitations of the game model, in part to show what it can and cannot hope to do.

The model of the game, it seems to me, is radically incomplete, and parasitic in a number of ways. To begin with, there is the idea that when we are inside of a game, we grant the objectives of the game a sort of conditional validity—we act as though they matter. Now, the playing of games is only a small fraction of our activities, and games stand out against a background of non-game endeavors and practices. That is why it is not hard to understand what it means to act, inside of a game, 'as though' the objectives of the game mattered: we are modeling our activity inside the game on more familiar, more pervasive, non-game related ways of acting—we are engaged in a sort of make-believe. This means that, conceptually, what it means to play a game is posterior to what it means to engage in a non-game activity. Doing a proper job of exhibiting diligence within the game means acting, with respect to the objectives of the game, as though it was not a game, as though it was an ordinary, non-game related activity. That is one way in which games are parasitical on non-games. And it means that there is something slightly uneasy in the prospect of saying, as the Stoics seem to want to say, that all of the activities in our life—all of the concrete doings and pursuings and avoidings—are part of a large game, the game of acting as though indifferents matter. There is not only the fact that a derivative and marginal sort of activity—playing a game—is now occupying all of our waking hours. There is also the concern that, if we stress the 'as though' in that last claim, and ask whose activity we are being asked to model, we seem to get the strange result that we ought to act towards indifferents, within the game, as if we shared the false beliefs of people who mistakenly think that indifferents are really good or bad.

Furthermore, in real life games tend to be parasitic on non-games even in the details of the game's activities and objectives. Historically, most games have evolved because they train people in real skills that are worth having—non-game-related skills that allow us to do a better job of securing indifferents for ourselves and our community. It is no accident that many ancient games inculcated war-fighting skills, and evolved out of military practice. But then the value that running in armor has, internally to the Olympic athletic event of running in armor, depends on the value that real running in armor has outside of any game, on the battlefield. This means that games do not in general give us a good model of how an activity that would otherwise be pointless or indifferent can be elevated to a rationally worthwhile activity by its role in a game—the direction is usually the opposite, that activities win their roles in games because they are activities that have a real, non-derivative value outside games (or are closely related to such activities). When the ancient athletic javelin-thrower asked why it made sense to practice for the javelin-event, he did not have to rest content with the claim that it made sense inside of the practice of athletic javelin-events, though outside of that practice it was indifferent. Quite the opposite, any appeal to the existence of a game-like institution of javelin-events would only be a brief way-station along the direct justificatory path from the need to be able to throw javelins in battle, to the rationality of practicing this skill in non-lethal settings.

This is a fact about game-internal activities that the Stoics cannot help themselves to; Epictetus' use of the ball-game would be vitiated if he finished off by saying 'and the reason it is important for them to play the game gracefully and with skill is because this trains their hand–eye coordination, and this in turn has a statistically significant effect on their ability to perform in battle and in commerce, thereby increasing their personal income and their community's GDP'. These last considerations are supposed to be utterly indifferent outside the game; they cannot be used to ground our engagement with indifferents inside the game. In order to make the point it is supposed to make about the diligent and conscientious treatment of ultimately indifferent things, the model of the game must show how the activities within the game derive all of their point from considerations internal to the game, without needing to derive any of their worth from the worth of that kind of activity outside of games. Epictetus' ball-game must show us how it matters to take health seriously, even though health doesn't matter in the big picture; but in the more typical case, what matters inside of some game is exactly something that matters in the big picture.

And in this sense, these are facts about games that the Stoics are helping themselves to, illegitimately. The non-arbitrary nature of

Final Ends ~ 149

many games and their internal activities and objectives is part of what tempts us to concede to the Stoics that a practice that is justified within a game has been adequately justified, tout court. This, though, is the most important way in which games are parasitic on non-games: whenever a justification of some activity is given in terms of its role in a game, this automatically invites the further question, how a game of this sort, with these rules and these objectives, gains its justification in human affairs at large. Now, the answer need not come in the hard-bitten instrumentalist terms exemplified by the javelin contest, or more intellectually by the chess match that sharpens wits for more serious encounters. It may be that the game earns its keep merely by providing idle delight, and would not be as delightful if it did not employ these rules governing these activities. There can be many kinds of answers to the question of what justifies the existence of a particular game with the rules and activities that constitute it. My point here is simply that some such answer must be available if the game itself is to have any hope of justifying activities that are internal to it. By itself, the justification of a game-internal practice in terms of the game it is internal to is a clear exercise in buck-passing; far from putting a stop to the demand for justification, it makes the need for a justification all the more pressing.

This line of thought should not, I think, make us reject the Stoic appeal to games. Rather, it gives us reason to hope that the appeal was meant to do less work than it might seem. The model of the game does answer the charge raised in the last passage from Plutarch, that it is irrational to pursue things one believes to be indifferent; at least in some cases, there is no irrationality in acting this way, and the model of the game shows us one kind of case. Now we are faced with the follow-up question of what makes it rational for us to engage in this particular game—the game of treating indifferent diligently—and we see immediately that the appeal to games has exhausted its utility. But the Stoics have many more things that they can say at this point, which can avoid a further appeal to games, but also avoid granting indifferents some non-conditional value. When we ask why it makes sense to play a game in which we act as though indifferents matter, the answer does not have to be that some day the game will end and we'll be scrapping for indifferents in earnest—that would be a satisfactory sort of answer from the structural standpoint, but it is not one the Stoics can endorse. Instead, for instance, they can say that our attention to indifferents mirrors Zeus' own providential attention to a cosmos whose contents he too believes are indifferent, and that we have good reason to imitate Zeus. Or they can say that this way of relating to indifferents is the one specified in our nature, and that we always have reason to act in accordance with our nature. Or that wisdom and virtue need some substrate and material for their manifestation; that acting wisely is always a matter of doing some concrete actions wisely, and that these concrete actions—the ones of diligently selecting and disselecting—are the ones that permit the virtues their greatest scope for display. Answers of this sort would pick up where the appeal to games must leave off; it is not clear exactly what answer of this sort the Stoics would endorse, but it is more charitable to suppose they intended to offer one at this point, than to suppose that they thought the appeal to the game all by itself could obviate the need for further answers.

NOTES

1. 'Experience' here must be equivalent to knowledge, since we are discussing the beliefs of Sages; and indeed Cicero's translation of this formula (*de Finibus* 3.31 = SVF 3.15 = LS 64A = IG2 II–102) employs the word '*scientia*', suggesting that he was familiar with a version that used 'knowledge' (*episteme*) rather than 'experience'.
2. *DL* 7.87–88 = SVF 3.4, 1.555 = LS 63C = IG2 II–94.
3. Stobaeus 2.75–76 = SVF 1.179, 1.552, 3.12 = LS 63B, 58K = IG2 II–95.6.
4. *DL* 7.64 = SVF 2.183 = LS 33G = IG2 II–3.
5. This move can be buttressed by claiming that the end must be consistency, since Stobaeus follows the short formula by (1) equating it with 'living according to one harmonious reason' and (2) saying that 'those who live inconsistently are miserable'. But 'harmonious' (*sumphônon*) simply means 'in harmony with—,' i.e. itself or something else external to it; it is just as conceptually incomplete as 'in agreement with—'. That the second, external option is right is shown at *DL*

7.88 = IG2 11–94, which says that our inner state must be in 'harmony' (*sumphônia*) with the will of Zeus; conformity is the issue, not consistency. And the word translated 'inconsistently' really means more generally 'in conflict', and, as with 'agreement' and 'harmony', is open to completion either by an internal standard ('in conflict with themselves / their own views' = inconsistently) or by an external standard ('in conflict with nature / Zeus, etc.—not in agreement with nature'). So neither of these texts gives support for the internal 'consistency' reading.

6. Note also that Plato felt he had to add the explicit reflexive complement 'with themselves', even though he used 'agree' in the middle voice—the middle here has no different force from the active. So the fact that the Stoics used 'to agree' in the middle voice does not provide independent reason to interpret the word reflexively when it lacks an explicit reflexive complement.

7. Explicit attributions of expanded form to Zeno in *DL* 7.87 = IG2 11–94 (made more weighty by the citation to his treatise 'On the Nature of Human Beings') and Cicero in *de Finibus* 4.14, both collected together with a few later and less weighty sources (Lactantius and Philo) in *SVF* 1.179. Against this, only one explicit claim that Cleanthes added the complement 'to nature', in Stobaeus 2.76.3 = *SVF* 3.12 = LS 63B = IG2 11–95.6. In *DL* 7.89 = *SVF* 1.555 = LS 63C = IG2 11–94 we learn that by 'nature', Chrysippus understood both universal nature and human nature, whereas Cleanthes understood universal nature alone. This report does not show that Cleanthes introduced the 'to nature' complement, and suggests on the contrary that he is credited only with an interpretation of it, and one that Chrysippus contested, which is just what we would expect if the words themselves came from Zeno.

8. E.g. LS vol. i, translating *DL* 7.89 = *SVF* 3.39 = LS 61A = IG2 11–94.

9. Champions of 'consistency' will probably agree that the word should be understood uniformly in the account of the end and in the account of virtue, but will want 'consistency' to be the winner that takes all. Stobaeus 2.76 = *SVF* 3.3 = IG2 II–95.6b tells us that 'homologia' in the sense of virtue (the final good or *telikon agathon*) should be understood by referring it back to the predicate 'to live *homologoumenôs*' (which is the 'predicate correlated with' the *homologoumenos bios*, and thus is the third sense of *telos* in this passage). Since it was the settled opinion of at least Cleanthes and Chrysippus, and probably Zeno, that 'to live *homologoumenôs*' requires the complement 'with nature', it follows that to refer our understanding of *homologia* back to this means understanding *homologia* as 'agreement with nature', not as 'consistency'.

10. It is pursued with philosophical finesse and creativity in Engberg-Pedersen (1990), a book that is interesting and admirable in spite of what I take to be its thoroughly misguided reading of Stoicism.

11. The attribution of particular positions and criticisms to particular Stoics and their opponents is a matter of ongoing controversy, as is, consequently, the exact sequence of point and counterpoint—see Long (1967), Striker (1986), and Schofield (2003). (Carneades the Academic was certainly a pivotal figure in the

opposition, but we have his objections only at second or third hand through Plutarch, Cicero, and others.) My account here is intended to give a flavor of the kind of dialectical exchange that was involved, without attempting to detail the steps in the exchange.

12. *de Finibus* 4.78 = LS 64L.
13. Plutarch *Comm. Not.* 1070F = LS 64C.
14. Plutarch *Comm. Not.* 1071D–F = LS 64C—my translation rearranges some clauses.
15. Epictetus *Discourses* 2.5.1–4, 15–16, 20–21. 'sensitivity' translates *eugnômosunê*, more literally courtesy or considerateness. I take it that the reference is to a virtue of ball-players that involves understanding and relating to other players and their abilities in a sensitive way. Seneca *de Ben.* 2.17.3–4 attributes a very similar discussion of ball-playing to Chrysippus, which emphasizes the way that skillful players calibrate their efforts to the skill of the people with whom they are playing.
16. Striker (1991), Barney (2003).

Oikeiôsis *and Others*

We have so far not addressed the question how the Stoics wanted to incorporate my relations to other people into their account of my end. This was laid out in their theory of *oikeiôsis*. This term has so far eluded successful translation in critical discussions—unsuccessful candidates include 'appropriation', 'affinity', and 'familiarization'— and we may as well introduce the transliterated Greek as a technical term. As with most issues in Stoicism, we have no surviving, complete systematic treatises on the topic of *oikeiôsis*. What we have is the typical mixture of passing references in Cicero and Seneca, hostile discussions in anti-Stoic polemicists such as Plutarch and Alexander of Aphrodisias, a treatise from a genuine Stoic, Hierocles, that was probably quite helpful some millennia ago but has been reduced to a few shreds of papyrus, and the normal meager allowance from Diogenes Laertius.[1]

These texts tell us about a process called *oikeiôsis*, whereby things are rendered *oikeion* to human beings. Etymology tells us that the process-word, adjective, and related verbs all come from the word for a house or household, *oikos*, so we might expect the adjective *oikeion* to mean 'having to do with the household'; and so it does. But it also means, more broadly, having to do with the family or with kin, and it can even just indicate something with which one feels some affinity, affiliation, or familiarity, something that one takes as one's own in any sense. Usage, I think, suggests that the etymological links to the house and household were seldom salient to the user's mind, any more than our use of the word 'familiar' puts us immediately in mind of families.

Let us begin with Seneca and Diogenes Laertius.

Each period of life has its own constitution, one for the baby, and another for the boy, one for the youth, and another for the old man. They are all put into a relation of *oikeiôsis* with that constitution in which they exist:[2]

They say that an animal's first impulse is to preserve itself, because it is made *oikeion* to itself by nature from the start, as Chrysippus says in the first book of 'On Ends', saying that the first *oikeion* thing for each animal is its own constitution and its awareness of it... They say that nature made no distinction between plants and animals: even in plants nature governs (though without impulse and perception) and even in us there are some vegetative processes. When impulse has been added on top [sc. of the vegetative nature] in the case of animals, which make use of it to move towards things that are *oikeion*, then 'what accords with nature' is regulated by what accords with impulse. And when reason is given to rational animals for more perfect direction, then 'what accords with nature' for these animals has correctly turned into 'living in accordance with reason'. For reason has come in as the craftsman of impulse.[3]

Both of these texts refer to a sort of ordered hierarchy of animating principles or constitutions in different kinds of living things, or in one living thing as it matures. Unlike Plato and Aristotle, the Stoics did not say that plants have 'souls', but rather that they have 'natures' as their animating principles.[4] The animal begins its life as a plant-like fetus in the womb or egg, and thus has only a 'nature', which is transformed into a soul at the time of the animal's birth (or hatching or what have you). A human fetus also begins with a plant-like 'nature' in the womb, acquires an animal soul at birth, and then at the age of fourteen has its nature transformed a second time into reason, or a rational soul.[5]

The Diogenes passage is significant because it illuminates the Stoics' standard formula for the ethical end, namely living in accordance with nature. The word 'nature', of course, is endlessly ambiguous, but here a more focused and even purposeful ambiguity is in play, namely the fact that 'nature' can be used as a generic term that covers the souls of animals, the reason of adult human beings, and the natures, in a more specific sense, of plants. Thus what it means for each of these kinds of things to live in accordance with nature will vary with the kind of nature that it has. When an animal acquires a soul, it acquires perception and impulse, that is, the ability to sense its environment and pursue objects in it. Thus what it means for something of that sort to 'live according to nature' has to be cashed out in terms of its living according to impulse. Likewise for the adult human; since it has a rational soul or reason for its nature now, we specify what it is for *that* sort of thing to live according to nature by saying that it lives according to reason.

When the animal at birth, or the human being at various ages, is said to feel *oikeion* to itself or its constitution, the claim seems to be that its impulses are now organized towards preserving itself in the state in which it finds itself.[6] There seems to be a sort of built-in plasticity of concern; the animal's impulses seem designed to protect and conserve the welfare of something or another, but they gain their specific task only once the organism has identified what sort of a thing it is, and what sort of constitution it has. That settled, *oikeiôsis* dictates that the animal should be concerned to take care of itself on those terms.

This picture is put to polemical use in the Stoic argument that only virtue is good, whereas things like food and health are all indifferents. It makes sense that food, health, and so on are essential to maintaining the constitution of an animal, but a rational being is constituted by reason, and its impulses ought to be directed towards the maintenance of that reason, by acting rationally, that is, virtuously. I come to see my reason as the thing that is my own or *oikeion* to me, the thing whose welfare is my primary concern, such that if my reason is in good shape then I am in good shape. My final end, my summum bonum, is determined by the kind of thing I am; *oikeiôsis* is involved in my directing my impulse towards the preservation of that thing I recognize myself to be.

156 ~ **Oikeiôsis *and Others***

Other texts employ the language of *oikeiôsis* in relation to other people, making it the foundation of justice. Plutarch quotes the Stoics as saying

We are made *oikeion* to ourselves as soon as we come into existence, and our parts, and our own offspring.[7]

Cicero, in a discussion of *oikeiôsis*, says

They think it is important to understand that it comes about by nature that children are loved by their parents, and that it is from this beginning that we pursue the completed universal community of the human race.[8]

An anonymous commentator says that the Stoics derived justice somehow from *oikeiôsis*:

As for those who introduce justice on the basis of *oikeiôsis*, if they say that it is equal for oneself and for the furthest Mysian, then justice is preserved, but it will be . . . contrary to the evidence.[9]

Hierocles the Stoic gives us a long account, made vivid by the image of concentric circles, of how we ought to treat all people as though they were more closely related to us:

Each one of us is as it were entirely encompassed by many circles, smaller circles enclosed by larger ones, based on our different and unequal dispositions relative to each other. The first and closest circle is the one which a person has drawn as though around a center, his own mind. This circle encloses the body and anything taken for the sake of the body. For it is virtually the smallest circle, and almost touches the center itself. Next, the second one further removed from the center but enclosing the first circle; this contains parents, siblings, wife, and children. The third one has in it uncles and aunts, grandparents, nephews, nieces, and cousins. The next circle includes the other relatives, and this is followed by the circle of local residents, then the circle of fellow-tribesmen, next that of fellow-citizens, and then in the same way the circle of people from neighbouring towns, and the circle of fellow-countrymen. The outermost and largest circle, which encompasses all the rest, is that of the whole human race. Once these have all been surveyed, it is the task of a well tempered man, in his proper treatment of each group, to draw the circles together somehow towards the center, and to keep zealously transferring those from the enclosing circles into the

Oikeiôsis *and Others* ~ 157

enclosed ones . . . It is incumbent on us to respect people from the third circle as if they were those from the second, and again to respect our other relatives as if they were those from the third circle. For although the greater distance in blood will remove some affection, we must still try hard to assimilate them. The right point will be reached if, through our own initiative, we reduce the distance of the relationship with each person. The main procedure for this has been stated. But we should do more, in the terms of address we use, calling cousins 'brothers', and uncles and aunts 'fathers and mothers' . . . For this mode of address would be no slight mark of our affection for them all, and it would also stimulate and intensify the indicated contraction of the circles.[10]

It is worth noting that the paradigm case of what it is to take another human being as *oikeion* is the relation that a parent feels towards their children. It is surely conceptual priority rather than temporal priority that Cicero and Plutarch have in mind when they put the parental bond at the origin of justice—they are not claiming that adults cannot feel the pull of justice until they have reproduced.

So we learn from all of this that it is possible to feel *oikeion* towards oneself and others, that we feel this way as the result of a process that is natural in some sense (whenever the ancients say 'natural', it's time to hold onto your wallet), and that this process plays some role in the individual's discovery of their final end, and in the origins of justice. But what it means to take someone or something to be *oikeion*, and what follows from that fact for one's treatment of them, is not made as clear by the evidence as one would like. I propose that what it means to take something to be *oikeion* is that one treats it as an object of concern. In particular, when you think of something as *oikeion*, you think of its welfare as giving you reasons to act.

One advantage of this proposal is that it allows us to discern a unity in the notion of *oikeiôsis*, in contrast with the near consensus among critics that there are two separate kinds of *oikeiôsis*, to oneself and to others. We should take it that there is something like an open question, even in my own case, what I should care about, or where I should locate my sense of my own welfare. My impulses, my motivations to action, are directed towards the welfare of whatever

I take to be *oikeion*, but some further work has to be done in order for me to correctly identify what is in fact *oikeion* to me. The fact that in my own case this process is said to be natural should not make us overlook that there is, nonetheless, a process.

On this view, the question of *oikeiôsis* is distinct from, and antecedent to, the question of my end. One of the central topics of ancient ethical discussion was, as we have seen, the identification of a substantive account of the agent's end or good or summum bonum. It is a matter for ethical and (quasi-) empirical dispute whether or not I should take pleasure, honor, virtue, or what have you, to be part of my good. But we should not rush to assimilate the discussion of the *oikeion* to the discussion of the good. In fact, I think they are orthogonal; when we investigate the *oikeion*, or come to think of something as being *oikeion* or not, we are not taking a stand on the summum bonum, but on the cui bono, as the lawyers say: the recipients or beneficiaries of the good. When we add something to the list of things that are *oikeion* to us, whether it is our soul, our reason, our cousin, or our fellow citizen, we are not elaborating our conception of what is good for us, we are expanding our sense of whose welfare matters to us. If my reason matters to me, then what is beneficial to reason comes to be important to me; if I include my cousin within my sphere of direct concerns, then my cousin's welfare becomes important to me.

Before exploring the further ramifications of this theory, it is worth noting that the elements of the Stoic theory of *oikeiôsis* can be found in Book V of Plato's *Republic*, in the section that Socrates refers to as the 'second wave'.

The second wave is the section in which Socrates famously, and scandalously, proposes legislation about sex and reproduction among the guardians, abolishing marriage and nuclear families, and arguing that all mating should be arranged by lotteries which are deviously rigged for eugenic purposes. But the real subject matter and point of the second wave is not sex or reproduction; we can see this if we look at it as a whole. The beginning of the second wave is clearly flagged at 457c, and the third wave is announced at 473c. But the discussion of reproduction and family structure only occupies the first nine pages

Oikeiôsis *and Others* ~ 159

of the second wave, until 466; the second half of the second wave turns to a discussion of how the guardians should wage war. Whatever the second wave as a whole is about, it should be something that unites these apparently disparate topics of reproduction and warfare.

We can start to see a unifying theme if we look past the details of the sex-lotteries, to ask what their point is. What are they meant to accomplish? What is Plato trying to achieve by abolishing the nuclear family, replacing stable parent–child relationships with this looser, city-wide network of quasi-familial ties? The unifying thread is exactly the notion of the *oikeion*. The point of the abolition of nuclear families is to reconfigure the citizens' attitudes about which people are *oikeion* to them—the beneficial result of destroying the nuclear household, the *oikos*, is that the entire city will be a unified *oikos*. Instead of treating only one's biological kin as near and dear, one will treat all the other citizens as one's brother, sisters, parents, and children. But then this also turns out to be the message of Socrates' discussion of war, too; we need to extend our sense of kinship beyond the city, so that it encompasses all of the Greek cities, even those with whom we sometimes go to war.

Let's look at the relevant passages:

461e–462c   This, then, Glaucon, is how the guardians of your city have their wives and children in common. We must now confirm that this arrangement is both consistent with the rest of the constitution and by far the best . . . Is there any greater evil we can mention for a city than that which tears it apart and makes it many instead of one? Or any greater good than that which binds it together and makes it one? And when, as far as possible, all the citizens rejoice and are pained by the same successes and failures, doesn't this sharing of pleasures and pains bind the city together? Then is the best-governed city the one in which most people say 'mine' and 'not mine' about the same things in the same way?

462cd   What about the city that is most like a single person? For example, when one of our fingers gets hurt, the entire community pervading the body with the soul, organized into a single coordination under its ruling part, feels it, and the entire community is pained together at the same time and as a whole, though it is a part that is hurt, and that's why we say 'the person is hurt', in respect of their finger.

463be   Can you tell me whether a ruler in those other [sc. non-ideal] cities could address some of his co-rulers as his kinsmen (*oikeion*) and others as outsiders? And doesn't he consider his kinsman (*oikeion*) to be his own, and doesn't he address him as such, while he considers the outsider not to be his own? [But when a ruler in our city meets another of the ruling class,] he'll hold that he's meeting a brother or sister, a father or mother, a son or daughter, or some ancestor or descendant of theirs ... Will the law require merely that they use the kinship names (*oikeia onomata*), or that they also act in accordance with the names, giving these 'fathers' the respect, solicitude, and obedience legally due to fathers? ... When any one of our citizens is doing well or badly, they'll say that 'mine' is doing well or that 'mine' is doing badly.

464d   Our plan will make them genuine guardians, and prevent them from tearing the city apart by applying the word 'mine' to different things; ... they will have the same belief about what is their own (*oikeion*), will all aim at the same thing, and as much as possible be pained and pleased by the same things.

470b   It seems to me that as we have two names, 'war' (*polemos*— between cities) and 'civil war' (*stasis*—within cities), so there are two things and the names apply to two kinds of disagreements arising in them. The two things I'm referring to are what is one's own (*oikeion*) and akin on the one hand, and what's foreign and strange, on the other. The name 'civil war' applies to hostilities with one's own (*oikeion*), while 'war' applies to hostilities with strangers.

471ab   Then won't our citizens consider differences among Greeks [sc. in different cities]—since they are their own (*oikeion*)—to be a case of civil war [*stasis*], and refuse to call it 'war' [*polemos*]? ... They must treat barbarians the way Greeks [sc. of rival cities] currently treat each other.

So the point of the second wave, in the allegory of the city, is to implement a massive social engineering of one's sense of the *oikeion*. The goal is to unify the city by making everyone feel *oikeion* about everyone, since nothing is more divisive than having splinter-groups of *oikeion*-feeling, which is inevitable when people feel this sort of affinity and concern only for the members of their own family.

What would a Stoic find in the Second Wave?[11] To begin with, they would find the idea that people have an ability to see others as akin to them, as part of 'me and mine', and to feel a powerful sympathy on that basis. When you think of someone as *oikeion*, you are pained by their pain and pleased by their pleasure. A Stoic reader of the Second Wave would also see the proposal that this sense of the *oikeion* is highly plastic, that it can and should be redirected, manipulated, and engineered. They would read that the central, natural, and default object that we take to be *oikeion* is our biological family—good or bad, we take them to be part of me and mine, and we are inclined to share their pains and pleasures. They would find the analogy of the pain in the finger, illustrating how the model of the *oikeion*, of 'mine and not mine', can be applied to an individual's body parts, and also emphasizing, in vivid terms, the kind of direct, automatic, and unconscious sympathy that I am being asked to feel for the welfare of others. They would find normative proposals that we extend our sense of me and mine outward, smearing our feelings of *oikeiôsis* into ever wider circles. Plato tells us that we should think of all of the citizens around us in the way that we used to think of our blood relatives, calling all of the people in our city 'father', 'sister', 'uncle' and so on, and treating them accordingly. Furthermore, we should think of Greeks in other states the way that we used to think of Greeks in our own city. Here there is a very clear and direct foreshadowing of the concentric circles of Hierocles' discussion.

Although the fragment does not mention *oikeiôsis* explicitly, we can see it operating in the background of this report of a treatise by Zeno that he named after Plato's *Republic*:

Indeed, the much-admired 'Republic' of the founder of the Stoic sect, Zeno, is all directed towards this one summary point: that we ought not to dwell[12] in cities or in districts, dividing ourselves up into local systems of justice, but instead come to think of all human beings as fellow citizens of the same district, making a single life in this single cosmos, like a herd that pastures together and is ruled in common by a common law.[13]

The hypothesis that what it means to think of something as *oikeion* is that you include it among those things whose welfare gives you reasons to act could use some more specifying—what kind of reasons does it give you, and what are the relations between those reasons and other reasons you might have to act? Furthermore, what do we mean by 'welfare', since, as we have seen, the Stoics make a sharp distinction between the genuine good of virtue, and the merely promoted selective value of health, food, and so on?

In particular, would we be justified in saying that when you think of someone as *oikeion* you take it that their welfare gives you reasons to act that do not need to operate, even indirectly, through consider-ations of your own welfare? Is seeing other people as *oikeion*, for instance, like seeing them as an end in themselves?

It seems to me that we can say a few useful things straight off the bat. First, there is surely something right about saying that *oikeiôsis* has something to do with treating others in a more impartial manner. On the other hand, it is clear that what we are being offered falls far short of what some partisans of impartiality might want. The kind of concern that *oikeiôsis* can deliver will never be a matter of being motivated to benefit others regardless of the fact of their otherness. Quite the opposite; we do not help the other people qua other, but qua our own, *oikeion*, 'mine'. I am emphatically not being asked to transcend my partiality towards those I conceive of as my own, but rather to expand the extension of that concept. Still, the outcome is supposed to emulate impartiality to a large extent; I am supposed to feel *oikeion* towards everyone in my city, according to Plato, or towards the entire human race, according to the Stoa. Hierocles concedes to the anti-Stoic critics quoted in the Anonymous commen-tary that the result of using diffused partiality to emulate impartiality will be imperfect; we are likely to feel closer to some than others.

How worrisome this is depends in part on what sort of 'founda-tion' for justice *oikeiôsis* is meant to provide, and what sort of 'derivation' of justice is being attempted. If the normative facts about justice are supposed to be derivable from our feelings of *oikeiôsis*—along the lines of saying that we owe consideration to others just in proportion with our feeling of kinship with them—then the derivation will be manifestly inadequate, as the Anonymous commentator points out. But if the normative facts are fixed elsewhere—if we can independently secure the claim that justice demands the impartial treatment of all human beings, for instance—then *oikeiôsis* can still do some extremely useful work in providing the raw materials for making it psychologically possible to respond to this sort of norm. A human psychology that altogether lacked this ability to view others as near and dear, or had it in a form that precluded the expansion of one's near and dear beyond a narrow and biologically constrained set of blood relations, would then owe us an even more difficult, probably less plausible story about how things like us are supposed to be able to respond to the demands of justice.

Having seen all this, suppose that we ask whether the Stoic moral psychology was essentially egoistical or not—is it possible for me to be motivated by a concern for someone else's welfare, without this concern running through considerations of my own welfare? The answer will be complex, depending on whether the welfare in question involves goods or indifferents.

I have a direct and unmediated concern for my own happiness, and so for whatever I think will be constitutive or productive of it, that is, whatever I take, rightly or wrongly, to be a good. If I view something as a good, then I will not be able to treat my getting it or losing it as a matter of indifference—that is why even the loving father in Epictetus will come to plan for his son's death if he thinks that property or sex is good.[14] But this is also why, once I come to see that sex and property are not good, and that virtue alone is good, my attitude towards other people's virtue will be frankly uncharitable, as when Epictetus says to the person who is concerned about his servant's state of virtue 'it is better for your servant to become vicious than for you to become unhappy'.[15]

The fact that my attitude towards my own good and happiness is irredeemably self-centered turns out to have fewer consequences than might be expected, however, because of the fact that only my virtue is productive of my good. If I correctly understand the nature of indifferents, then it turns out that the essentially first-person orientation of my concern for goods will not prevent me from being motivated in unselfish ways when it comes to the distribution of indifferents. If I truly see the food as indifferent, that is, as not necessary for my good or even incrementally productive of it, then an important barrier to my sharing it with others will have been lowered.

Here we can see that the criticisms of Antiochus miss an important point: the Stoics think that the difference between calling something a 'good' and calling it a 'promoted indifferent' is far from a matter of superficial terminology; this difference in conception makes a vast difference for whether we can come to feel the sort of indifference towards it that will allow us to share it impartially with others. Once I think of it as a good, there is no way for me not to take it to be vital to my happiness. Perhaps if there is enough food and to spare I can think of food as a good and still share the unneeded surplus with others. But I will not be able to share the last bit of scarce food with others, not if I think of it as a good that I need for my happiness. On the other hand, when I combine my knowledge that the food is indifferent, with my enlarged sense that all other people are *oikeion* to me, then I can come to be moved by their need for food just as directly as I am moved by my own need for food.

There is still a sense in which my concern for the (indifferent-related) welfare of others runs through my concern for my own (happiness-related) good. But even here, there is a surprising element of impartiality, as a result of the fact that my concern for my *own* indifferent-related welfare must also run through my concern for my happiness. Why do I feed the stranger? There is no way to provide a full analysis of my motivations for doing this without mentioning the fact that it conduces to my virtue, and so to my happiness. But there is no other story I can tell about why I feed myself, either. If we stay at the level of indifferents—inside the game, as it were—then my concerns for the welfare of others can come to operate in me with the same directness and immediacy that my concerns for my

Oikeiôsis *and Others* ~ 165

own welfare do. I can come to see the fact of his hunger as giving me a reason of exactly the same sort as the fact of my hunger. In other words, not a very strong reason at all—since I think of my own hunger as a matter of indifference, and think that it will not really matter in any way to my happiness whether I get some food or not. That is what I think about his hunger as well. Still, I know how my pursuit of my own happiness, when combined with my knowledge of nature and the workings of nature, makes certain other activities rational, and among these are not only my pursuit of my own food, but my concern for the provision of food to this stranger.

From this perspective, we can see the distinction in value between goods and indifferents as a response to the expectation of egoistical eudaimonism in the account of the agent's psychology. It's a way of granting to the Socratic tradition that, when it comes to questions of real value and goodness, our motivation is irredeemably self-regarding, while at the same time making possible a wide range of apparently other-regarding behavior.

We can structure the resulting picture as a series of good news / bad news jokes.

(1) Here's the bad news: people are irredeemably selfish and self-centered about any value that they think really matters.

Here's the good news—people can come to see that not much matters—nothing at all, except virtue.

Again:

(2) Here's the good news: people can come to act with perfect impartiality about the distribution of food, wealth, and the rest of the so-called 'goods'.

Here's the bad news: they are capable of such selfless generosity only on the condition that they think none of those things are really good.

It is natural to come to the Stoics with the assumption that our desires for food, wealth, and so on are intrinsically gluttonous, self-centered, and in need of repression. The slogan that virtue is the only good then sounds like a defiant attempt to put those fleshly desires in their place—they cannot be rehabilitated, but they can be pushed out of the center of our attention, expelled from their central and controlling domination over our actions, by the constant insistence that they do not deserve our vehement pursuit.

But the curious result of examining *oikeiôsis* is that we have found that desires of this sort are much more amenable to domestication than we had thought—indeed, it seems that in principle the ravening lion of hunger for food can be transformed into a very lamb of impartial distribution. From this perspective, the one desire that is completely incapable of reformation—the one drive that must always smell of old Adam— is our desire for the good. Whatever we take to be good, we thereupon pursue with a selfishness and intensity both insatiable and unsociable. It wasn't hunger that made the beast ravenous, it was the belief that food was a good; shorn of that illusion, the beast can pasture peacefully with the rest of the herd. And now the claim that only virtue is good acts not so much to disparage the value of things other than virtue, as to keep them safely out of the reach of this devouring maw, the desire for the good and what we take to be good.

So just as we had first thought, there is a large and vicious dog in the picture, and it must be kept kenneled for our safety and for the safety of others. And just as we had thought, 'virtue is the only good' is the device written on its cage, the principle that keeps it confined to a small space where it cannot hurt ourselves or others. But this dog is not the dog of sensual appetites, it is the dog of desire for the good, that intrinsically selfish and vehement desire that refuses to share any bone it is given. When it roamed free and seized things at will, it made food its good, and wealth and health and honor, and it snarled and snapped at anyone who tried to take them away. Now safely caged, its only bone is virtue, which it can gnaw without harm to others. Outside its kennel, the desires for food and health and wealth may safely graze, since these desires are moderate and un-intense, mere selections of the indifferent, not relentless strivings for the good.

1. On Hierocles see Inwood (1984). On *oikeiôsis* in general, see Striker (1983).
2. *Seneca Ep.* 121 = LS 57B = IG2 II–107.
3. *DL* 7.85 = *SVF* 3.178 = LS 57A = IG2 II–94 trans. modified from LS.
4. Origen *de Principiis* 3.2.2–3 = *SVF* 2.988 = LS 53A = IG2 II–25; Hierocles 1.5–33, 4.48–53 = LS 53B; note that the word LS translate 'physique' in these contexts is the same word they translate 'nature' everywhere else, sc. *phusis*. Their desire to avoid ambiguity is understandable, but I prefer to highlight the importance of using 'nature' to refer both to one kind of animating principle (those proper to plants or embryos) as well as generically to any sort of animating principle, including a soul or reason.
5. *DL* 7.55 = *SVF* 3. Diogenes 17 = LS 33H = IG2 II–3.
6. Alexander of Aphrodisias reports the Stoics as saying that the first thing that is *oikeion* to the animal is itself, but he then comments that 'the more sophisticated-seeming among them say that what is *oikeion* to us is rather our constitution and the preservation of it'. (*Mantissa* 150 = *SVF* 3.183).
7. Plutarch *Sto. Rep.* 1038B = *SVF* 3.179 = LS 57E = IG2 II–114.
8. Cicero *de Finibus* 3.62 = *SVF* 3.340 = LS 57F = IG2 II–103.
9. Anon. in *Theaetetum* 5 = LS 57H.
10. Hierocles in Stobaeus 4.671–673 = LS 57G, translation from LS.
11. There is little doubt that Zeno read Plato's *Republic*—he wrote a treatise of his own entitled 'The Republic'. There is no doubt whatsoever that Chrysippus read Plato's *Republic*, because Plutarch quotes verbatim a passage in which Chrysippus criticizes the views of Cephalus from *Republic I* (Plutarch *Sto. Rep.*1040AB = *SVF* 3.313).
12. 'Dwell' here renders *oikômen*, the verb related to *oikeion*, so that Zeno is also saying 'we should not treat as *oikeion* only these cities and districts'.
13. Plutarch *de Alex. virt.* 329AB = *SVF* 1.262 = LS 67A.
14. For the same thought cf. also Epictetus 4.5.30–32: 'This is the nature of each thing: to pursue the good and flee the bad . . . If these things [sc. external indifferents] are good, then the father is no friend to his son, nor the brother to the brother: everything around us is full of enemies, conspirators, and sneaks. But if a properly functioning prohairesis is the only good, then where is there any longer room for conflict or contention?'
15. *Encheiridion* 12.

II

What Makes an Action Befitting?

One of the most influential legacies of the Stoic system was their theory of the *kathêkon*, or, as the word is variously translated, 'duties', 'offices', 'proper functions', 'appropriate actions', or 'befitting actions'. I shall employ this last term, as having the fewest misleading connotations.

In some sense that we shall now explore, these befitting actions are the ones that we ought to do. They are both the actions that people who are already virtuous do, and also the ones that we make progress towards virtue by doing. They also set standards for failure; we are making an error if we do something contrary to the befitting.

At least some of the Stoic examples make this seem like a straight-forward and familiar view. For instance, they say that it is befitting to honor one's parents and country, and that to neglect one's parents, or to despise one's country, is contrary to the befitting.

The Definition of the Befitting

The Stoics tell us some other important things about befitting actions. For instance, we are given a definition of them:

A befitting action is one which, once done, has a reasonable justification.[1]

This definition requires unpacking. To begin with, what makes a justification a reasonable one is that it conforms to the standards of reason that are set by Sages—in this context, it might be better to say 'well-reasoned', rather than 'reasonable'.

In particular, the reference to a reasonable or well-reasoned justification is not intended to make it easier for an action to be a befitting one, or for ordinary, non-virtuous people to discover them. In contemporary Anglophone jurisprudence, the 'reasonable person' is used as a standard of judgment for deciding whether a defendant acted rashly, irresponsibly, negligently, and so on. It is part and parcel of this use of the term 'reasonable' that most ordinary people are reasonable, and that reasonable people can disagree about courses of action. In fact, in most cases there will be several different courses of action that are all roughly 'reasonable' in this legal sense. But the Stoics' use of the 'well-reasoned' is not intended to introduce this sort of room for disagreement or toleration of various alternatives. It is the Sage's perfect and infallible reason that sets the standard for what is 'reasonable', and it is the Sage's action, or what the Sage would have done, which sets the standard for a reasonable action, and thus for the befitting action.[2]

Second, there is no reason to think that the reasonable justification that makes an action a befitting one need ever be articulated, uttered, or even contemplated by anyone, whether the person who performed the action or someone else.[3] It must simply be available in principle. This point is reinforced by the passages that tell us that even irrational animals and plants perform befitting actions.[4] For some of the things that plants and animals do, there is a well-reasoned justification available, though of course they could never articulate it themselves.

Befitting and Perfected

Furthermore, they say that the actions of virtuous people are all befitting ones.[5] But they are a special class of befitting actions; when a

Sage performs a befitting action, it may also be called a perfectly befitting action, or a perfected action.[6] Although both Sages and non-Sages perform instances of the genus 'befitting actions', only Sages perform instances of the species 'perfectly befitting actions'. In light of the fact that the generic category of befitting actions applies equally to the actions of Sages and non-Sages, befitting actions are sometimes called 'middle actions'.[7]

This pattern should look familiar to us from the case of epistemology, where both Sages and non-Sages were said to have episodes of *katalêpsis*, but only in the case of Sages did these constitute episodes of knowledge. In the case of non-Sages, the name that was applied to their episodes of *katalêpsis* seemed somehow unfairly condemnatory; even though the judgments were true, and involved assents to impressions that were not only true but were such as could not come from false origins, the Stoics nevertheless lumped together these judgments along with the non-Sage's false and accidentally true judgments, calling them all 'opinions'.

Here too, something similar applies: when a non-Sage performs a befitting action, it receives the same name as when the non-Sage performs an action contrary to what is befitting: both are labeled 'errors'. Indeed, everything that the non-Sage does is an error, even when it is exactly what a Sage would have done in parallel circumstances. Not only is it labeled an error, it is also said to be done badly and viciously, and done in accordance with all the vices.[8] And since there is good reason to suspect that all of the people alive in Chrysippus' time and ours are non-Sages, we can conclude that all of Chrysippus' actions were vicious errors, and all of Mother Teresa's actions were vicious errors, and so on.

The rationale for this strange method of categorization is the same with actions as it was with judgments; what the Stoics want to emphasize is the difference between a mental disposition that is completely incapable of error, and a mental disposition that is capable of error because of its inconsistency and irrationality. The fact that a particular judgment happens to be in conformity with the truth, or a particular action is in conformity with the befitting, is less import-

What Makes an Action Befitting? ~ 171

ant in their eyes than the fact that it is done from the very same mental state that, in altered circumstances, would have produced a false judgment or an action contrary to the befitting.[9]

The Difference in Terms of Impulse

We can describe the difference between a Sage's perfected befitting action and the non-Sage's merely befitting action in another way. Since we know that all actions stem from impulses, and all impulses are judgments or beliefs, we can describe the difference between the Sage's virtuous actions and the non-Sage's vicious actions in those terms as well:

a virtuous action is one whose impulse consists in a strong assent to a kataleptic impulsive impression;

a vicious action is one whose impulse involves either a weak assent or a non-kataleptic impulsive impression.

We have also seen that the Sage's virtue simply is their mind, that is, the totality of their dispositions to assent, and that the non-Sage's vice simply is their mind as well. Thus it is literally true that all of the Sage's actions are done from virtue, that is, that the causal source of the actions, and the impulses that produce them, is the Sage's mind. Its freedom from inconsistency and rashness makes every one of the Sage's assents strong, and guarantees that the Sage assents only to the kataleptic. And it is literally true that all of the non-Sage's actions are done from vice, that is, the causal source of those actions is the non-Sage's imperfect disposition. The non-Sage's unstable and contradictory mental contents render all of their assents weak ones, and cannot preclude their sometimes assenting to the non-kataleptic.

This difference of impulse and difference of disposition is sufficient to make the difference between virtuous and vicious action, even if the actions are identical to the outward eye:

The activities are all common, and they are differentiated only by arising from a craftsmanlike disposition or from an inexpert one. For the

172 ~ *What Makes an Action Befitting?*

characteristic function of the Sage is not 'attending to parents and generally honoring them'; the characteristic function of the Sage is doing this from wisdom. And just as 'bringing about a cure' is an activity common both to doctors and to laymen, but doing it as a physician would is the special mark of the expert, so too 'honoring parents' is an activity common both to the Sage and the non-Sage, but 'honoring parents from wisdom' is the special mark of the Sage. The Sage thus has an art of life, whose special function it is to perform each of the actions from the best disposition.[10]

The Lists of Befitting Actions

In addition to the definition, we are also given lists of various kinds of befitting actions, as mentioned above. To begin with, we have the lists which contrast befitting actions (e.g. honoring one's parents or country) and actions contrary to the befitting (e.g. neglecting one's parents or country), and actions that are neither befitting nor contrary to the befitting, which include picking up a twig, holding a pencil or scraper, and the like. Then another list contrasts those actions that are befitting without regard to circumstance and those that are befitting in light of circumstances. Taking care of one's health and one's sense-organs are said to be befitting without regard to circumstance, whereas mutilating oneself or throwing away one's possessions are said to be befitting in light of circumstances; and an analogous story applies to actions contrary to the befitting. Another list tells us that some befitting actions are always befitting, others are not always befitting. The action that is always befitting is to live according to virtue; actions that are sometimes but not always befitting include walking, asking and answering questions, and the like.[11]

It is important to keep in mind the great variety of befitting actions, so that we can reject the view that the theory of befitting actions has any special reference to actions that we owe to each other as human beings, or actions that are other-regarding, or virtuous in more familiar ways. This is also a clear lesson from the fact that plants and animals can perform befitting actions. What makes an action befitting is something about how it accords with the

What Makes an Action Befitting? ~ 173

nature of the agent and with the nature of the universe as that is revealed in the special circumstances of action that may arise. The nature of plants is such that they perform their befitting actions by photosynthesizing (let's say). The nature of humans is such that they perform their befitting actions by walking, by bending or stretching their fingers in certain ways, by asking and answering questions, by taking care of their health in some cases, by mutilating themselves in other cases, and so on. In addition, human nature involves interaction with other human beings, that is, it is social and communal, to an extent that the natural behavior of pine trees or polar bears is not. It is for that reason that, among the actions that are befitting for human beings, there are actions like honoring one's parents and one's country. But they have no privileged place in the system. If we come to this material thinking that the Stoics have a theory of 'duties', then we may think that actions like honoring one's parents are the central and paradigmatic cases of 'duties', that is, things that are due to other people, moral obligations and ethical demands. Then we may think that the other actions mentioned, e.g. taking care of one's health, should be included into the system as secondary or derivative instances of 'duty', perhaps 'duties to oneself'. But this would be to get the picture backwards. What is typical of a befitting action—whether it involves people other than the agent or not, and indeed whether the agent is a person or not—is that it somehow is in keeping with the agent's nature. Bending one's finger in the right way, or walking and talking in the right way, are no less central expression's of the agent's nature than returning deposits and keeping promises.

The Psychological Ubiquity of 'Befitting'

We can reinforce this line of thought by recalling a point made in the discussion of impulse. An important text tells us that what is essential to the content of an impulsive impression is the fact that it represents its actions as, in a certain sense, the thing to do.[12] The word that is used in this text is the same one that I have been translating as 'befitting', that is, *kathêkon*. The evidence shows that it is this very thought that does the motivating; what sets our limbs in motion, so to speak, is the fact that we assent to the impression that our action is *kathêkon* or befitting. Now to judge from the theory of impulse, this would seem to be an absolutely ubiquitous feature of all the actions performed by all people. It is not only those with constabulary duties to be done who think that what they are doing is befitting; this very same thought also motivates the burglar who's a-burgling, and the cut-throat who is occupied in crime. Epictetus explicitly says that there is only one source of impulse to action, namely the thought that something is befitting, and that it is this thought that motivates robbers, thieves, and adulterers, along with everyone else.[13] But then it seems that any conception of their own action which we attribute to every agent, on the occasion of every one of their actions, cannot be the thought that they are doing their *duty*, for surely it is essential to that notion that actions done from duty should contrast with actions done from other considerations or motives. In order for a moral psychology to have the notion of an agent's performing an action from the thought that it is a duty, it must also be possible within that psychology for agents to perform actions without that thought. Since, within Stoic moral psychology, every action is conceived of as befitting, and it is not possible to perform actions without that thought, it follows that acting because one conceives of one's action as befitting is not the same as acting from duty.

Of course, it is one thing for the burglar to think that a bit of burglary is befitting just now, that is, the thing to be done, and a different thing for the burglar to be right about that point—the burglar is almost certainly wrong. In the psychological theory, every agent conceives of their action as befitting and assents to it on that basis; it is exactly that judgment that motivates them. In the ethical theory, many of those judgments turn out to be wrong. It's the difference between how ethically imperfect agents view the action from the inside, as it were, and how the correct account of ethics views the action from the outside.

Setting up the problem

The Case of the Progressor

It should be noted that in describing the vicious and virtuous actions, we have not said anything about the agent's explicit motives or reflections; the virtuous agent, performing perfected actions, is not necessarily thinking different thoughts from the vicious agent, performing errors that are externally the same. Indeed, Chrysippus describes a case exactly like this, where a vicious agent is doing exactly what a virtuous agent would be doing, and having thoughts that differ only in the way that a non-Sage's true and *kataleptic* judgments differ from a Sage's knowledgeable judgments, that is, in the firmness of their assent. What he describes is a Progressor—a vicious person or non-Sage who is making progress towards virtue—who is furthermore very close to the moment when their state of complete vice, misery, and ignorance will be transformed into a state of complete virtue, happiness, and freedom from anything but knowledge:

The Progressor on the verge [sc. of Sagehood] performs absolutely all of the befitting actions, and omits none of them. His life is not yet happy, but happiness will eventuate for him when these middle actions [i.e. befitting actions] acquire firmness and the status of dispositions and their own characteristic fixity.[14]

Here we are given a carefully calibrated assessment of the minimal difference between a (particular kind of) non-Sage, all of whose actions are errors and vicious actions, and a Sage, all of whose actions are perfected actions and virtuous actions. The relevance of happiness, of course, is that it is a marker for virtue; the Progressor's life is not yet happy because he is still vicious, but happiness will come exactly when virtue does, that is, when the actions acquire firmness, fixity, and so on.

It may seem strange that the Progressor's actions still count as vicious, and the Sage's actions count as virtuous, when they are performing actions that are externally the same, and with impulses whose contents are the same. It will seem less strange if we

176 ~ *What Makes an Action Befitting?*

remember that for the Stoics, virtue literally is knowledge. Now the question is how one person can know something, and the other fail to know it, when they both believe the same thing—and here it should seem obvious that this is possible, both in our own views of knowledge and in Stoic epistemology as well. The case of the Progressor is exactly parallel to the epistemological case in which we might have a non-Sage all of whose beliefs are mere opinions and not knowledge, but who is only assenting to *kataleptically* true impressions, and compare it to a Sage who has nothing but knowledge. If the non-Sage and the Sage are assenting to the very same true and *kataleptic* impressions, why does the Sage have knowledge where the non-Sage does not? Because the Sage's assent is strong, and the non-Sage's assent is weak, where that means: because the Sage's disposition to assent is so stable and reliable that no matter what circumstance they find themselves in they will never assent to anything non-*kataleptic*, never be taken in, never accept an impression that is inconsistent with the totality of their beliefs, and so on.

The epistemologically imperfect non-Sage, by contrast, may well be assenting to all and only the same impressions as the Sage, but their disposition to assent is not completely stable and reliable. They responded appropriately to the truth in this context, and if the circumstances had been slightly different they still might have got it right, but in sufficiently exotic circumstances they would have taken a deceptive impression for a true one, or an obscure impression for a clear one, and assented to something non-*kataleptic*. Their faculty of assent, that is, still needs to take on a certain stability and fixity, and become a completely reliable disposition.

What the Progressor Shows

This is an important passage, because it rules out certain ways of distinguishing virtuous action from vicious action within Stoicism. There are other ethical systems in which a vicious person and a virtuous person may be performing exactly parallel actions, for example, returning the correct amount of change to a customer who cannot count, where the difference that makes one action virtuous and the other action vicious is held to reside in the motives or intentions of the two agents. The vicious agent, for instance, might be doing the honest thing because they hadn't realized this was an opportune moment to cheat, or because they realized it, but did not think the small gain in coins was worth the risk to their commercial reputation. The virtuous person, on the other hand, would be acting virtuously exactly to the extent that they were doing the virtuous thing because it was virtuous, or for the sake of virtue. The thoughts running through the two agents' heads would differ in a characteristic way; if we could somehow overhear their motives and intentions, we would find a distinct difference of content, with one of them making a grudging calculation of self-interest, and the other motivated by the pure light of duty.

This is clearly not the account adopted by Stoicism. Not only can a virtuous action and a vicious action (provided that it is a befitting one) look exactly the same from the outside, that is, as far as the external, observable behavior goes, it is also the case that the two actions can be accompanied by the very same thoughts, intentions, and motives, or the same sequence of impressions and corresponding propositions. Whatever the Sage is thinking in performing their perfected action, the non-Sage may be thinking in performing their vicious error. The difference lies neither in their actual actions nor in their actual thoughts, but in the thoughts they would have been having, and the actions they would have been performing, in sufficiently altered circumstances. That is what the focus on fixity and firmness shows us.

Of course, this is a very unusual case—progressors on the verge of Sagehood are presumably almost as rare as Sages themselves. In the more typical case of contrasting virtuous and vicious behavior, a mere comparison of the external behavior will show that the non-Sage did something different from what the Sage would have done, i.e. that the non-Sage did something contrary to what is befitting. There will also be many cases in which the non-Sage performs a vicious action that is also a befitting one, i.e. in external conformity with what the Sage would have done, but in which the non-Sage is thinking very different thoughts in the course of performing it—perhaps assenting to unclear truths, or assenting to falsehoods. A very common case of this last sort will be when the non-Sage does what the Sage would have done, for instance, eating some food when that is befitting, but the non-Sage will have the false belief that the food is a good thing; their motivation will be an emotion. All of these are cases in which the Stoic judgment that one action is virtuous and the other is vicious looks more like familiar judgments made in other ethical systems. But those grosser differences—differences in external action, or in the content of the impressions—do not go to the heart of the difference, they do not show us the essence of what makes one action virtuous and one action vicious. That, it turns out, is completely a matter of the fixity of the agent's disposition.

But then if it is possible for a virtuous action and a vicious action to be accompanied by the same thoughts, motives and intentions, this might show us one of two very different things. It might show us that one can have, to speak loosely, extremely virtuous thoughts—self-sacrificing thoughts, thoughts about what justice requires, thoughts about the value of acting for the sake of virtue alone—and yet not succeed in acting virtuously because one's character lacks the requisite fixity. Perhaps those are the kind of thoughts that both the Sage and the progressor on the verge are having, and the progressor loses out only because of his weak assent—only because of thoughts he *would* have had in a sufficiently different context. Or it might show us that one can have, again to speak loosely, thoughts which are not the least bit virtuous—thoughts which make no reference to virtue, in which explicit considerations of the various virtues and what they require make no appearance—and yet succeed in acting virtuously because one's character has the requisite fixity. Chrysippus' example of the progressor on the verge guarantees that virtuous and vicious thoughts can have the same propositional content, but we would still like to know what that content is. The best way to figure out the content of these various agents' thoughts is by considering the thoughts that lead up to their actions, by focusing on the

What Makes an Action Befitting? ~ 179

deliberations that lead agents to act, and seeing what considerations feature in them. This will be our task in the next two chapters.

NOTES

1. *DL* 7.107 = *SVF* 3.493 = IG2 ɪɪ–94; Stobaeus 2.85 = *SVF* 3.494 = LS 59B = IG2 ɪɪ–95.8. *SE AM* 7.158 = *SVF* 3.284 = LS 69B = IG2 ɪɪɪ–18 presents itself as a definition of perfected action, but still gives us confirmation of the definition of the befitting action.
2. I thus disagree with the claim that the befitting action 'is a particular action or activity, the ethical grounding of which, in the case of humans, is "reason", but not necessarily "right reason, the foundation of right actions"'. For this fallible sense of "reasonable", cf. 40F' (LS vol. 1.365). The text referred to is the anecdote of Sphaerus and the pomegranates, discussed above. I have argued in Brennan (1996) that the reference to the 'reasonable' does not indicate any standard of reason that is 'fallible' or less rigorous than the Sage's right reason.
3. I thus disagree with the claim that the befitting action 'must require that its agent act on the promptings of reason, that is, be rationally motivated to do what is appropriate' (LS vol. 1.367) I believe that a vicious agent who eats when it is befitting, even if motivated by gluttony rather than a sense of what is appropriate, has still performed a befitting action—at any rate, I do not see any evidence to the contrary. The evidence about plants and animals certainly suggests that no particular motivation is essential. And if it were, then we ought to have a distinction in Stoicism between performing a befitting action, and performing an action that conforms to what is befitting, but is not a befitting action. (Philo *de Cherubim* 14 = *SVF* 3.513 = LS 59H is rightly discounted by LS—on Philo's thorough-going unreliability as a source for Stoic doctrine see von Arnim's strictures in *SVF* ɪ.xɪx). It seems to me that befittingness in impulses parallels truth in impressions, i.e. it is purely a matter of external conformity, whereas considerations of the agent's thoughts or mindset come in with the difference between the befitting and the perfectly befitting, as with the difference between opinion and knowledge.
4. *DL* 7.107 = *SVF* 3.493 = IG2 ɪɪ–94; Stobaeus 2.85 = *SVF* 3.494 = LS 59B = IG2 ɪɪ–95.8.
5. Stobaeus 2.66.14 = *SVF* 3.560 = LS 61G = IG2 ɪɪ–95.5b10.
6. 'Perfectly befitting action' translates '*teleion kathêkon*'; 'perfected action' translates '*katorthôma*'.
7. Cicero *Acad. Post.* 1.37 = *SVF* 1.237, Cicero *de Fin.* 3.58 = *SVF* 3.498 = LS59F, though the reference to middle actions is not translated in their volume 1. Distinguish this from the mistaken view that 'middle actions' means befitting

actions done by progressors, or by well-intentioned non-Sages, and that they are middle in the sense of being better than vicious actions, though not as good as the Sage's perfected actions. There is no such class of actions; every action is either vicious, if done by a non-Sage, or virtuous, if done by a Sage—and there is no third class of people, either (since progressors are non-Sages). Middle actions are not intermediate in the sense of belonging to neither, but in the characteristically Stoic sense of straddling both, i.e. being a type which has tokens of both kinds. The case is again like *katalêpsis*, which some texts say is 'on the border between' or 'intermediate between' knowledge and opinion, but which more careful texts clearly show divides its instances between these two types exhaustively and without remainder.

8. Stobaeus 2.66 = *SVF* 3.560 = LS 61G3 = IG2 ii–95.5b10; also at Stobaeus 2.105 = *SVF* 3.661 = IG2 ii–95.11k. The label is even more prejudicial in Greek; what I have translated 'error' is a word sometimes used for 'sin' and related to the standard New Testament word for 'sin'. My decision to use 'error' here probably errs on the side of caution, but 'sin' would be too misleading in other directions.

9. 'It is an equally grave error for the captain to allow the ship to sink, whether it contains straw or gold.' (Cicero *Paradoxa Stoicorum* §20). We are inclined to think that the loss of some straw is a trivial thing, but when we see it as the outcome of the very same psychological state that would have led to the loss of some gold, had gold been on board, then we come to see why the loss of the straw is just as bad. That's the Stoic argument; but are they entitled to it? Doesn't the very structure of this argument depend on its being self-evident and uncontroversial that the loss of gold is a more serious thing than the loss of the straw? If we ask why sinking the straw-filled ship is bad, we're told its badness flows from the badness of the state of mind. When we next ask why the state of mind is bad, the Stoics do not try to persuade us of its badness by saying it could lead to the loss of straw, or mud, or something of that sort—they say that it's bad because it could have led to the loss of some gold. Can the Stoics argue that their reliance on a scale of values that ranks gold above straw is merely intended to convince non-Stoics? Or if they insist on the official view, that straw and gold are both indifferent things, though demoted and promoted respectively, could we perhaps use an argument of the same structure to show that the state of mind is really indifferent, too, rather than bad—a very un-Stoic conclusion—since it could have led to the loss of something promoted like gold, or something demoted like enemy soldiers or contagious plague-victims?

10. *SE AM* 9.200 = *SVF* 3.516 = LS 59G.

11. *DL* 7.108–109 = *SVF* 3.493–496 = LS 59E = IG2 ii–94.

12. Stobaeus 2.86 = *SVF* 3.169 = LS 53Q = IG2 ii–95.9.

13. Epictetus *Discourses* 1.18.1–5; cf *Encheiridion* 42: 'whenever someone slanders or mistreats you, remember that he does what he does in the belief that it is befitting'.

14. Stobaeus 5.906,18–907,5 = *SVF* 3.510 = LS 59 i = IG2 ii–97.

12

Discovering the Befitting: Two Models

How do Stoics decide what to do? Here are two quotations, both from Cicero, that seem to point in opposite ways on some fundamental issues:

The final end specified by the Stoics, 'to live in agreement with nature', has the following meaning, in my opinion: always to conform to virtue, and as for the other things which are according to nature, to select them if they do not conflict with virtue.[1]

Since it is by nature that all love themselves, it belongs just as much to the non-Sage as to the Sage to take the things that are according to nature, and reject the things contrary to nature. The befitting action, then, is a thing common both to Sages and non-Sages, from which it follows that the befitting action deals with what we call 'intermediate' things. But since these intermediate things form the basis of all befitting actions, there is good ground for saying that it is to these things that all of our deliberations are referred.

And among these deliberations are those concerning the departure from life or remaining alive: when one's circumstances contain a preponderance of things in accordance with nature, it is befitting to remain alive; when one possesses or sees in prospect a majority of the contrary things, it is befitting to depart from life. From which it is apparent that it is sometimes befitting even for the Sage to leave life, despite being happy, and befitting even for the non-Sage to remain alive, despite being wretched.

For good and evil, as we have often said, arise afterwards: what falls directly under the judgment and selection of the Sage are the primary things in accordance with nature and contrary to nature, and it is these that are like the material substrate of wisdom.[2]

The first quote sketches out an algorithm for deliberation in which we pursue things that are according to nature—presumably the promoted indifferents—while always keeping an eye out for the demands of virtue. In fact, Cicero rather clumsily makes us attend to virtue twice, since his phrasing is equivalent to saying '(1), always act according to virtue, and for the rest, (2), pursue things according to nature, provided that you (3), always act according to virtue.' But that inelegance aside, it is clear that there are two very different kinds of considerations that must go into any decision about action, and it is also clear that one of them, sc. the one concerning virtue, will always trump the other.

The second quote offers a decision-procedure in which explicit considerations of virtue play no role: we are told that 'all of our deliberations are referred' to intermediate things, that is, indifferents; 'what falls directly under the judgment and selection of the Sage are the primary things in accordance with nature and contrary to nature'. And the reference to suicide gives a concrete example of this: in deciding whether to kill oneself or not, neither Sages nor non-Sages should give any weight to their own virtue. Despite the fact that virtue is the only good and vice the only bad, those considerations should never enter into one's deliberations; when one has or foresees having a preponderance of things according to nature, one should remain alive—regardless of one's vice—and when one has or foresees having a preponderance of things contrary to nature, one should kill oneself—regardless of one's virtue.

There is a great difference between the second picture, which I shall call 'Indifferents-Only' deliberation, and the first picture, which I shall call 'Salva Virtute' deliberation, (from the Latin phrase meaning 'provided that virtue is preserved').[3] Does virtue have a role in our deliberations or not? Ought we to attend only to indifferents, pursuing the promoted and avoiding the demoted, or should we do that only after we have satisfied the requirements of virtue? I shall consider the claims of both pictures, before offering a resolution of the two.

Salva Virtute

Consider how the members of a rival school, the Epicureans, would deliberate about an action.[4] The Epicureans declared that the end of action is the maximization of the agent's pleasure—pleasure is the only good, pain the only evil, and everything else (for example, the virtues) has value only to the extent that it contributes to pleasure or reduces pain. The end is a happy life, or a life of maximum pleasure; the role of virtue is to provide that maximization of pleasure, whether by arranging for the smooth and efficient provision of pleasures, or by reducing the stress and anxiety that accompanies vice. Accordingly, the practical algorithm is clean and straightforward: when faced with any practical decision to make, one surveys courses of action to see which one delivers the maximum pleasure and minimum pain. Virtuous behavior, the Epicureans assure us, will also be produced by this method, but as a sort of side-benefit: given the facts about what pleasure and pain are like, especially pleasure and pain of the soul, a decision based on these grounds will also lead to performance of the virtuous action.[5]

Having been told that the only good for the Stoics is virtue, and that the end is a life according to virtue, or living in accordance with virtue, it is easy to suppose that the analogous Stoic algorithm will lead to virtuous behavior even more directly and transparently: one will simply survey the courses of action and choose the one that is the most virtuous. This supposition is further encouraged by the Stoic insistence that the values that might conflict with virtue, or that might lead us to choose an action other than the virtuous action, are in fact not goods at all. If health and wealth and so on are not good, and do not contribute to our end, then it seems we can wholly dismiss them from our practical considerations. Virtue alone is good; virtue alone benefits us and makes us happy; a strict attention to our happiness will thus require us only to attend to virtue.

This line of thought is fundamentally wrong as an account of Stoicism, but before turning to its diagnosis and correction it is worth examining several of the more common ways in which this wrong thought can be extended. In particular, we can start with this picture of the deliberative centrality of virtue, and then take any of several approaches to introducing considerations of the indifferents—since, if we want to say something about Stoic ethics, it is clear that we do need to say something about indifferents in this context.

One thought would be that the demands of virtue are central and overriding, but so easily met that in many circumstances there will still be further decisions to be made about what to do, even after we are committed to doing something virtuous. So, for instance, if I find myself in a situation in which I could murder someone, or abstain from murdering someone, then considerations of virtue will show immediately that I should abstain from the murder. But there are many ways of abstaining from the murder, many of which would leave virtue equally satisfied. So, I might abstain and have a walk, I might abstain and read a sentimental novel, or I might abstain and gorge myself on unhealthy food. On the assumption that none of these options has more in its favor from the standpoint of virtue, it seems that there is a further decision to be made, which must be made on a further basis. And here, it seems, we have a role for the indifferents: once the considerations of virtue have been dealt with, any further guidance is to be sought by considering where the preponderance of promoted indifferents lie. It's on this basis that I will decide to walk for my health rather than reading the trash novel or eating the junk food. I decide to walk, because this option provides me with the greatest amount of the promoted indifferents.

We can give this deliberative structure a slightly different look, if we imagine that I begin by deliberating in terms of indifferents,

Discovering the Befitting: Two Models ~ 185

attempting to maximize the promoteds and minimize the demoteds. Then, after I order all of the possible courses of actions by the amount of promoted indifferents that they yield, I then prune off from the top of the list any of the options that conflict with considerations of virtue. So, beginning purely from considerations of indifferents, I make up a rank-ordering which shows that my greatest amount of health, wealth, and so on, is to be got by committing murder and eating a healthy breakfast, my second-greatest is to be had by committing murder and reading a sentimental novel, my third greatest is to be had by abstaining from murder and eating a healthy breakfast, and so on down the list. In assembling this rank ordering, I do not attend to virtue, only indifferents. But after I have made up the whole amoral list, I strike out all of the courses of action that conflict with virtue, and choose from those options that remain the one that delivers the most of the promoted indifferents.

Despite the fact that we have reversed the sequence of events—whether I think about virtue first, and then indifferents, or indifferents first, and then virtue—the two deliberative structures are effectively equivalent, in that they will always give the same prescriptions in the same situations. This is because virtue is given logical priority, deliberative priority, over indifferents, whether it comes first in time or not.

Another way to incorporate indifferents would be to rank them by their suitability or aptitude or instrumental utility for performing acts of virtue. Here is a quote from an author who takes this view:

First came those things which are an integral part of 'life according to nature'—that is, of virtue—for instance, the exercises consisting in the examination of conscience and in attention to oneself, which contribute to the practice of moral life. The value of these things was considered to be absolute. In second place came those things which could help the practice of virtue in a secondary way. Taken by themselves, these things are neither good nor bad, but are indifferent with regard to moral good. Possessing them and exercising them, however, allows us to practice better the moral life. Examples would include health, which makes it possible for us to do our duty; and wealth, if it allows us to come to the aid of our fellow man. These second-rank values do not have the absolute value which pertains only to the moral good, but they can be ranked in hierarchical order according to the closeness of their relationship to the moral good.[6]

On this picture, too, considerations of virtue have deliberative priority—the worth of virtuous actions is 'considered to be absolute'. But if such considerations leave the agent's course under-determined, and indifferents must be consulted as well, then they are consulted not as a mere value to maximize for its own sake (as in the first picture), but as instrumental aids to the performance of virtuous actions, things that 'help the practice of virtue'—the promoted indifferent 'allows us to practice better the moral life'; it 'makes it possible for us to do our duty'.

There are a number of things wrong with these pictures. It may well be that they are philosophically coherent, and that someone has advocated them, or could advocate them. But the Stoics certainly did not. To begin with, these interpretations suppose that the actions that the Sage performs can be divided into two groups: virtuous actions of a familiar kind, like examining one's conscience, coming to the aid of our fellow man, saving drowning children, and the like; and indifferent actions of a familiar kind, such as eating healthy food, brushing one's teeth, earning money, walking and talking, and the like. But the Stoics are quite explicit about the fact that the Sage only performs one kind of action, namely virtuous ones, whether the Sage is examining his conscience, aiding his fellow man, rescuing children, eating, or brushing his teeth. It is not that the Sage is performing a virtuous action when assisting his fellow man, but doing a merely promoted action when he brushes his teeth; the action of brushing his teeth, like all the rest of the Sage's actions, is a virtuous action.[7] And it is just as virtuous as the examinings, assistings, and rescuings— the Stoics deny that one virtuous action is more virtuous than another, and this is one of the areas in which this denial makes a difference.[8]

Hand in hand with this is their denial that any vicious action is any more vicious than any other, along with their insistence that all actions of the non-Sage are vicious actions and errors. So when the non-Sage steals something he is performing a vicious action, but it is no more vicious than when he brushes his teeth, or earns money, or rescues someone from drowning. No matter what nice thoughts may run through the non-Sage's head as he dives into the icy depths to pull out the floundering child, no matter whether he only hopes to cash in on a hero's fame or does his good deed and disappears into the anonymous night, his action is just as vicious as the robber's or murderer's more familiar crime.

Nor is tooth-brushing choiceworthy in a 'second rank' because it preserves our health, and thus makes us better able to save drowning children; we cannot divide actions into those that are virtuous in themselves, and others that are indirectly or instrumentally valuable, because they facilitate actions of the first sort. It cannot be right to say that 'health makes it possible for us to do our duty', for there cannot be some duty whose performance depends in this way on the Sage's being healthy. If there were, then disease would make it impossible for us to do that duty, in which case, the Sage's virtue would depend on remaining healthy. So too with the use of money 'to come to the aid of our fellow man'; if there were some aspect of the 'moral life' which required this sort of thing as a part of virtue, then the Sage's ability to be virtuous would depend on their possession of money. Quite the opposite; the Sage is completely independent of all such things. The Sage will be equally virtuous with or without money, with or without health; the Stoics made this amply clear in their disagreements with the Peripatetics. It was the followers of Aristotle who said that a virtuous person must have resources with which to manifest and actualize their virtue, as for instance money with which to be liberal. The Stoics insisted that the relation between promoted indifferents like money and health and the true good of virtue was nothing like that.[9]

A general problem here is simply the fact that all of the Sage's actions are virtuous, and all of the non-Sage's actions are vicious. This means, on the one hand, that it becomes trivially easy for a non-Sage to deliberate: in order to do the virtuous thing, one should simply do what a Sage would do. On the other hand, it is impossible for the non-Sage to follow up on this thought, since even if they could tell what virtuous action the Sage would perform in this circumstance, they could not perform it, or any other virtuous action, from the kind of Sagely disposition that would succeed in making it a virtuous action. Their action may be externally equivalent, and their thoughts may even sound the same, but a virtuous action will not result.

Now that is not an insuperable bar to figuring out what to do, when we remember that the non-Sage can at least perform the befitting action, which will be observationally equivalent to the Sage's befitting and virtuous action, though failing to be virtuous for reasons having to do with their respective psychic conditions. Indeed, the non-Sage *can* perform such an action, and the non-Sage *should* perform such an action; the befitting action is exactly the one that it is incumbent on all agents, Sages and non-Sages alike, to perform (whether the action performed will be befitting and virtuous, as with the Sage's perfected action, or befitting and vicious, as with the non-Sage's error). This attempt at observational conformity to the Sage's virtuous action might make sense of Cicero's phrasing of the *Salva Virtute* model, when he talks of 'conforming to virtue' and avoiding 'conflict with virtue'.

The deeper problem can be seen by examining the Sage's own deliberation. The Sage can be confident that whatever action they decide on will be the virtuous action; they are infallibly virtuous in their actions. But that does not show us, or them, how they can arrive at the specification of the virtuous action in this situation. By knowing that the virtuous action is the one that the Sage will perform, we still have not come any closer to putting any content into the Sage's own deliberations.

At this point we might look once again to the lists of befitting actions and unbefitting actions for assistance. Here is one of the fullest and most informative ones:

Befitting actions are those that reason requires us to do, for instance honoring our parents, brothers, and country, and keeping company with friends. Contrary to the befitting are those actions that reason requires us not to do, for instance neglecting our parents, treating our brothers with contempt, not

Discovering the Befitting: Two Models ~ 189

spending time with friends, despising our country, and the like. Neither befitting nor contrary are those things that reason neither requires us to do nor forbids us to do, for instance picking up a twig, holding a stylus or scraper, and things like this.

Some actions are befitting without regard to circumstance and some are befitting in light of circumstances. Taking care of one's health and one's sense-organs are befitting without regard to circumstance, whereas mutilating oneself or throwing away one's possessions are befitting in light of circumstances; and an analogous story applies to actions contrary to the befitting.

Some befitting actions are always befitting, others are not always befitting. It is always befitting to live according to virtue; it is not always befitting to walk, ask and answer questions, and the like. And so too for actions contrary to the befitting.[10]

One thing that is immediately clear is that the presence of an action-type on a list of befitting actions does not by itself indicate that every instance of that action is befitting; many types of actions will have instances that are sometimes befitting and sometimes not befitting, or contrary to the befitting. Walking, for instance; this is listed as an action that is not always befitting, but this strongly suggests that sometimes it will be. Indeed, we know it will sometimes be befitting, since we know that some cases of walking count as perfectly befitting actions, that is, when the Sage walks wisely.[11]

The same variability will affect those actions that are said to be 'befitting without regard to circumstance'—here too, it is clear that some instances of that type will not be befitting, and that 'without regard to circumstance' cannot mean the same as 'in all circumstances'. For in some circumstances, the befitting thing to do is to mutilate oneself, in which case taking care of one's health and organs in those circumstances would be contrary to the befitting.

Even the claim that actions like holding a pencil or a scraper are neither befitting nor contrary to the befitting is somewhat misleading. For we also know that bending or stretching one's finger can be a perfectly befitting action, if done by a Sage, in which case it seems likely that holding a pencil or a scraper can also be a perfectly befitting action.[12] Indeed, that likelihood is made a certainty by those passages that tell us that everything the Sage does—every one of the Sage's actions, no matter how trivial—is a perfected action, and thus a befitting action.[13]

Given the difficulties in the interpretation of this list, it seems unclear whether we can take even the first instances of befitting actions—honoring one's parents and country, for instance—as actions every one of whose instances is befitting. For there seem to be cases in which the befitting thing is to betray one's parents, or even kill them.[14]

If we are looking for some ground-level considerations of virtue from which to start a *Salva Virtute* deliberation, then it seems that this list will not provide us with very solid guidance either. For the only action that it mentions as being 'always befitting' is the action of 'living according to virtue'. And that is a singularly unhelpful principle to start from if one wants to find out what it is virtuous to do. If we are attempting to deliberate in the *Salva Virtute* way, then we need some concrete, action-guiding advice about what agrees with virtue and what conflicts with virtue, advice that we can apply in new cases, that we can be sure will apply to all cases. The lists of befitting actions have not provided it.

We might look for help in the fact that the Stoics sometimes talked in terms of laws—universal moral laws that apply to all rational agents. Chrysippus began his treatise 'On the Law' with a sort of hymn to it:

Law is the king of all things, divine and human. It must be the overseer of fine things and base things, leading them and ruling, and acting as a norm of just and unjust things, and prescribing for naturally political animals the things that are to be done, and forbidding the things that are not to be done.[15]

Law is also mentioned in one specification of the final end or summum bonum:

The end is to live in accordance with nature—both one's own nature and the nature of the wholes—doing none of the things that are forbidden by the

Law that is common, which is the same thing as the Right Reason that pervades all things, and is the same as Zeus.[16]

Now Sages live in conformity with this Law, exercising Right Reason in all they do. Indeed, the Sage's Reason simply is the Law, as one text tells us:

The law is the highest reason, implanted in nature, ordering which things are to be done and forbidding their contraries. This same reason, when it is in a confirmed and perfected human mind [i.e. the mind of a Sage], is law.[17]

The trouble is that we have learned no more about the content of this law by finding out that the Sage always obeys it. It might be that the Sage always obeys the law in the trivial or vacuous sense that whatever the Sage does is thereby the law. Or it might be that the Sage obeys the law by following Zeus, but that what Zeus wills on any occasion is different from what he wills on other occasions— there might not be any fixed content to the will of Zeus that one could transfer from one deliberation to the next. On one occasion, Zeus, Reason, and the Law dictate that I should preserve my health, on another occasion they dictate that I should neglect it. Indeed, we have a passage from Chrysippus that says this very thing:

This is why Chrysippus was right to say: 'As long as what is coming is unclear to me, I always stick with what is most naturally suited for getting what is according to nature. For it was God himself that fashioned me to be the sort of thing that selects it. Whereas if I had known that being ill now was fated for me, then I would have had an impulse towards that. For the foot, too, if it had any wits, would have an impulse towards getting muddy.'[19]

Sometimes Zeus wills that we should be healthy, and sometimes Zeus wills that we should be ill. Our understanding of the Stoic equation of virtuous behavior, the will of Zeus, and the 'Law that is Common' should not start from the assumption that by 'law' the Stoics must have meant invariable general regularities, and then conclude that Zeus in his normative role is similarly invariable. Rather, we should start from the evident variability of Zeus's will, and assume that the 'law' the Sage follows will be just that variable, and just that incapable of antecedent specification—that it is really not much like a law at all. Those who instead try to invent laws for the Sage to follow seem to be doing so, at times, from some thought that the essence of virtuous behavior, in all lands and eras, is the conscious subordination of one's inclinations to the dictates of law qua law; and from what we have seen so far, this may simply not be a Stoic thought.

To see how the Stoics might have arrived at a different conception of the law, we should consider the lessons that the Stoics might have drawn from a reading of Plato's *Statesman*.[20] That dialogue argues that we cannot have two beliefs that are antecedently attractive:

(1) The law is a system of general principles.
(2) The law is always correct.

The *Statesman* argues that human affairs are so variable, so subject to 'the winds, and whatever else comes from Zeus, contrary to expectation and the usual events' (*Statesman* 295d), that systems of general principles will inevitably support the wrong prescription for action in some circumstances, and so must sometimes be over-ridden by the particular injunctions of ethical experts, in particular the 'kingly ruler' (*Statesman* 294a). This figure has a complete knowledge of the good in every circumstance, and is compared to a god. In a conscious paradox, Plato described the expert who over-rides the general principles as someone who 'establishes their expertise as law' (*Statesman* 297a); not the general regularities, but the particular prescriptions of the expert, are the true and genuine law. Since expert and kingly rulers of this sort are hard to find—they are in fact as rare as Stoic Sages will later be—Plato argues that the second-best system is to have rulers who follow established laws, not attempting to override them with inexpert improvisations.

In line with this dialogue, the Stoics opted to retain the view that the law is always correct, and rejected the view that the law is a system of general principles. Thus in Stoic parlance, 'law' does not refer to a system of general principles, but to the particular injunctions of ethical experts. This is clear from their official definition of 'law'. Nothing about the standard Stoic definition of law says anything about generality or universality; it simply says that a law is a prescription or imperative (*prostaktikon*) that prescribes (*prostattei*) or forbids action.[20] There is strong lexical and philological evidence to think that the Stoics took this idea from the *Statesman*.[21] In the *Statesman*, the word 'prescribe' (*prostattein*) is exactly the word that is repeatedly applied, not to the orders codified in the general and 'law-like' principles that are followed in the second-best constitution, but to the exceptional, anomalous over-riding prescriptions of the kingly expert.[22] The essential nature of the law, in Stoicism, is that it prescribes, that is, issues imperative orders or commands, and the act of prescribing carries no assumption of generality or 'law-likeness'; a reader of the *Statesman* would assume that a prescription is an imperative or order, which, if anything, is more likely to be an ad hoc, one-off order that contravenes a standing system of general principles. Thus the centrality of 'law' to Stoic ethics has nothing to do with any interest in general, universal, or 'law-like' moral principles.[23]

This outcome may surprise us less if we keep in mind the experience of Socrates, whose depiction in the Platonic dialogues had such an important influence on the Stoics. His ethical inquiries led him to believe that virtuous action cannot be produced merely by acting in accordance with general rules phrased in observational terms. The only rules that we might bring with us into a new situation will either be exceptionless but too vague, as for instance 'be courageous', and 'don't commit injustice', or adequately determinate but no more productive of virtue than the opposite, as for instance 'never retreat in battle' or 'always return deposits'. Courage will sometimes require standing one's place in battle, but sometimes will require retreat or some other action; justice will sometimes require returning deposits, but sometimes will forbid it.[24]

Indifferents-Only

Our attempt to make sense out of the *Salva Virtute* model has foundered on our inability to give any content to the notion of doing the 'virtuous thing', beyond saying that the virtuous action is whatever the Sage will actually do.

The Indifferents-Only model offers us a way out of this bind, by proposing that virtue is not mentioned among the inputs to deliberation. The deliberation will eventuate in the specification of a virtuous action—that is exactly what we are looking for, after all—but it will start by describing the various courses of action purely in terms of how various indifferents—promoted and demoted—are distributed.

We have already seen one piece of evidence for this view—the claim in Cicero's *de Finibus* 3.60 that 'all of our deliberations are referred' to intermediate things, that is, indifferents, and that 'what falls directly under the judgment and selection of the Sage are the primary things in accordance with nature and contrary to nature'. That claim is illustrated by the case of suicide, in which the deliberation is spelled out very explicitly: 'when one's circumstances contain a preponderance of things in accordance with nature, it is befitting to remain alive; when one possesses or sees in prospect a majority of the contrary things, it is befitting to depart from life'.

This case is especially relevant for the present discussion, since it seems fairly clear that preserving one's life is an action that would be befitting on most occasions, whereas ending one's life is also befitting on some occasion. In terms of the earlier list, we can certainly say that neither preserving nor ending will be one of the actions that is 'always befitting', and if the comparison to general health and the preservation of one's sense-organs is any guide, it seems likely that preserving one's life will be an action that is 'befitting without regard to circumstances', whereas suicide will be an action that is 'befitting in light of circumstances'. But how can we tell, when we find ourselves in any particular circumstances, whether it is befitting in these circumstances or not? It won't help to say that it is befitting just in case it conforms to virtue, since that merely repackages the very thing we don't know.

Thus the discussion of suicide gives us evidence for the Indifferents-Only model, and also shows us its superiority to the *Salva Virtute* model for deliberating about an actual situation. To decide whether

Discovering the Befitting: Two Models ~ 195

to remain alive or not, one should simply look at the present and future expected distribution of indifferents, and stay if the balance preponderates towards the promoted ones, or depart if it preponderates towards the demoted ones. And once we have established that it is befitting, in this case, to depart (or to stay), we thereby know what virtue requires, as well—we have identified the virtuous action, by deliberating from inputs that did not beg the question.

But we will find other evidence for the Indifferents-Only model, too, when we consider how Chrysippus reacted to a suggestion that we ignore the difference between promoted and demoted indifferents, a view put forward by a dissident Stoic named Aristo.[25] Cicero has his Chrysippean spokesman argue for the existence of promoted and demoted indifferents by saying:

If there were no difference between things, the whole of life would be thrown into chaos, as it is by Aristo. Wisdom would have no role or function, since there would be no difference whatsoever between any of the things that pertain to the conduct of life, and so no method of choosing could properly be applied.[26]

On the Indifferents-Only view, we may take the present claim quite literally; if there were no distinctions among indifferents, then wisdom would have lost its function, exactly because the function of wisdom is simply to select among indifferents, that is, to consider indifferents qua indifferents, and arrive at plans of action on those terms alone. The virtues do not each have a double function, both calculating about indifferents, and also keeping in mind the antecedent and over-riding constraints of ethical considerations that the *Salva Virtute* model presupposed ('don't lie' etc.). Had that been true, then Aristo's insistence on complete indifference would have left virtue with half of its function intact; it would still keep on telling us not to lie, not to kill, and so on. But there are no such antecedent and over-riding ethical considerations; the virtues start merely from descriptions of indifferents, and arrive at decisions about action from those bases.

This also seems like the most sensible way to understand several of the Stoic formulae for the end, especially those of Diogenes of

Babylon and Antipater of Tarsus. These were the heads of the Stoic school directly after Chrysippus, and we have ample reason to believe that their views on central topics in ethics were meant to agree with his.

Diogenes said that the end is 'to reason well in the selection of things according to nature'.[27] Antipater said the end is 'to live unceasingly selecting the things that are according to reason, and disselecting the things that are contrary to reason'. He would also often phrase it as follows: 'to do everything that accords with oneself, unceasingly and unswervingly, towards the acquisition of the things that are promoted according to nature'.[28]

Unlike Cicero's paraphrase of the Stoic end in the *Salva Virtute* formula, these formulations of the end make no reference to virtue of any kind. They describe the end as reasonable activity in the selection of things in accordance with nature. On the Indifferents-Only view, we can take them at their word: what the Sage does is simply to view his situation in terms of indifferents, value them accurately in those terms, arrive at a course of action, and then act. Acting so, he attains his end, and is happy, and is also at the same time virtuous.[29]

Indeed, this line of consideration suggests the deepest problem for the *Salva Virtute* model; for 'virtue' in Stoicism is not the name of a set of rules, but rather another name for the Sage's soul.[30] Virtue simply is the Sage's soul, which is also the same as wisdom, that is, it simply consists in the Sage's knowledge of goods, bads, and indifferents.[31] So there is no work for a *Salva Virtute* clause to do; whatever plan of action the Sage arrives at on the basis of their understanding of the various values involved, will already be a plan that reflects their wisdom, and so is in accordance with their virtue.

Selection, as was mentioned earlier, is in the first instance a kind of impulse: an impulse directed towards the promoted indifferents which values them accurately as promoteds, not mistakenly as goods. We saw earlier that the Sage has impulses of this kind, and this is borne out by the evidence from Diogenes and Antipater. But Sages also have *eupatheiai*, which are impulses towards the good per se. We can see what their role is in the Indifferents-Only model; they play no role in deliberating about which action should be undertaken, but once the deliberation has identified an action as the befitting one, the Sage will also recognize their performance of it as a virtuous action, and thus a good. At that point they can be motivated to pursue it by the eupathic impulse of volition, that is, the virtuous analogue of desire for the good, that is, the constituted by their continued future virtue. The second, eupathic, impulse ratifies, but cannot redirect, the first, selective impulse.[32]

In light of the amount of evidence that considerations of virtue do not figure in Stoic deliberations, it is hard to see how Cicero can have been right to propose his *Salva Virtute* model. In a previous discussion of this material, in which I sided squarely with the Indifferents-Only model, I proposed that Cicero was simply mistaken, and that we should not treat his enunciation of the *Salva Virtute* formula in *de Officiis* 3.13 as evidence for an authentic Stoic view.[33] In the next chapter, I want to retract that charge. Cicero is still slightly confused, I think, but there is more truth to Cicero's *Salva Virtute* model than the Indifferents-Only model allows.

NOTES

My progress towards my current view has been roundabout, and I have acquired several important debts. I was working mainly under the influence of Inwood (1985) and Cooper (1989) when I wrote and delivered Brennan (1998b), which had many arguments against *Salva Virtute* and espoused the Indifferents-Only view. My thoughts from this phase can also be seen in Brennan (2003). Rachel Barney delivered a commentary on Brennan (1998b) and developed her comments into her own Barney (2003), which sharpened up the question but ended in *aporia*—she agreed in rejecting *Salva Virtute*, but raised problems for Indifferents-Only as well. A reading of her paper led me to re-read Cicero's *de Officiis* with new eyes, and I came to think my earlier view was fundamentally wrong. In this chapter and the next, I am covering ground that Barney and I have gone over in common, and then taking up and modifying one of the options she discarded—what she calls the 'Degrees of Nature' view, and rejects as unworkable. Her arguments against that view do not strike me as insuperable, and her assemblage of the evidence for it has spurred me on to make it work. These chapters are thus a friendly return toss in our on-going game of ball; it is a pleasure to play with an expert (Seneca *de Ben.* 2.17.3; *Epictetus* 2.5.15). At one crucial juncture, a long-forgotten conversation with Charles Brittain also helped me to answer one of Barney's arguments against *Salva Virtute*.

1. Cicero *de Officiis* 3.13.
2. Cicero *de Fin.* 3.60 = *SVF* 3.763 = LS 66G.
3. The Latin phrase is from Bonhöffer (1968), 195. The label 'Indifferents Only' was coined by Barney (2003) in order to describe my position in her comments on my paper, 'Demoralizing the Stoics'.
4. E.g. *Principal Doctrine* xxv = LS 21E = IG2 1–5.
5. *Principal Doctrine* v = IG2 1–5.
6. Hadot (2001), 215.
7. All Sage's actions are virtuous: Stobaeus 2.65.12 = *SVF* 3.557, all of non-Sage's actions vicious: Stobaeus 2.66.14 = *SVF* 3.560 = IG2 II–95.5b10; the Sage's walking is virtuous: Stobaeus 2.96.18 = *SVF* 3.501 = IG2 II–95.11e; the Sage straightens his finger bravely: Plutarch *Sto. Rep.* 1038F = *SVF* 3.211; the Sage holds out his finger wisely: Plutarch *Comm. Not.* 1068F = *SVF* 3.627; the Sage waggles his finger in accordance with the dictates of reason: Clement *Paedag* 2.224 = *SVF* 3.730 (these finger-fragments are clearly intended to provide examples of the most trivial and apparently inconsequential actions an agent can take).
8. Stobaeus 2.7.106.21 = *SVF* 3.528 = IG2 II–95.11l. Unfortunately IG2 mistranslates the middle portion of this paragraph. The section reading ' . . . and it is no more possible to say that the one is a falsehood than to say that the other is; but the falseness in each is not equally false, and those who are in error are not equally in error', should read: 'and it is not possible to say that the one of them is more a falsehood than the other; but it is not the case that: the false is equally false, but those in error are not equally in error'. The argument is as follows: all false propositions are equally false; if all false propositions are equally false, then all who are in error are equally in error; therefore all who are in error are equally in error. (I have phrased the major premiss as a conditional for clarity, though in the original it is phrased as a negated conjunction.) And if all who are in error are equally in error, then all vicious actions are equally vicious, since all arise from error.
9. Alexander of Aphrodisias, a late Peripatetic critic of the Stoics, offers several arguments of the general form: if virtue is the selection of promoted indifferents, then virtue must have available the promoted indifferents in order to select them. But it cannot provide them itself—virtue does not guarantee a supply of food—so it is not self-sufficient (see *Mantissa* 159–168, excerpted in *SVF* 3.67, 3.764, 3.767). This would be a problem for the Stoics if virtue really did consist in successfully acquiring food, health, and so on. But (a) the success of the selection does not depend on actual acquisition of the thing selected, and (b) for any distribution of promoted and demoted things available, there is a virtuous way

to select and avoid those things, even if it simply consists in avoiding the demoted things by killing oneself.

10. DL 7.108–109 = SVF 3.493-496 = LS 59E = IG2 II–94.

11. Stobaeus 2.96 = SVF 3.501= LS 59M = IG2 II–95.11e.

12. Plutarch *Sto. Rep.* 1038F = SVF 3.211; Plutarch *Comm. Not.* 1068F = SVF 3.627

13. DL 7.125 = SVF 3.561 = IG2 II–94; Stobaeus 2.65 = SVF 3.557 = IG2 II–95.5b8; Stobaeus 2.66 = SVF 3.560 = IG2 II–95.5b10. LS vol. 1.367 deny that 'picking up a twig and similarly trivial doings are either right or wrong'. They suggest that 'some activities are too trivial to qualify as actions, and thus as amenable to moral appraisal in any sense'. This seems to overlook both the finger-fragments discussed above, and the fundamental role of impulse as both the originator of action and the anchor of moral significance. Picking up a twig is an action exactly because it stems from and manifests an impulse to pick up a twig, and this impulse in turn stems from and manifests one's entire psychic disposition, i.e. one's virtue or vice. True, under the general description 'picking up a twig', reason will neither dictate nor forbid it, but every particular instance will either be virtuous or vicious, and among some of the vicious instances there will also be some that are contrary to the befitting.

14. Cicero *de Officiis* 3.90; Cicero *Paradoxa Stoicorum* §24.

15. Marcian 1 = SVF 3.314 = LS 67R.

16. DL 7.87 = SVF 3.4 = LS 63C = IG2 II–94.

17. Cicero *de Legibus* 1.6,18 = SVF 3.315.

18. Epictetus, *Discourses* 2.6.9 = SVF 3.191 = LS 58J = IG2 II–98.

19. An incidental piece of evidence that the Stoics were familiar with the *Statesman* may be found in Origen *Contra Celsum* 1.37 = SVF 2.739, which seems to report a Stoic reworking of the myth of the Earthborn from *Statesman* 271a.

20. Cicero *de Legibus* 1.6,18 = SVF 3.315; Philo *de Joseph* 11.46 = SVF 3.323; Stobaeus 2.7.96 = SVF 3.613. And compare the purely linguistic discussions of the imperative mood (*prostaktikon*) in DL 7.66 = SVF 2.186 = IG2 II–3, SE AM 8.70 = SVF 2.187, where the examples are of the emphatically non-law-like sort, e.g. 'you now, go the river Inachus!' 'come here, dear lady!'

21. Sedley (1999b), 129 mentions the *Statesman's* discussion of the failure of universal laws, but draws precisely the opposite conclusion from the comparison. He claims that no one in the Hellenistic period was worried about the adequacy of general principles. 'The Stoics, certainly, held that the virtues are exact sciences . . . and therefore had no trouble in supposing that ethical norms could be followed all the way down into sets of exact rules for every situation-type.'

22. *Statesman* 294de, 295a, 295b, 295c, 295d, 296a, 305d. Contrast the use of *epitattein* at 294b and 294d to refer to the covering-law generalizations that turn out to need amendment. That Zeno had read the *Statesman* is also suggested by his description of the human race as a 'herd' (Plut. *De Alex. virt.* 329A = SVF 1.262 = LS 67A).

23. Given the Stoic fondness for near-etymologies, it may also be that the description of law as a *prostatês* in the fragment of 'On the Law', is a further reflection

of *Statesman's* influence, so that it should not be translated 'overseer' as above but e.g. 'prescriber'. So too, perhaps, with the claim in *DL* 7.86 = *SVF* 3.178 = LS 57A = IG2 II–94 that reason exercises *prostasia* over impulse because it is the 'craftsman' (*tekhnîtês*) of impulse—as in the *Statesman* 297a, the *technê* of reason, knowing the good in detail, produces particular prescriptions (*prostattei*) that over-ride the second-best law of mere animal impulse. Neither *prostatês* nor *prostasia* is genuinely derived from *prostattein*, i.e. 'to prescribe', but the Stoics may have wanted to suggest a connection, i.e. that 'law must be the prescriber of fine things and base things' in the fragment of 'On the Law', and that 'reason exercises imperative/prescriptive control over impulse' in the Diogenes Laertius passage. Plato himself puns in this way, treating forms of *epitattein* (to prescribe) and *epistates* (overseer) as equivalent at Statesman 260b and 292b, and juxtaposing them at 261c.

24. *Laches* 191c, *Republic* 331c.
25. Cf. White (1985).
26. *de Fin.* 3.50 = *SVF* I. Aristo.365, translation modified from Woolf. Cf. also *de Fin.* 4.69 and Cicero *de Off.* 1.6 = *SVF* I. Aristo.363, discussing Aristo along with Pyrrho and Erillus: they are debarred from offering philosophical contributions to the theory of the befitting, because of their advocacy of the complete indifference of ordinary things, i.e. their assertion that we cannot even distinguish health from disease as 'promoted' versus 'demoted'. 'And yet', says Cicero, 'they would have had some standing in the dispute about the befitting, if only they had accepted some principle of selection or distinction between things, which would have provided a means of approach for the discovery of befitting actions.'
27. *DL* 7.88 = *SVF* 3. Diogenes 45 = IG2 II–94; Stobaeus 2.76.12 = *SVF* 3. Diogenes 44 = LS 58K = IG2 II–95.6a.
28. Stobaeus 2.76.14 = *SVF* 3. Antipater 57 = LS 58K = IG2 II–95.6a.
29. Cooper (1989) puts this view well: 'Thus, according to the Stoics moral virtue . . . is as it were a purely formal condition: it consists in one's reason's being correctly informed about . . . things other than virtue itself . . . and shaping one's impulses to action in accordance with that knowledge. All the specific, substantive content of this state of mind—everything that determines what the virtuous person wants, cares about, makes an object of pursuit or avoidance in his actions etc.—is drawn from the list of preferred and avoided things [i.e. promoted and demoted indifferents] . . . Thus to pursue the good in which virtuous action consists is to pursue a purely formal end; one pursues it in pursuing some other, concrete goal . . . '
30. *DL* 7.89 = *SVF* 3.39 = LS 61A = IG2 II–94.
31. Stobaeus 2.59 = *SVF* 3.262 = LS 61H = IG2 II–95.5b1.
32. In Brennan (1998b) I argued that the Sage's virtue-oriented thoughts and eupathic impulses 'are always posterior to a round of deliberation that is (a) phrased only in terms of indifferents, and (b) completely sufficient to determine the Sage's course of action and motivate the Sage to its

accomplishment. So the Sage, just by deliberating about indifferents, identifies a course of action and arrives at a selective impulse, and that impulse is sufficient for the action that ensues. Only now that the virtuous action has been identified can considerations of virtue come into play, and only now can the Sage's conception of the action as a virtuous action elicit a eupathic impulse: and none of the new virtue-oriented considerations or impulses that arise at this second round of deliberation are in a position to change or even influence the course of action that the Sage settled on at the first round. Where Barney worries about overdetermination, I prefer to think of the second, virtue-oriented impulse as ratifying the first, indifferent-oriented impulse.' I still think this is correct, if we replace the narrow focus on 'indifferents' with the wider range of concerns identified in the next chapter, that is, indifferents plus other people's property plus communal welfare. Barney (2003) endorses 'deliberative sufficiency' and 'unrevisability', and talks of the eupathic impulse 'supervening' on the selection—I think 'ratification' may raise fewer problems than supervenience.

33. See Brennan (2003), fn.52.

13

Discovering the Befitting: A Better Model

In the last chapter I presented what I called the *Salva Virtute* model of deliberation and criticized it in the course of introducing a rival alternative, the Indifferents-Only model. But that model, too, is not without problems.

Problems for the Indifferents-Only Model

To begin with, it is unclear how a mere consideration of the promoted and demoted indifferents could lead to some of the actions that Sages are known to undertake. For instance, we are told that the Sage may commit suicide 'if he suffers intolerable pain, mutilation, or incurable disease'; and it is easy enough to see how the Sage might arrive at this decision using the Indifferents-Only model.[1] But the same sentence tells us that he will commit suicide on behalf of his country, or on behalf of his friends, and it is harder to see how a calculation of the present and prospective promoted and demoted indifferents could lead to that choice.[2]

Secondly, there is a perplexing distance between this picture of the Sage, surveying the stocks of promoted and demoted indifferents like a close-fisted grocer taking inventory, and the picture of the Sage as a lover of virtue. What of the idea that virtue alone is good, that it alone is beautiful and fine? What of the Sage's noble unconcern for everything indifferent? The view of the Sage that we find in later Stoic texts—Seneca, Epictetus, Marcus—seems somehow different from the view offered by the Indifferents-Only model, and in a way that makes it difficult even to see what developments or distortions could have led from one to the other. These later authors do not seem to know about the mercenary, calculating Indifferents-Only model, and they seem closer in spirit, at any rate, to the *Salva Virtute* agent who consciously puts virtue and its demands ahead of any market-basket of indifferents.[3] If Cicero completely failed to understand Chrysippus, he failed in a way that was either very influential, or at least reflected an important shifting of the school's fundamental principles and self-understanding, one that itself demands further explanation.

Other Evidence against Indifferents-Only Model

But as it happens, we cannot dismiss Cicero's *Salva Virtute* formula in *de Officiis* 3.13 as a simple one-off aberration from early Stoic orthodoxy, because there are several other texts that express principles roughly equivalent to it. Here is another one from the *de Officiis*:

Nor indeed should we condemn the accumulation of private property, provided that it does not harm anyone; but we must always avoid injustice.[4]

If we think of the 'accumulation of private property' as the part that corresponds to the selection of things according to nature, and the 'not harming anyone' and 'avoiding injustice' as the *Salva Virtute* clauses, then we have the same structure here as at 3.13: we may pursue the selection of promoted indifferents like private property, but always provided that virtue and justice are preserved. It might be suggested that this second text from the *de Officiis* is only a second reflection of the influence of Panaetius, a Stoic several generations after Chrysippus; but a similar sentiment is voiced in the *de Finibus*, which is usually assumed to be more purely Chrysippean, and it appears only a few pages after the text that gave us the Indifferents-Only model:

> Some say that the Sage will consider his friend's interests to be equally important to him as his own interests, others say that the Sage's own interests will be more important to him. All the same, even this latter group says that it is alien to justice to deprive someone else in order to acquire for oneself.
>
> (*de Finibus* 3.70)

Thus the Sage may pursue his interests, and perhaps even pursue his own interests more diligently than his friend's; but he must not pursue his own interests by depriving other people of their possessions,[5] since to do that would be unjust. Again we have the contrast between the pursuit of indifferents, that is, things according to nature, and the constraints of justice.

Another formula that is very like Cicero's *Salva Virtute* phrasing comes from his quotation of a contemporary Stoic named Hecato (*de Officiis* 3.63):

> Sages should attend to the interests of their intimates—for we do not want prosperity only for ourselves, but for our children, relatives, friends, and especially our country—while doing nothing contrary to the customs, laws, and institutions.[6]

Here again, there is one part of the formula that corresponds to selecting the things according to nature, that is, the 'attending to our interests', where this is then glossed in terms of prosperity.[7] And there is a second part of the formula that mentions the constraint that we must do nothing contrary to the customs, laws, and institutions of our country. Hecato was a student of Panaetius, and the *de Officiis* quotes his treatises at several points; perhaps then we can exonerate Cicero of misunderstanding his sources, but say that Panaetius and Hecato were the ones who pushed the course of Stoic doctrine away from the Chrysippean Indifferents-Only model.

Discovering the Befitting: A Better Model ~ 205

Chrysippus' Footrace

But this hypothesis is scotched by the striking fact that there is a passage of Chrysippus that expresses the same thought:

Runners in a race ought to compete and strive to win as hard as they can, but by no means should they trip their competitors or give them a shove. So too in life; it is not wrong for each person to seek after the things useful for life; but to do so by depriving someone else is not just.[8]

Here again there is a two-part structure, both in the metaphor of the racers, and in the literal application: runners ought to strive as hard as they can, and people ought to seek after 'the things useful for life'; those are the considerations that parallel Cicero's talk of 'selecting the things according to nature', or Hecato's talk of 'attending to interests'. But runners must observe the rules of the race, not commit fouls by tripping and shoving others, and ordinary agents must observe the rules of property, not increasing their own prosperity by depriving others of what belongs to them. Those are the parts that correspond to Cicero's injunction that 'virtue be preserved'.

It is one thing to contemplate dismissing Cicero's words when he may be merely interpreting Stoicism; what Chrysippus himself says cannot be dismissed. Our job is now to see how the footrace fragment can be interpreted to give a coherent picture of Stoic deliberation, and how it can answer the various challenges that have been posed to the two previous models.

It is worth recalling that Cicero offers his *Salva Virtute* formulation as an interpretation of the well-attested Stoic formula that the end is 'to live in agreement with nature'.

The final end specified by the Stoics, 'to live in agreement with nature', has the following meaning, in my opinion: always to conform to virtue, and as for the other things which are according to nature, to select them if they do not conflict with virtue.

(*de Officiis* 3.13)

This suggests that Cicero thought that both parts of his two-part deliberative structure could somehow be understood as involving agreement with nature—both the part that explicitly advocates selecting 'the things according to nature', and the part that restricts that selection by reference to virtue. If we follow up this hint by looking for passages that relate just action to conformity to nature, we find an amazing bounty of them in the *de Officiis*:

For one human being to deprive another in order to increase their welfare at the cost of the other person's welfare is more contrary to nature than death, poverty, pain, or any other things that can happen to one's body or one's external possessions.

For, to begin with, it destroys human communal living and society. For if we are each at the ready to plunder and carry off another's advantages for the sake of our own, that will necessarily demolish the thing that is in fact most according to nature, namely the social life of human beings.

(de Officiis 3.21)

So actions contrary to justice are 'more contrary to nature' than death, while the social life of human beings is 'most according to nature'. Similar thoughts occur at 3.26, 3.28, 3.30, 3.32, 3.35, and less explicitly at 3.46, 1.146, and 1.159. It is in accordance with nature for me to eat food, for instance, and contrary to nature for me to starve. But if I deliberate in terms of what is according to nature and what is not, I will not take food from another person in order to have more food, or even in order to avoid death. For doing so will never put me in a better position vis-à-vis what is according to nature; it is *more* contrary to nature to take the food from another person than to starve.[9]

This does not mean that the status quo in private property is inviolable. It will sometimes be according to nature for me to take someone else's food, provided that I do it for the common welfare, and not for my own:

If for the sake of your own advantage you take something from someone, even someone completely useless to the community, then you have acted inhumanely, and contrary to nature. But if you are capable of providing a great deal of welfare to your country and to human society by remaining alive, and if you do it for that purpose, then it is not forbidden to take it from them. Otherwise, each person must bear their own disadvantage rather than deprive someone else of their advantage; for disease, poverty, and other

Discovering the Befitting: A Better Model ~ 207

demoteds are not more contrary to nature than pursuing and taking what belongs to someone else. But it is also contrary to nature to disregard the common welfare; indeed, it is unjust.

(de Officiis 3.29–30)

So, the general rule is that A cannot take B's property for A's advantage, even if B is completely useless. But if the welfare of the whole community can be advanced in this way, then A is justified in confiscating B's property for the sake of the common welfare (though not for A's welfare), and indeed would be acting unjustly not to do so. Cicero adds the charming caveat that one should not let one's estimate of one's own importance become a pretext for injustice! And indeed, this is a rule that will invite abuse. Nevertheless, it is at least a rule; it allows us to see how deliberation could have some sort of content. We can think about indifferents, but we can also think about the property-rights of other people, and we can think about the welfare of our country or humanity at large.[10]

These two further considerations are again juxtaposed in an important passage at *de Officiis* 1.31, in which Cicero reflects on the apparent lack of exceptionless, universal, and substantive moral laws. In the last chapter, I used this apparent lack as a stick with which to beat the *Salva Virtute* view; if the only rule that always applies is 'live according to virtue', then it seems that considerations of virtue cannot play a substantive role in a deliberation. Thus it is important to see that Cicero offers a more general principle which, he says, will cover even the apparent exceptions:

But occasions often arise when those actions that seem most appropriate to the just and good man— for instance, returning a deposit or keeping a promise—, are changed and become inappropriate to him. It sometimes happens that the just thing is to bypass the actions that belong to truthfulness and faithfulness, and not observe them. For such matters ought to be referred to the fundamentals of justice that I laid down at the beginning: first, that no one be harmed, and second, that the common utility be preserved.

(de Officiis 1.31)

It is worth noting that this formula for the 'fundamentals of justice' does not mention 'virtue', but rather 'harm' and 'utility', that is, matters of indifference.[11] Indeed, with the exception of Cicero's *Salva Virtute* formula, that seems to be true of every relevant text in the *de Officiis*—Chrysippus' footrace first talks about tripping and shoving, and then forbids depriving someone of their useful belongings, on the grounds that it is unjust. Hecato bids us observe the 'customs, laws, and institutions'. Another of the important considerations involves property-rights; indeed, when the last passage refers to 'the fundamentals of justice that I laid down at the beginning', it is referring to this earlier formulation:

The first function of justice is that no one should harm another unless he himself was unjustly harmed; next, that each person should use communal things as communal, and their own private things as their own. But no properties are private by nature, only by long occupation, as when the occupants found it uninhabited, or by victory in war, or law, bargain, sale, or lottery . . . For this reason, whichever of the naturally communal things belongs to someone, let them retain it: and if anyone else seeks to acquire it for their own, they are violating the law of human society.

(*de Officiis* 1.20–21)

Another text from the *de Finibus* reinforces the claim that property is in some sense conventional, but still has a status that makes any prejudicial transfer of ownership by force or fraud a matter of injustice:

Human nature is such that there is a sort of civil law in effect between each person and the human race: whoever preserves it is just, and whoever strays from it is unjust. The theater is a communal place; nevertheless, whichever seat a spectator is occupying is rightfully said to be their own. So too in the state or in the universe, it is not contrary to justice that each person's things should be their own.

(*de Finibus* 3.67)

A Greek text tells us a parallel story about marriage:

Those who follow Zeno of Citium's philosophy avoid adultery, because of communal life. For to seduce a woman who has been previously contracted to another man by law (*nomos*) is contrary to nature, as is destroying the household of another human being.[12]

Discovering the Befitting: A Better Model ~ 209

Here too the requirements of human society transform a conventional arrangement into a norm of nature. The Stoic position on the naturalness of monogamy is not clear—some texts say that Sages will marry, whereas others say that Sages will treat all other Sages as spouses in common, having children in common and 'doing away with jealousy'. But it would be consistent with their picture of the conventionality of property rights that they might well think that monogamy is in some sense a conventional arrangement, and still insist, as in this text, that a violation of an already constituted marriage is contrary to nature, and contrary to communal life.[13]

In the case of depriving someone else of what is theirs—the case that Chrysippus spotlights in his footrace—the agent will need to deliberate in terms of property, as well as indifferents, harm, welfare, and justice. But no reference to 'virtue' is made in any of these texts—except in the case of Cicero's formula at *de Officiis* 3.13. And the sense in which an appeal to justice is providing a concrete constraint on behavior is different from the sense in which I denied, in the previous chapter, that there was any work to be done by appealing to virtue. Virtue, I pointed out there, is officially just a name for the Sage's soul, or for the Sage's right reason or wisdom. It is also true that 'justice' is the name of one of the virtues, and that all of the virtues are in a sense the same thing, all of them being simply the Sage's soul viewed in different ways. But in the texts we are now examining, 'justice'— or more accurately, 'the just'—is not being used in that way. It is referring to certain arrangements of indifferents, even when the arrangements arose from accidents of history or convention. A large house is an indifferent thing, not a good, and the ownership of it is irreducibly arbitrary, not natural: but in light of facts about the ownership, even though they are constituted out of facts about indifferents through and through, there arise further facts about what it is 'just' to do or not do in regards to this house and its owner. The 'just' here is obviously a different thing from the state of a Sage's soul which we would call 'justice', that is, the virtue.[14]

I suspect the Cicero's *Salva Virtute* formulation really does make at least a terminological error, in exactly the respect in which it deviates from the picture that emerges from Chrysippus' footrace, Hecato's law-abiding benefactor, and the 'fundamentals of justice' laid down in *de Officiis* 1.31. The correct formulation should not mention virtue, and the agent's deliberations do not take place in terms of virtue. Instead, one deliberates about advantage and harm (where these are both matters of promoted and demoted indifferents), property-rights, laws, and customs, and the general utility of the whole country, society, or human race, where this utility is also a matter of indifferents—both the direct provision of, for example, deliverance from wild beasts (for which Hercules was famed), and the maintenance and preservation of the very institutions of social life that allow for human beings to live communally. It will be useful to have a label for the new kind of deliberation envisioned here, which shares its two-tier structure with Cicero's *Salva Virtute* model, but does not make the misleading reference to 'virtue'. Chrysippus tells us to run as fast as we like in pursuit of a first prize, but to avoid tripping or shoving our competitors; in honor of this image let us call the new model the 'No Shoving' model.

The No Shoving model seems to me largely to escape the charge of vacuousness or circularity that was lodged against the *Salva Virtute* model. My point is not that it will be an easy, algorithmic, or unambiguous matter to step through this three-round deliberation, in which my pursuit of my interest is curbed by my commitment to avoiding harm to others, especially the diminution of their lawful property, while both of these considerations can and should be overridden by the utility of the whole society. There will be ample room for confusion, self-dealing, and casuistry. But we at least have a range of considerations that can get a deliberation off the ground. An agent can reflect on whether their pursuit of some promoted indifferent will lead to harm to another individual or their property. They can reflect on whether their motivation involves the attempt to increase their welfare at the expense of someone else's. They can ask whether some special national or social crisis puts them in a position that justifies them in, for instance, taking a car to pursue a fleeing criminal. There is nothing mysterious about reflections and deliberations of these kinds.

Discovering the Befitting: A Better Model ~ 211

Furthermore, the overarching considerations advanced in Cicero's discussion of low-level variability, the 'fundamentals of justice', really do seem adequate to account for the exceptions in ethical behavior that are found in Stoic texts. In the last chapter I spoke as though the Sage's actions were completely unpredictable and inscrutable. We know, more or less by definition, that the Sage will do the virtuous thing, but whether the virtuous thing on this occasion will consist in preserving health or injuring it, honoring parents or betraying them, seemed impossible to figure out from any of the philosophical resources given to us. This told against the *Salva Virtute* view, since virtue could only play a regulative role in the agents' deliberations if they could know what virtue required, prior to finding out what the Sage would do.[15]

But I think this picture of the idiosyncratic, cryptic, and almost irrational behavior of the Sage is not borne out by a full examination of the texts. For instance, in arguing that it is not befitting without exception to honor your parents, I referred to a text in which we are told that it is sometimes befitting for children to betray their parents. Now I quote the text:

If the father attempts to become a tyrant, or to betray the country, should the son remain silent about it?

No indeed; he will plead with his father not to do it. If that doesn't stop him, then he will berate him and even threaten him. If after all this the affair is tending towards the destruction of the country, then he will put the safety of his country ahead of the safety of his father.

(*de Officiis* 3.90)

This does indeed seem to be a case in which the injunction to honor one's parents is suspended. But far from giving proof that there will always be further exceptions to any general ethical rule in Stoicism, this case turns out to be a fairly mechanical application of the 'fundamentals of justice' model, according to which the welfare of the community is always the over-riding consideration.

So too with the case I alluded to in which some children kill their parents. It comes up in a discussion of whether all errors are equally vicious:

Then is there no difference (someone will say) between killing a slave and killing your own father?

If you pose the cases without further specification this way then it is not easy to judge what they are like. If to kill one's parent were in and of itself a crime, then the Saguntines who preferred that their parents should die free rather than live as slaves would turn out to have been parricides. Therefore, it is sometimes possible to deprive a parent of life without crime; and it is often impossible to deprive a slave of life without injustice. It is not the nature of the action, but the rationale (*causa*) that makes the difference.

(Cicero Paradoxa Stoicorum §24)

The (presumably adult) children of the Saguntine elders deprived their parents of life when a long siege was ending in an imminent sack, but without crime, because of their rationale—the beliefs on which they acted and the impulses to which they assented. Had their rationale been the desire to advance their own welfare at the expense of their parents, then of course this action would be condemned as unjust. But instead, they seem to have decided to euthanize their parents on grounds parallel to those on which they probably decided to commit suicide themselves: they saw in prospect a preponderance of things contrary to nature (e.g. pain, death, slavery, etc.), and a dearth of things in accordance with nature, both for themselves and for their parents (remember Hecato's comment that we do not seek prosperity only for ourselves). Again there is nothing necessarily inscrutable or unfathomable about these ethical deliberations.[16] And this, it seems to me, provides a further confirmation for the picture of deliberation I am proposing.

The last chapter argued that the Stoics were not interested in general, law-like ethical principles, and motivated that claim in part by suggesting that they modeled their notion of 'law' on Plato's discussion in the *Statesman* of the particular, over-riding injunctions and prescriptions of the moral expert. The evidence we have just seen for stable, exceptionless 'fundamentals of justice' in Stoicism does not require us to retract the suggestion of influence, for in the *Statesman*, too, it is clear that the expert's ad hoc prescriptions are far from random or unprincipled; they are made according to the criterion of the advantage and salvation of the people in the city (296e–297a). And

Discovering the Befitting: A Better Model ~ 213

to the extent that the advantages, welfare, and so on of the whole community and its citizens can be cashed out in ordinary, indifferent ways that do not mention virtue, this criterion of justice can provide a basis for deliberating about what virtue requires which will be both contentful and non-circular.

The Aristo Argument, Again

On the other hand, the content of these deliberations is such that we can still make sense of Chrysippus' disagreement with Aristo. Chrysippus said that Aristo's abolition of the difference between promoted and demoted indifferents would leave wisdom without a function. In the last chapter, I drew another argument in favor of the Indifferents-Only model from Chrysippus' complaint. But in fact this text shows us only that a real distinction among indifferents is *necessary* for wisdom's function, not that the consideration of such indifferents is *sufficient* for it. And on the expanded model that we are considering now, there is still a very good point to Chrysippus' comment.

Think of Aristo's position as licensing the free substitution of the name of any indifferent into any ethical context, without alteration of ethical significance. If there is no difference between poverty and wealth, for instance—if poverty is not demoted and wealth promoted—then there is no ethical difference between 'he deprived me of my wealth' and 'he deprived me of my poverty'. If there is no difference between sound limbs and damaged ones—if health is not promoted and disease demoted—then there is no ethically significant difference between 'she caused my healthy leg to be diseased' and 'she caused my diseased leg to be healthy'.

If we adopted this picture, it is not only the straightforward weighing of promoted and demoted—as in the Indifferents-Only model—that would become incoherent. We would also not be able to make any sense of the idea that we are obliged not to harm others, or increase our welfare at the expense of theirs. On Aristo's picture, this would have the same ethical significance as saying 'we are obliged not to help others, or increase our poverty by alleviating theirs'. We would not be able to distinguish unprovoked attacks from unsolicited generosity. Nor would we be able to make sense of the idea that our country or human society as a whole has interests and a communal welfare that demands our attention. As the No Shoving model fleshes out those ideas, the references to harm, property, welfare, and utility all require a distinction between promoted and demoted indifferents. It is perfectly consistent to imagine Chrysippus espousing the No Shoving model, deliberating about more than merely indifferents, and still complaining that Aristo's leveling of the promoted/demoted distinction would throw the whole of life into confusion.

The fact that the bulk of the evidence points away from a *Salva Virtute* model, but towards the closely related No Shoving model, is important for a number of other reasons.

The Leveling Problem, Again

It means, for instance, that we will no longer have the leveling problem that resulted from the fact that all of the Sage's actions are virtuous, and all of the non-Sage's actions are vicious. The *Salva Virtute* model asked us to regulate our deliberations by the standard of virtue, and our only access to virtue was the behavior of the Sage. But the Sage's behavior did not provide us with a useful norm, because all of it was virtuous, even the most trivial parts, and yet none of it seemed to manifest any overall rationale for its virtue, or any general principle that we could transfer from case to case.

Now we are thinking about what is required, not by Virtue, but by various just arrangements, and the content of that thought comes, not from the mental disposition of an ideal agent, but from the welfare, property-rights, and community relations of ordinary people.

The Convergence of Indifferents-Only and No Shoving

Second, the move from *Salva Virtute* to No Shoving brings out more clearly what was right about the Indifferents-Only model, for two reasons.

Agreement on Exclusion of Agent's Own Virtue

In its own context, the claim in *de Finibus* 3.60 that agents deliberate only about indifferents is designed to make a fairly focused and limited point. It is meant to give emphatic stress to the apparently paradoxical point that virtue, the one thing that provides happiness, does not provide us with reasons to continue living, and that vice, the one thing that guarantees misery, does not provide us with reasons to kill ourselves. The agent's own status vis-à-vis virtue is irrelevant to their deliberations over living or dying. So the question of whether the deliberation may make reference to the virtue or vice, the justice or injustice, of *actions* or action-types is not central to the context; what is most centrally being denied is that the virtue or vice *of the agent who is deliberating* figures in their deliberations. That aspect of the Indifferents-Only model is preserved in the No Shoving model; we have added in the considerations of 'the just' and the 'fundamentals of justice' that the Indifferents-Only model left out, but there is still no room for self-conscious reflections about the agent's *own* virtue.

The same point can be made by juxtaposing some passages from the *de Officiis*, where it becomes clear that what is relevant to agents' deliberations is not their own vice or virtue, but their own utility, either to themselves or to the community as a whole—where again, this utility is not virtue masquerading under an assumed name, but plain old wealth, health, social welfare, and the ability to provide and increase the same for others.

If for the sake of your own advantage you take something from someone, even someone completely useless to the community, then you have acted inhumanely, and contrary to nature. But if you are capable of providing a great deal of welfare to your country and to human society by remaining alive, and if you do it for that purpose, then it is not forbidden to take it from them. Otherwise, each person must bear their own disadvantage rather than deprive someone else of their advantage; for disease, poverty, and other demoteds are not more contrary to nature than pursuing and taking what belongs to someone else. But it is also contrary to nature to disregard the common welfare; indeed, it is unjust.

(de Officiis. 3.29–30)

Here in *de Officiis* 3.29–30 the agent's own virtue or vice is not given any weight in the deliberation.[17] Rather, what makes the difference is whether the agent can provide utility and welfare to the community at large—where this involves the provision of promoted indifferents, or preservation from demoted indifferents, not virtue and vice. Now, sometimes a Sage will be able to provide utility of this sort, but it is not a necessary part of being a Sage, nor is it incompatible with being a non-Sage. From the mere fact that one person is a Sage and another is a non-Sage, we cannot straightaway infer anything about their relative utility to the community. That is why a different problem case in the *de Officiis* is answered by reference to property rights untrumped by considerations of utility:

'Suppose a non-Sage has taken hold of a timber from a sinking ship; should a Sage take it away, supposing the Sage can do it?'
    'No, for that would be an injustice.'

(de Officiis 3.89)

At first glance, this answer seems inconsistent with the earlier passage from *de Officiis* 3.29–30: why is it right for the agent in the first case to take the food, despite the fact that it is the other person's property, but not right to take the timber in this case? The difference is solely in terms of the common utility that the agent can provide; a non-Sage who can provide a great deal of utility is justified in taking the food, a Sage, despite the fact of being a Sage, is not justified in taking the plank in the absence of some explicit argument from utility. To make this lesson even clearer, Cicero passes on to a further hypothetical case:

'Alright, suppose one timber, two survivors, and both are Sages: should both of them try to take it from the other, or will one cede it to the other?'

Discovering the Befitting: A Better Model ~ 217

'One of them will cede it, of course, based on the fact that the other one's life makes a greater difference either to his country or to himself.'[18]

'But what if all that is equal between the two of them?'

'They are not going to wrestle over it; they'll draw lots, or play odd-and-even or what have you, and the one will cede to the other on that basis.'

(de Officiis 3.89–90)

Once again, the decision is based on utility, not virtue. Just as we learn from the *de Finibus*, I make no reference to my own virtue or lack of it in deciding on a course of action.

Agreement on 'More and Less Natural'

Secondly, we have seen that the No Shoving model can also be presented as a series of comparisons of what is more 'according to nature' and what is more 'contrary to nature'. We choose death rather than stealing a man's bread for our advantage, because that unjust deprivation is more contrary to nature even than death. We choose to confiscate the man's bread and give it to someone useful to the country, because it is more contrary to nature to neglect the welfare of the country than to neglect an individual's welfare.[19]

This version of the No Shoving model, in which the deliberation proceeds by choosing what is more in accordance with nature and avoiding what is more contrary to nature, is getting very close indeed to the Indifferents-Only model, except for the fact that one is expressed in terms of 'naturalness' and the other expressed in terms of 'indifference'.

But a second look at the *de Finibus* passage dispels even that difference. 'Indifferents-Only' was always something of a misnomer for the view expressed at *de Finibus* 3.60; it talks all the way through about things according to nature:

Since it is by nature that all love themselves, it belongs just as much to the non-Sage as to the Sage to take the things that are according to nature, and reject the things contrary to nature . . .

. . . when one's circumstances contain a preponderance of things in accordance with nature, it is befitting to remain alive; when one possesses or sees in prospect a majority of the contrary things, it is befitting to depart from life . . .

... what falls directly under the judgment and selection of the Sage are the primary things in accordance with nature and contrary to nature ... [20]

So there was always room in the so-called Indifferents-Only model for considerations other than indifferents, since it always was phrased in terms of naturalness and what is contrary to nature—it might more accurately have been called a 'Naturalness-Only' model. To the extent that those considerations can capture and represent the requirements of justice to others and the interests of our community, even the model of deliberation at *de Finibus* 3.60 can explain how a Sage might die on behalf of a friend, or for the sake of their country, as it says at *DL* 7.130.

Or to look at this from the other direction, it seems that without ever consulting the *de Officiis*, we could have used *de Finibus*. 3.60 and *DL* 7.130 as the premisses for a syllogism showing that the requirements of justice and society can be expressed as considerations of what is according to or contrary to nature. For *de Finibus*. 3.60, again, says that the entire decision about suicide will be made based on the present and future distribution of things according to nature and things contrary to nature; and Diogenes Laertius 7.130 says that the Sage will sometimes commit suicide for the sake of his country or his friends. Thus it follows, just from these two early sources, that the Sage's decision to commit suicide for the sake of their country or friends is the result of deliberations carried out in terms of things according to nature and contrary to nature. The Sage must reason that suicide is more according to nature than continued life, or that failing to kill himself would be more contrary to nature than death: when he looks into the future and sees a life in which he failed to act for the sake of his country or friends, he sees a 'preponderance of things contrary to nature'.

It is important to secure this kind of confirmation of the *de Officiis* picture in sources that are generally taken to represent an earlier stratum of Stoicism, in order to avoid any suspicion that the *de Officiis* represents only a late and unorthodox development by Panaetius or Hecato. Quite the opposite; even if we focused only on such early sources as Cicero's *de Finibus* and Diogenes Laertius there was a gap to be crossed between a theory of deliberation that seemed to forbid any terms other than promoted and demoted indifferents, and the kind of behavior that the Sage arrived at on the basis of those deliberations. The *de Officiis* shows us what had to be there all along.

We have arrived at a sort of synthesis of the first two views, then. The Indifferents-Only model has been replaced by a Naturalness-Only model, and this seems both more reflective of the actual contents of *de Finibus* 3.60, and also more theoretically adequate to generating the Sage's behavior. The *Salva Virtute* model has been replaced by the No Shoving model, where here too we have reason to think this is an improvement. And the two new models can be shown to be deliberatively equivalent—yielding the same prescriptions in the same circumstances—as a result of the bridging-principles between acting contrary to what is just, and acting contrary to nature. Neither one has any role for considerations of the agent's own virtue—that was an important lesson of the Indifferents-Only model, and a prime red-herring in the *Salva Virtute* model. Both models have integral roles for considerations of what is just, arising from the welfare, advantages, and property-rights of other agents, and the needs of the agent's country or human community as a whole—that was an important kernel of truth in the *Salva Virtute* model, but obscured by Cicero's unfortunate phrasing.

The Role of Virtue in Deliberation

One significant point about the synthesis that has emerged is the fact that it does not appeal to agents to forgo their own interests for the sake of virtue. It does sometimes ask agents to forgo the enlargement of their own stock of promoted indifferents if it would harm another agent, or for the sake of their country or community. But when it asks these sacrifices (as they might seem), it presents them as ways of improving one's situation in regard to what is natural, or at least avoiding actions that would be contrary to nature. What it does not do is to offer virtue or its rewards as compensation for the sacrifice; it neither makes the agent's own virtue a consideration, nor makes it a consideration that these actions would be virtuous.

And that is just as well, since the actions that I will do, if I do what I ought to do, will not be virtuous actions in any case, since I am not a Sage. I can and should do the befitting action, the action that is, more in accordance with nature, the action that respects other agents' welfare and property, and the action that preserves the community or the communal way of life. Indeed, I should do exactly what a Sage would do—their action sets the norm for my own. But when I do it, it will not be a virtuous action, since the virtuous action, that is, the perfectly befitting action, can only be done by a Sage. And when I do it, I will not reap any of the benefits of performing a virtuous action, since again it is simply not possible for me to perform a virtuous action. I may at some future date become a Sage and perform virtuous actions, but in the context of my current deliberation, given the current state of my soul, it is simply not open to me to perform a virtuous action.

This means that the promise of virtue's rewards could never have gotten a motivational grip on me in any case. The unique goodness that virtue delivers is simply not on offer for me, right now.

We could imagine a different theory in which it was easier for just anyone to perform the virtuous action—perhaps simply by refraining from this opportunity for theft—and in which performing the virtuous action had all of the benefits that it has in Stoicism, that is, that anyone who performs a virtuous action is perfectly happy, has the sum total of goodness, is a king, and so on. That theory might well have a deliberative structure that would ask me to consider the action's pay-off in terms of promoteds and demoteds, and then consider the action's pay-off in terms of the goodness that I would enjoy from the performance of the virtuous action. Here's what I would see: if I steal the bread, then I get a piece of bread, i.e. a small amount of some promoted indifferent, which is not a good and has no power to make me happier. If I refrain from stealing the bread, then by performing that virtuous action I immediately receive the genuine good of perfect happiness, wisdom, kingship, and so on.

We can see why this deliberative structure would have a very high rate of success at producing virtuous behavior: any agent who was minimally rational would choose the action that will deliver the genuine good (and in an unsurpassable quantity) rather than the action that will deliver an indifferent. Considerations of virtue would always win out.

But it should also be clear that a theory which started from this picture would have no use for an additional measure of value, 'agreement with nature', that could measure both the genuine good of virtue and the promoted indifference of bread.[21] Once I know that the virtuous action brings the summum bonum, perfect happiness, there is simply no role for an additional inducement: it could only seem idle or irrelevant to appeal to any lesser value. It would be like telling the prospective buyer of a Rembrandt that its value can also be measured in the form of several million returnable soft-drink cans—if the thing's supreme intrinsic value was somehow failing to move them, then this conversion into a debased currency would surely not move them either.

This line of thought should further persuade us that the appeal to what is 'more contrary to nature' or 'more in accordance with nature' is not functioning in the deliberative structure as a way of bringing the value of indifferents into comparison with the value of virtue, that is, the unique and supreme value of genuine goodness. That second value simply does not function in my deliberations—it cannot, since I'm not a Sage—and if it did, then it would not need any adventitious trapping of 'naturalness' in order to secure its ascendancy in my actions.[22]

Conversely, the fact that the deliberative trade-offs *are* sometimes presented as choices between what is more and less in accordance with nature should further persuade us that we were right to expel virtue from deliberations, and replace the *Salva Virtute* scheme with the No Shoving model. The values on offer are all indifferents, whether the indifferents of bread and death or the indifferents of keeping myself in accordance with nature and doing what I can for the welfare of the community. When certain arrangements of indifferents are said to be 'just', this may make us think that considerations of virtue have come on to the scene. But virtue and its special transcendent value are not playing any role in the deliberations at all.

This way of looking at my reasons for doing what is befitting will look very familiar to readers of Epictetus. He does not say things like, 'it is not easy to attend to wealth and also attend to virtue', but rather 'it is not easy to attend to externals and also keep your mind in a natural state' (*Ench.* 13). He does not say 'taking the bigger share of food gives you more of an indifferent, but gives you less virtue'; he says 'taking the bigger share of food may have value for your body, but for preserving the communal aspect of dining it has disvalue' (*Ench.* 36). He urges us to keep our mind in a natural state, rather than urging us to perform virtuous actions, because keeping our mind in a natural state is something we can actually do right now. And he explicitly tells us that there is no point in our attempting to desire noble things (that is, virtue), since they simply are not on offer for us yet (*Ench.* 2).[23]

On the other hand, simply keeping my mind in a natural state, in a consistent, firm and unshakable way, is both sufficient for becoming a Sage and for being a Sage—though since we know how hard those tasks are, we know how hard it is to keep my mind in a natural state with that sort of consistency. Still, there is nothing in the progress towards Sagehood, or the activity of being a Sage, that consists in something other than keeping one's mind in a natural state. In particular, there is no stage at which explicit thoughts about virtue need to play a role in determining which action I should next pursue. Nor do they acquire any role in the determination of action, even once I have become a Sage. Sages deliberate as non-Sages do, attending to the values of indifferents and the demands of others' welfare, and determining a course of action on that basis. Once they have discovered the befitting action in that way, then their selective impulse will be sufficient to produce it. Since it will also be a virtuous action in their case, and thus a genuine good, their eupathic desire for the good will also ratify their first-order selection of the befitting—the two impulses will go in tandem. And as was spelled out in the last chapter, the desire for virtue will play the same role in the Sage's choice of toast for breakfast that it does in their dying for their country.

In an earlier chapter, we saw the Stoics employing the image of a game as a way of explaining how my actions can be sensibly aimed at indifferents, even though my end is something outside of that game, namely attaining the good of virtue. In this context, it is worth pointing out that my deliberations all take place within the game, and are based on considerations drawn exclusively from within the game. Crossing the finish-line ahead of my competitors is a goal internal to the game of footraces; tripping and shoving are fouls internal to the game of footraces (they are permissible in some other games). My piece of bread has value, but only within the game; your property rights have a claim on me, but only within the game. The considerations of virtue and its absolute value are all external to this; it is their job to explain why we should have any interest in playing this game, with this set of internal ends, these rules for getting points and these regulations for fouls and penalties.

If we have acquired a better sense of the considerations that a Stoic employs in deciding what to do, we have also acquired a clearer sense of why Stoic ethical thought is prone to the indecisions and waffles that it invites. I am justified in considering my own welfare and my own stock of the things that are useful for life; I also have an obligation to enhance the welfare of those I take to be within the sphere of my concern as that is expanded by the process of *oikeiôsis*— and to the extent that the *oikeiôsis* is successful, I will feel a positive desire to help them, viewing their welfare as part of 'me and mine'. But even those outside what I take to be that sphere have a claim on me, inasmuch as it is unjust to disadvantage them in order to enhance my advantages or the advantages of those whom I consider 'me and mine'—unjust in light of its violation of the 'conventions, laws, and traditions' of the human community in which we find ourselves. And I ought also to be considering the welfare of the country, community, and society as a whole.

This is exactly the plurality of concerns that we should expect if we want to explain the kind of casuistry we see in our most explicit Stoic texts—the *de Officiis*, and Seneca's treatises like the *de Beneficiis*. Is it befitting for me to give a gift to my cousin? In its favor is the fact that my own private stock of advantage is not thereby increased. But it may profit 'me and mine' to the detriment of the greater social welfare. And whether my cousin is part of 'me and mine' or someone outside that sphere can shift, it seems, depending on whether I compare him to my brother or to a tax-collector. And to what extent is my obligation to other people fulfilled by a pro forma observance of the 'laws and customs', as opposed to an analysis that considers the good of the whole community or the strengthening of communal life?[24]

We may also be able to explain why it has seemed to many readers that the doctrine of the befitting, i.e. the *kathêkon*, had a special relation to our duties to others. Of course, all of the considerations that go into my deliberation, as well as all of the impulses that issue from it, will include claims that such and such is or might be the *kathêkon* thing to do. Once again, even my vicious desire to eat the last piece of cake, or to desert my comrades in battle, will consist in impulses that describe the action as 'the thing to do', that is, as the befitting or *kathêkon*. My desire for the cake will (falsely) attribute to it the value of absolute goodness, and on that basis my eating of it will seem like the befitting action; my fear of injury and death will attribute to them the value of absolute badness, and make avoiding them seem like the obvious thing to do.

But if we direct our attention only to the tolerably decent impulses of respectable agents, and divide them up into three groups, sc. my selection of promoted indifferents for myself, my forbearance from infringing on other's welfare, and my regard for the communal welfare, then it looks as though the first group of impulses includes a clear reference to a value, that is, the selective value or axia that promoted indifferents enjoy. My impulses in the other two cases—for example, my impulse to stay and protect my comrades despite the danger—are presumably specimens of selection, since they look neither like emotions nor like *eupatheiai*.[25] And yet they are not selections that are easily analyzed as cases in which I select for myself some of the selective value of promoted indifferents. It's one thing to say that my eating a moderate and dispassionate breakfast is a selection of the promoted indifferent of food; but the failure of the original, narrow-focused Indifferents-Only model was exactly tied up in the implausibility of saying that my risking my life for my friends could be the result of a totting-up of promoteds and demoteds and their selective value.

So this particular impulse does not seem to be a matter of thinking that something is a good of such a sort that it's befitting that...; or thinking that something is a bad of such a sort that it is befitting that...; or thinking that it is a promoted indifferent of such a sort that it is befitting that... In other words, the judgment that it is *kathêkon* does not seem to mention any antecedent judgment of value, for example, good or bad or promoted or demoted. This impulse seems to consist simply in the thought that it is *kathêkon*, *tout court*. So if we ask what led people to overlook the clear evidence of the ubiquity of the *kathêkon* or befitting in all motivation, and what led them to think that the befitting or *kathêkon* named a special sort of consideration or motivation, for instance, a selfless or other-regarding motivation, then it may be just this fact: that in many self-regarding impulses, for example, my gluttonous desire for food as a good or my more moderate selection of food as an indifferent, there is an explicit reference to a value which I acquire for myself, and the judgment that the action is *kathêkon* somehow arises from that value, whereas in these other-regarding cases there does not seem to be a value that I acquire for myself, and the judgment that the action is *kathêkon* is not based on any antecedent assessment of value.

NOTES

1. *DL* 7.130, trans. from Hicks (1925).
2. This is related to the problem that Barney (2003) raises, that the Indifferents-Only model (which she generally endorses) cannot account for what she calls 'Regulan' behavior, on the self-sacrificing virtue of the Roman hero Regulus, celebrated in *de Officiis* 3.99 et seq., who voluntarily brought about his own death by torture in order to help his country.
3. My complaint here parallels a complaint that Posidonius leveled at certain formulations of the Stoic end that gave too prominent an emphasis to the orientation towards indifferents; see Galen *PHP* 5.6.10 = *SVF* 3.12 = LS 64I.
4. *de Officiis* 1.25

5. That the 'interests' pursued here involve indifferents rather than the goods of virtue and virtuous action is made clear by the injunction against augmenting your advantages by depriving another of their own. Virtue is clearly not a negotiable instrument whose title can be conveyed from one possessor to another.

6. See below on Hecato's quotation of the possibly Platonic *Epistle* 9.

7. Another echo of the same thought occurs at *de Off.* 1.43, in a discussion of liberality: 'we must see that we are using liberality in such a way that it benefits our friends, but harms no one'. *Nocere* here as in 1.42 as passim in *de Officiis* does *not* translate *blaptein* in the strict sense of 'injuring someone's real good, that is, their virtue'. Although *blaptein* in Stoicism is typically a word that involves real goods rather than indifferents, and although *nocere* often translates it in other texts, it is clear that the hurts and harms referred to by *nocere* in the *de Officiis* are all simple demoted indifferents (e.g. 2.14 on destructive wild animals).

8. *de Officiis* 3.42. Can we be confident that this passage really originated with Chrysippus? Yes, for two reasons. One, there is the external consideration that Cicero introduces it by saying '*Scite Chrysippus, ut multa*', i.e. 'Chrysippus puts it neatly, as he so often does.' This promises a verbatim quotation, and there is no reason to doubt Cicero's word. Secondly, there is the internal consideration that Chrysippus frequently employed athletic analogies of this sort, especially drawn from running (e.g. Galen PHP 4.2.10–18 = *SVF* 3.462 = LS 65J, also *SVF* 3.473, 476, 478, 699)—perhaps because, as the ancient tradition tells us, he himself had been a runner in his youth (*DL* 7.179 = *SVF* 2.1 = IG2 II–I).

9. Here I am especially grateful to Barney (2003) for showing me both that it was an option to take 'according to nature' in a more extended sense than merely 'promoted indifference', and that this is a strategy employed throughout the *de Officiis*. Barney argues that this strategy was never employed by the early Stoics (e.g. Chrysippus) and would not have worked; I believe I have answered her arguments below.

10. The story of Brutus and Collatinus at *de Officiis* 3.40 is another case in which A's apparent injustice to B ('it might have seemed that he acted unjustly') is justified by the need to consult the interests of the country. Does this mean that the Stoics thought the preservation of the current regime trumped every other ethical consideration? Even if the regime itself is immoral? Their view is not clear enough here, but at least in one case Cicero does allow us to distinguish between the welfare of the people and the welfare of the current regime in power. *De Officiis* 2.26 and 3.32 advocate the murder of a tyrant for the sake of the people at large. So if the government consists in a wicked tyrant, then the mere interests of its stability—and the tyrant at issue, Phalaris of Sicily, was a very well entrenched and stable one—does not confer any special ethical status on it.

11. At *de Officiis* 1.85 the Stoics attempt to find Platonic support for these two principles. 'Plato's two precepts' of good governance are first that rulers should look to the utility of the people and forget their own advantage, and second that they should care for the state as a whole rather than advancing the interests of one part at the expense of another. The mapping onto the

'fundamentals' formula is not as clear as it might be, but plausible, i.e. that the first injunction addresses the natural tendency to purely first-person aggrandizement, and the second addresses the tendency to make one's sense of *oikeiôsis* stop short of the whole community. The interest in finding Platonic support (here from the *Republic*) may come from Panaetius and Posidonius. See also the use of the formula from the possibly Platonic *Epistle* 9 'we are not born for ourselves alone' at *de Officiis* 1.22, which is recalled in Hecato's phrase at 3.63 (*non nobis solum/neque solum nobis*), where [Plato]'s list, not quoted at 1.22, continues 'but rather our country, parents, and other friends each claim a part' (*Ep.* 9 358a4–6), and Hecato's continues 'but rather we want prosperity for our children, relatives, friends, and country.' This Platonic or pseudo-Platonic foreshadowing of *oikeiôsis* is intriguing, and the epistle does not otherwise sound Stoic (indeed, the use of *katalambanein* is clearly not Stoic).

12. Origen *contra Celsum* 7.63 p.739 = *SVF* 1.244.

13. Sage will marry: *DL* 7.121 = *SVF* 1.270 = IG2 II–94, Stobaeus 2.7.109.10 = *SVF* 3.686 = IG2 II–95.11m; Sages have children in common *DL* 7.131 = *SVF* 3.728, *SVF* 1.269 = IG2 II–94. And see Seneca *de Beneficiis* 2.35: 'We deny that the Sage can suffer any damage, but if someone knocks him down with a fist he will be penalized for the damages; we deny that anything belongs to the non-Sage, but if someone takes something from a non-Sage by stealth we will convict him of theft.'

14. At the level of vocabulary, all of Cicero's references to '*ius*' are presumably translations of *to dikaion*, not *hê dikaiosunê*. It may be that these words were distinguished in the same way that the 'true' and 'truth' (*to alêthes/hê alêtheia*) were distinguished (*SE AM* 7.38 = *SVF* 2.132 = IG2 II-39, paraphrased at *SE PH* 2.81 = LS 33P). 'True' is a word applied to individual incorporeal propositions, e.g. that it is day, and there are thus as many instances of 'the true' as there are true propositions, but 'truth' applies to a single body, and is merely another name for the Sage's soul (which is a body), inasmuch as it is infallible. Like that pair, it may be 'the just' is an incorporeal, propositional entity ('it is just that . . . '), whereas 'justice' is a body, i.e. the Sage's soul in a certain disposition. There is thus the same difference between saying that the Sage always pursues justice (i.e. the virtue, as a psychic state), and the Sage always pursues the just, as there would be between saying that the Sage's mind always corresponds to the truth (*alêtheia*) and that it always corresponds to the true (*to alêthes*): the first is vacuous; the second has content. Being told to believe in accordance with 'the truth' would be unhelpful; we know that whatever the Sage believes is in accordance with 'the Truth', just as whatever a Sage does is in accordance with Virtue (these being two further synonyms for the Sage's soul), but we have learned nothing further about how to find out which belief is true or which action is just, or about how Sages themselves could ever deliberate about these things. But looking for 'the true' or 'the just', i.e. particular true propositions or just arrangements, can give us a purchase on the matter that is independent of the vacuous and tautological reference to the Sage's mind, and allows us to make forward progress.

15. I found philosophical nourishment for thinking about this topic, though no interpretive assistance, from Hooker (2000).

16. A further case in point: Origen tells us that the Stoics said that incest is indifferent, despite the fact that one ought not to do such things in established political systems. 'And as a hypothetical case, to show the indifference of it, they make the Sage and his daughter the sole survivors after the human race has been destroyed. And they ask whether it would be befitting for the father to have sex with the daughter so as to avoid the extinction of the whole human race' (*Contra Celsum* 4.45 = *SVF* 3.743). We may infer that the answer was 'yes' from Origen's loud displeasure (though a father of the church ought to have known Genesis 19:30). Thus we learn that incest is indifferent 'in its own right' (*tôi idiôi logôi*); that in established communities one ought not to do it, i.e. it is not befitting to do it contrary to the 'laws, customs, and institutions'; and that when an exceptional circumstance arises in which it is befitting to do it, this fact is amply explained by the appeal to the general utility and welfare of the human community (i.e. its need for preservation). This apparent exception, then, is also covered by the 'fundamentals of justice' formula. It is also worth noting that what makes it befitting in this case—the fact that the survival of the race depends on it—has nothing to do with the man's being a Sage, and the same rationale would make it obligatory for a pair of non-Sages in the same fix to do the same thing. The Stoics employed the Sage in the hypothetical to clarify the issues; if we ask 'would the non-Sage have sex with his daughter?', the answer is that he might well, but for any number of reasons irrelevant to what makes it befitting, or he might not, despite the fact that it is befitting. Asking 'would the Sage have sex with his daughter?' guarantees that a 'yes' answer will track the real issue of befittingness. This is a good example of how it can come to appear, misleadingly, that Sages are allowed to do things that non-Sages may not do.

17. It is true that the case is introduced at the beginning of 3.29 by asking whether a Sage might take the bread from someone useless to society, and summed up in 3.31 by saying that the necessities of life may be legitimately transferred from the useless person to 'a man who is wise, good, and strong', where this might well describe a Sage. But when the solution to the case is given in 3.30, no reference is made to the useful person's being a Sage; Cicero says 'if you are the sort of person who can provide a great deal of utility etc.'. In addition, the caveat that people who invoke this rule should be careful of self-deception would be superfluous if it only applied to Sages. Finally, if what licensed the taking of the bread in this case was not the relative utility of the two people but their relative virtue, i.e. the fact that it was a Sage who took it from a non-Sage, then this case would be inconsistent with the claim in 3.89 that the Sage is not justified in taking the plank from the non-Sage.

18. What could it mean to say that Sage A's life makes a greater difference to Sage A, than Sage B's life makes to Sage B? This sub-question simply reverts to the question of suicide at *de Fin.* 3.60: 'when one's circumstances contain a

preponderance of things in accordance with nature, it is befitting to remain alive; when one possesses or sees in prospect a majority of the contrary things, it is befitting to depart from life.' And here we have set aside the question of the agent's virtue, and of their utility to society at large, so that the question really is simply: which Sage is enjoying, or can expect (if granted use of the timber) to enjoy, a greater amount of the promoted indifferents, or a greater ratio of the promoted to demoted?

19. Cf. *de Finibus* 3.64 on preferring the common utility to our own.

20. *de Finibus* 3.60 = SVF 3.763 = LS 66G.

21. As a point of translation, it is not clear whether Cicero's *Salva Virtute* formulation in *de Officiis* 3.13 says that virtue is in accordance with nature or not (though this is clearly stated in other parts of the *de Officiis*). ' . . . always to conform to virtue, and as for the other things which are according to nature, . . . ' might mean 'the other things which, like virtue, are according to nature', or it might mean 'the other things, i.e. those that, unlike virtue, are according to nature'.

22. This is meant to answer the concern in Barney (2003) that if the Stoics said a virtuous action was 'more according to nature' than a promoted indifferent like health, the rigid partition between the value of true goodness and the value of promoted indifference would collapse, leaving the Stoics with an Antiochean or Peripatetic theory. It is true that the Sage's actions have the higher sort of value, but the non-Sage's do not, even when they are done in conformity with the dictates of justice or other virtues. This confusion between virtuous action and action in conformity with virtue may help to excuse Cicero's anomalous reference to virtue in *de Officiis* 3.13.

23. There is another intriguing Ciceronian anticipation of an Epictetan idiom when he talks about an unrepentantly vicious agent 'destroying the human being in the human being' (*de Officiis* 3.26), cf. Epictetus 2.9.3 on 'destroying the human being.'

24. I have in mind here the disagreements that Hecato recorded between Diogenes and Antipater in 3.91 et seq. I take it that Diogenes' advocacy of minimal compliance with the law is a reflection of the view that property-claims are conventional rather than natural, and grounded in particular systems of 'laws, traditions, and customs'. Antipater's view emphasizes the claims of human society and communal living as a whole. It is a mistake to think of either Diogenes or Antipater as being more 'cynical', 'mercenary' or 'self-interested' than the other; both of them draw their considerations—of the property-claims of others vs. the good of the whole society—from the two parts of the 'fundamentals of justice' formula from 1.31.

25. This is guaranteed, I think, both by the *telos*-formulae of Diogenes and Antipater (see above in Chapter 8), and also by the reference in Hierocles of the 'selection of the befitting' (*eklogê tôn kathêkontôn*) Stobaeus 4.502.

Stoic texts on goods are collected at LS 60; texts on indifferents are collected at LS 58; and texts on the end are collected at LS 63 and 64. *Oikeiôsis* is rendered by 'appropriateness' in LS and treated in chapter 57; it is rendered by 'the congenial' in IG2 (see their index for guidance to the texts).

For contrasting approaches to the Stoic theory of goods and ends see Long (1974/1986) and Annas (1993). Irwin (1986) definitively establishes that the Stoics were not Aristotelians. Brunschwig (1986) makes more progress by comparing the Stoics with the Epicureans.

The theory of *oikeiôsis* has received many treatments. See Long (1970), Pembroke (1971), White (1979), Striker (1983), Inwood (1984), Inwood (1985), 190–202. The book-length treatment by Engberg-Pedersen (1990) is impressive but, I believe, wholly misguided.

My approach here differs from many approaches that place *oikeiôsis* in the context of the search for the good or the final end; for more conventional recent treatments see Inwood and Donini (1999).

Befitting actions (*kathêkonta*) are called 'proper functions' in LS and the texts are collected in chapter 59. IG2 calls them 'appropriate acts' (see their index for guidance to texts); this means that 'appropriate' in IG2 and 'appropriate' in LS are translating two different things.

Befitting actions are covered in practically every discussion of Stoic ethics. My emphasis on deliberation arose out of my earliest piece on Stoicism, Brennan (1996) and was sharpened by debate with Cooper (1989) and Barney (2003), but it also has points of contact with a separate debate between Mitsis (1993), (1999), and Inwood (1999).

Discovering the Befitting: A Better Model ~ 231

In several areas of current controversy about Stoic ethics it is possible to discern a recurrent debate between those who are inclined to a more naturalistic reading of the ethics and those who are inclined to a more rationalistic reading of it. Naturalists emphasize the role of metaphysics, cosmology, theology, and anthropology in providing the foundations for ethics. Rationalists emphasize the role of reason, rational consistency, rules, and considerations of autonomy. I tend to side with Long, White, and Inwood in following the naturalistic camp. Annas, Engberg-Pedersen, Irwin, and Mitsis have followed the rationalist camp. Striker is an unaligned independent; Schofield (2003) tries to offer compromise formulae.

The reader who finishes the middle third of my book and wants to take the next steps into studying Stoic ethics should begin by devoting time to the relevant portions of LS or IG2, or better yet to *SVF* if Greek and Latin are accessible. For good overviews of the whole field, at a slightly greater level of difficulty, I recommend Long (1974/1986) and Striker (1991). Slightly older but still useful are Rist (1969), Sandbach (1975), and Bonhöffer (1968). Long (1971), Rist (1978), and Schofield and Striker (1986) are excellent collections of articles which are still valuable. Algra et al. (1999), Ierodiakonou (1999) and Inwood (2003) are the most up-to-date collections of essays by various hands.

PART IV

Fate

14

God and Fate

The Stoics believed that every event that occurs in the cosmos—from the most important to the most trivial—was fated to occur, and determined to occur.[1] It all occurs in accordance with the plan of Zeus, and it is all bound to occur, by the bonds of Necessity. The Roman empire was fated to fall, and you were fated to read this page. And, yes, you were even fated to have the last thought you had. You might think that the Stoics would have put a fire-wall between external physical events, for example, my taking a walk, and internal mental events, like my assenting to an impression, or my taking a certain attitude towards what happens externally. Indeed, there are even parts of Epictetus that might look as though he is saying something like that. But as we will see later, there is no difference between the outer world and the inner world of the mind, so far as the determination of fate goes.

When events are controlled by Fate—which the Stoics tell us is also the same thing as Necessity, and Zeus, and Providence—they are not influenced from a distance, or controlled from on high, as though pulled by the strings of divine puppet-masters.[2] Instead, Fate goes to work in every portion of every object's being. Each object is a combination of inert matter, and vivifying breath, the 'spirit' which is another name for Fate. (This spirit or *pneuma* is still corporeal and material.) Whenever an object causes something, its causal power is the same thing as Fate.[3] But this does not mean that the cause of each thing is not divine; it is divine, for Zeus is in all things, too. There is a huge, comprehensive master-plan, controlling all events in the past, present and future, and this is Fate, and Zeus and the Cause.[4] There is also a cause of that leaf's fluttering there, which is a portion of Fate, a portion of Zeus, and a portion of the Cause of the cosmos. It has always been true, as far back as you care to go, that that same leaf would have to flutter just now, in exactly the way it did. It is true, already, that you will die on a certain day, saying certain words, when the day-light in your room has modulated to a certain shade of pale yellow. You will die having done all the things you were always fated to do, and nothing else. You will die a happy person, because you will die a virtuous Sage—if it is fated for you to become a Sage. Or you will die a wretched, miserable, confused non-Sage, if that is fated. The numbers strongly suggest misery as the more likely course, but Fate does not defer to probabilities—you will do what you are fated to do, whether it is the more likely course or the less likely course.

Given how much trouble the Stoics brought on themselves by taking this view of fate, we might well wonder why they bothered. Indeed, most of this section will be taken up with attacks on the Stoic position launched by other philosophers—especially the Academics—and the Stoics' efforts to respond. I think those efforts are characteristically brilliant, resourceful, and influential—they always deepen our understanding of the issues at hand. I also think they fail to rescue the Stoics from the hole they dug for themselves. The fact that their views on fate produced insurmountable difficulties for them only makes it more curious that they should have adopted those views to begin with (of course it is tempting to say: 'they were fated to'—but it doesn't help).

It seems fairly clear that the Stoic understanding of fate was intended, at least in part, to play some role in helping individuals to take a different view of their lives. Understanding events—especially misfortunes—as the result of fate could help us to see why we should not be disturbed by them:

236 ~ *God and Fate*

Sages are content with events, on the grounds that everything happens according to fate.[5]

Whenever you are blaming providence, reflect on it and you will recognize that the thing happened in accordance with reason.[6]

Such is the nature of the cosmos, and such it was, and is, and will be; and what happens cannot happen otherwise than as it now is . . . If you make the attempt to incline your mind to these things, and to persuade yourself to accept the necessary things willingly, then you will live your life most moderately and harmoniously.[7]

But we should not suppose that the Stoics adopted their views on fate merely to help them out of a bind in ethics. Critics do sometimes write as though the Stoics taught us to believe in fate so that we could attain tranquility. Here is one critic's summation of the view:

We must be indifferent to death, pain, and illness, and even the loss of our dearest relatives must not touch us. For all this not only belongs to the external world, but also happens through Divine Providence, which is always good.[8]

It seems to me that this sort of view gets two different things wrong. First of all, it suggests that we could use our beliefs about Zeus and fate in order to alter our beliefs about what is truly good and bad; but Epictetus, at least, quite clearly thinks this is not psychologically possible. Piety cannot teach us to be resigned to misfortunes; quite the opposite, we must already accept that what occurs is not bad for us, if we are to have any hope of being pious:

Let's switch back to calling health, life, and other external things 'goods'. Now: is it possible for someone who is 'harmed' and fails to get his 'goods' to be happy? It is not possible. Then how can I still do what I should towards Zeus? If I am 'harmed', and losing my 'goods', then I think he is not taking care of me. And what do I care about Him, if he can't help me? What do I care about him, if he is willing to let me get into my present situation? Then I start to hate God. All this follows once we suppose that external things are goods.

(1.22.13–16)

It is a universal rule—so don't kid yourself!—that every animal identifies with nothing more than with its own self-interest. If anything seems to be getting in the way of that, no matter if it's a brother or father or child or lover, then the animal hates it, accuses it, and curses it. If the gods seem to be getting in the way of our self-interest, then we revile them, too, and knock down their statues and burn their temples.

(2.22.15–17)

It is not in human nature to put up with being stripped of what we think is good, or to put up with encountering what we think is bad. [If external things happen which I think are bad], I sit down and groan and shout abuse at Zeus and the other gods. If they are not taking care of me, then what do I care about them? 'But in that case', you say, 'you would be impious!' True, but I would be no worse than I already AM! [i.e. since my belief that externals are good is just as bad as impiety]. The point is, unless we make piety and self-interest coincide, there is no way for piety to survive—in anyone.

(1.27.12–14)

Thus the Stoics would not have seen any point in trying to adopt a particular view about divine determination in order to change our mind about what is good and bad. The ethical point, that nothing but virtue is good, must be secured first, and independently, before the theological point can be secured.[9]

Second, the putative ethical motivation for determinism suggests that we should conclude that what happens is good, because it was caused to happen by a good agent. But in fact, what happens is not good, it is only indifferent. The Stoics are happy to say that Zeus is good; but they do not say that any external events are good, even if they are all produced by the will of Zeus. (Nor do we need to think that they are *good*, in order to safeguard our piety; we merely must avoid thinking they are *bad*.) But not only is the arrangement of externals around us indifferent—that is, this amount of food here, that amount of life there, sickness for you, health for him, and so on—it is also the case that any other arrangement of externals that Zeus *could* have provided would have been *equally* indifferent—no arrangement would have made them any better or worse than any other arrangement. The externals around us did not have to be

238 ~ *God and Fate*

exactly the way that they are *now* in order for them to be indifferent. Nor did Zeus need to arrange them in exactly this way in order for them to be indifferent. Now matter how Zeus might have arranged them—or even if Zeus had not arranged them—or even if a hateful and malevolent anti-Zeus had arranged them—it would still be the case that the externals around us are indifferent. The fact that they are indifferent derives from wholly other sources—it derives from the kind of creatures we are, and what our good consists in. Thus, for this second reason, it seems very unlikely to me that the Stoics adopted the deterministic outlook in order to counsel us to resignation.

But if Zeus's management of the world is not directed towards selecting the one arrangement that is *better* than the others—if the actual world is not, in that sense, the *best* of all possible worlds—there is still one respect in which this world surpasses any other possible arrangement: it is the most reasonable, the most rational, of all possible worlds. As we saw earlier, the thing that is truly good for us—our virtue—consists in our responding wisely and rationally to the indifferent things that we encounter. So too with Zeus; Zeus's goodness consists in his maximally wise and rational arrangement of the indifferents that make up the cosmos as a whole. But these reflections are either too little to provide consolation, if one still believes that the events that happened to you are bad, or they are not needed for consolation if one understands that the events are indifferent.

And as we will see, the Stoic theory of fate is so closely connected to other parts of their system—their logic, their physics, metaphysics and theology, and their entire picture of the cosmos—that it would be a distortion to say that they adopted the view to score any particular point in the ethical realm. The Stoic boast of systematicity and rigor is nowhere better exemplified than in the wide-ranging connections that surround the theory of fate.

But these views on fate left the Stoics open to a variety of attacks. In the chapters that follow we shall examine in detail the two strategies for attacking the Stoic theory of fate:

God and Fate ~ 239

(1) The argument that fate makes personal responsibility incoherent, that is, that we cannot meaningfully praise or blame people for their actions, if what they did was fated;

(2) The argument that fate makes personal effort incoherent, that is, that there is no point in our making an effort to achieve things, if what will happen is already fated.

The first point involves our judgments of people's past behavior; the second involves our planning for the future. So we might think of them as the retrospective problem and the prospective problem. After we have spent two chapters looking at these two problems, we will look at some of the historical consequences of the Stoic theory of fate, especially as it was represented in Epictetus.

NOTES

I could not have written this part, nor would I have attempted it, without the immense assistance provided by Bobzien (1998a). She has brought order, clarity, rigor, and understanding, to a topic that has long been a sink of ignorance and confusion, and I am indebted both to her book and to our conversations for much of what I say here. I venture to write on this topic, so soon after the appearance of her book, primarily because we are addressing different audiences; in attempting to make the results of her dense and erudite tome accessible to a non-specialist audience, I am playing Epictetus to her Chrysippus. But I have also not hesitated to disagree with her on many points of interpretation, and I depart from her scholarly restraint by expressing more speculative views about the philosophical significance of the Stoic system.

1. *DL* 7.149 = *SVF* 2.915 = IG2 II–20; Cicero de Fato 20 = *SVF* 2.952 = LS 38G = IG2 I–15; Stobaeus 1.79.5 = *SVF* 2.913 = LS 55M.

2. Fate is nature, reason, and god: *DL* 7.135 = *SVF* 1.102 = LS 46B = IG2 II–20; Alexander of Aphrodisias *de Fato* cp. 22 p. 191, 30 Bruns et seq. = *SVF* 2.945 = LS 55N; Fate is the reason of Zeus, and Necessity: Plutarch *Sto. Rep.* 1056B = *SVF* 2.997 = LS 55R = IG2 II–91; Fate is nature and providence; Aëtius 1.27.5 = *SVF* 1.176; what happens according to Fate happens according to Providence Alexander of Aphrodisias *Quaestiones* 1.4 = *SVF* 2.962; the cosmos is called Zeus,

Fate, and Providence: Arius Didymus apud Eusebium *praep. Evang.* 15.15 p. 817.6 = *SVF* 2.528

3. Fate is a network of causes: Aëtius 1.28.4 = *SVF* 2.917 = LS 55J = IG2 11–79; Aëtius 1.27.3 = *SVF* 2.976; every cause is pneumatic: Aëtius 1.11.5 = *SVF* 2.340 = LS 55G; the cosmos is unified by a single all-pervasive pneuma Alex. Aphr. *De mixtione* 216 = *SVF* 2.473 = LS 48c.

4. Past present and future in Stobaeus 1.79 = *SVF* 2.913 = LS 55M.

5. pseudo-Plutarch, *de Fato* 574e = *SVF* 2.912 = IG2 11–77.

6. Epictetus 3.17.1-2.

7. Musonius Rufus, fr. 42 Hense. Musonius is still difficult to find in English, other than in Lutz (1947).

8. von Fritz (1970).

9. This is not a claim about logic. So far as logic goes, the position is symmetrical, as Epictetus shows: piety and the belief that externals are good and bad are *incompatible* with each other, and thus the negation of either can be inferred from the other. (And thus, too, we see why all non-Sages are impious). If one could be perfectly persuaded of the theological point without having any views on the ethical point, then the theology could be used to derive the ethics. But Epictetus seems to think that is not a psychologically possible route to take from folly to wisdom; one cannot be *more* certain of God's goodness than one is of the external world's indifference.

15

Necessity and Responsibility

There is a natural tendency to feel that any doctrine of Fate deprives individuals of responsibility for their actions. This, in turn, seems to make it pointless to blame them for what they did, or to praise them either. It doesn't take much sophisticated logical training to lay out the basics of an argument like this; all you have to do is say 'don't blame me; Fate made me do it!'

However, simple arguments get simple replies. It is said that one of Zeno's slaves stole something from the household, and was about to be whipped for it. 'But I was *fated* to steal!' he said, as he was led away. 'Yes, and to be whipped, too', replied Zeno.[1] If we want to move beyond one-liners, then we need to think more carefully about the relations between fate, causation, necessity, and human action. The Stoics and their opponents can help us to do this.

Here as often, fruitful disagreement takes place against a background of considerable agreement. The Stoics and their opponents agree on several important principles that connect up the topics of moral assessment, human agency, and necessity. They agree, first of all, that an agent cannot be blamed for an action unless *that* agent did it, rather than something else, and chose to do it, knowingly, rather than doing it unintentionally or through some misunderstanding. This idea is usually put by saying that one can sensibly praise or blame an action only if the action is 'up to' the agent. Secondly, they agree that an action is not 'up to us' if it was necessary for us to do what we did. Combining these two principles, we find a third point of common agreement: one can sensibly praise or blame an action only if it was not necessary that the agent should perform it.

Furthermore, all sides agree that there are some human actions that one can sensibly praise or blame, that is, there are some that really deserve praise or blame, as opposed to the actions that should be ignored, forgiven, or treated as evidence of some sort of incompetence on the agent's part, like insanity or intoxication. Now we have the following common ground for both parties:

(1) There are some actions that agents perform which deserve praise and blame

(2) No action deserves praise and blame unless it was 'up to' the agent

(3) No action is 'up to' the agent if it was necessary for the agent to perform it

(4) So, there are some actions that agents perform without it being necessary for the agents to perform them.

Most of the debate then turns on whether the Stoics can consistently deny that agents are necessitated to do what they do. The question is especially pressing, since the core of the Stoic position on fate and determinism is contained in two further principles: that every event has a cause; and that every event happens by fate.[2]

For the Stoics, these are as it were two sides of one principle, since whatever happens by Fate has Fate for its cause, and whatever is caused was caused by Fate. The opponents of the Stoics then claim that the Stoics must agree that everything that happens, happens by necessity, and thus that there are no actions that are really open to moral assessment. So the main ground of contention between the Stoics and their opponents are the following two principles, accepted by their opponents and rejected by the Stoics:

Necessity and Responsibility ~ 243

(CN) if something is caused to happen, then it happens by necessity

(FN) If something happens by Fate, then it happens by necessity.

In this chapter, then, we will look at two anti-Stoic arguments. The first claims that the Stoic acceptance of divination and fate commits them to the conclusion that everything happens by necessity. Because of the example used, I shall call this the Fabius Argument. We will see how Chrysippus responds to this argument by claiming that divination does not make events necessary.

The second anti-Stoic argument claims that their view of causation entails that nothing we do is really 'up to us', and so nothing we do can justifiably be praised or blamed. Chrysippus responds to this by distinguishing how our actions are caused.

After we have looked at those arguments, we will be in a position to take a broader view of the significance of the Stoic position on Fate and its relation to moral responsibility.

Two Anti-Stoic Arguments against Fate

Against Fate 1: The Fabius Argument, that Divination Makes All Events Necessary

The Background on Divination:

Divination was the ancient practice of predicting the future on the basis of events in nature, which were treated as signs of things to come. The practice was very thoroughly woven into the fabric of Greek culture; in Homer and the tragedians people draw inferences about the future from the flight of birds in the sky or from a sneeze, as well as from the inspection of sacrificial victims.[3] Certain people were supposed to be especially skilled at this sort of inference—seers, diviners, prophets—and it was widely thought that these people practiced a codifiable art or science that had rules and principles, not unlike mathematics or medicine. Of course it was also a well-known fact that many prophets were charlatans, and that many prophecies were wrong, even those uttered by the sincere and scrupulous seers. But the same was, and still is, true in the case of medicine—many alleged medical experts are unscrupulous rogues, and even the pillars of the profession make mistakes in diagnosis and treatment on a daily basis. The doctors give someone two months to live, and they die in two days instead—or in two decades. These imperfections in the practitioners and in the predictions do not undermine our confidence that there really is a body of science called 'medicine', with rules and principles that can be more and less skillfully employed. The ancient attitude towards divination was, for the most part, like this: no lack of skepticism about particular prophets and prophesies, but a general acceptance that the future may be read from the present, if the signs are treated with sufficient skill.

The Stoics had this conventional view of divination, and added to it only the further point that in order for there to be an art or science of this sort, there must be rules and laws that link the present to the future: the signs must be signs of an underlying causal order. It is not that the shape of a sheep's liver today is the cause of the army's victory tomorrow, but both are caused by the same network of causes, in such a way that if the liver had been differently shaped, then whatever caused the different shape would cause a different outcome for tomorrow's battle as well. In order for divination to work, that is, the future events must already be determined to occur, before they occur.

Cicero presents the Fabius Argument

Well, if there is a science of divination, then what sorts of theorems does it employ? In every science the scientists make use of theorems in their work, and I can't believe things are different for the people who use divination to predict the future. So there are theorems of divination, and they go like this: 'If anyone is born at the rising of the star Sirius (to make up an example), then he will not die at sea.' But you'd better watch out, Chrysippus, or you'll be giving up the struggle you have with Diodorus the great logician. For if that is a true conditional sentence—i.e.,

'if anyone is born at the rising of the star Sirius, then he will not die at sea,'

—then so is this one:

'if Fabius is born at the rising of Sirius, then Fabius will not die at sea.'

So there is a conflict between

'Fabius was born at the rising of Sirius,' and

'Fabius will die at sea.'

But since it is stipulated as certain that Fabius *was* born at the rising of Sirius, then there is a conflict between

'Fabius exists' and 'Fabius will die at sea.'

So the following will also be a conjunction of incompatibilities:

'both: Fabius exists, and Fabius will die at sea'

which can thus never happen as it is stated. So it turns out that the statement:

'Fabius will die at sea'

belongs to the class of things that cannot possibly happen. So, any false statement about the future describes something that cannot possibly happen.[4]

We should look more closely at the details of this argument, and at how Chrysippus responds to it. But first, we should review the reasons why its conclusion is unacceptable to the Stoics. They agree, to begin with, that divination can tell us at least some things about the future. We might not be able to ask the oracle for an answer to every possible question about the future, but a question like 'will Fabius die at sea?' would be a pretty typical question to ask an oracle (especially if you are Fabius), and the Stoics would agree that divination can provide an answer like 'Fabius will not die at sea.' They think, furthermore, that genuine divination is infallible: if the oracle says that Fabius will not die at sea, then Fabius will not die at sea. However, the Stoics want to claim that future events are not necessary, because they agree that if an event is necessary, it is not 'up to us'. To make room for events that are 'up to us', even though they are predicted to happen, the Stoics must insist that other things *could* have happened, even if they do not happen. The oracle truly predicts that Fabius will not die at sea, and a statement that Fabius will die at sea is false. But even though it is false, it is still possible. The oracle says, truly, that I will buy a certain piece of land, and so it is false that I will not buy that piece of land. But the oracle does not make it *necessary* that I buy the piece of land. My not buying the land is still a possibility, and so when I do buy it, my action is still 'up to me'.

The anti-Stoic argument tries to deprive the Stoics of that position, by claiming that if divination is a science, then any statement that contradicts a prediction is actually *impossible*, not merely false. So the things that I am predicted to do are not really 'up to me'. The crucial move is to claim that the 'theorems' of divination express a necessary connection between their two parts. That is what is meant by references to 'conflict', which I shall shortly explain.

The Stoic theory of logic is one of their most brilliant contributions to the history of philosophy. Although they owed part of their inspiration to the true originator of formal logic, Aristotle, they also set out in completely original directions, and developed their logic into a far more rigorous and powerful system than even Aristotle's had been. Aristotelian logic somehow became more popular towards the declining days of Greek philosophy—the reasons for *that* are a fascinating story in their own right—and Stoic logic lay misunderstood and unappreciated until the end of the nineteenth century when propositional logic was independently reinvented by Gottlob Frege. It was only after considerable progress had been made in the modern reinvention of propositional logic that scholars came to realize that Stoic logic was its true precursor. Even in the twenty-first century, new discoveries in modern logic are still enabling us to understand corners of Stoic logic that are unclear, and every discovery gives us further reason to admire them—and Chrysippus in particular, who by all reports was here again the real creator of the Stoic system.

The Stoics gave great attention to the meaning of such logical terms as 'and', 'or', and 'if', and developed criteria for the truth of propositions containing such connectives. Their criterion for 'if . . . then . . .' sentences, which we call 'conditionals', was as follows: 'if p, then q' is true just in case there is a conflict between p and the negation of q. Examples help most: 'if Fred is a human being, then Fred is an animal' is true just in case there is a conflict (as there is) between 'Fred is a human being', and 'Fred is not an animal'. On the other hand, 'if Fred is tall, then Fred is a good basketball player' is not a true conditional, on the Stoic view, because there is no conflict between 'Fred is tall' and 'Fred is not a good basketball player'. There are lots of tall people, after all, who are not good at basketball.

Suppose we have a true conditional, like 'if Hilda stole the jewels, then Hilda is not trustworthy'. The truth of this conditional reflects the fact that there is a conflict between the two propositions 'Hilda stole the jewels' and 'Hilda is trustworthy'.[5] These can't both be true; trustworthy people do not steal jewels, and jewel-thieves are not trustworthy. On the other hand, the fact that the conditional is true does not tell us whether Hilda is a jewel thief or not. Of the two statements 'Hilda stole the jewels' and 'Hilda is trustworthy', only one can be true; but we don't yet know which. Maybe she is a thief, and not trustworthy; or maybe she is trustworthy, and no thief: the conditional tells us there is a conflict, but not how to resolve it. On the other hand, if we found out that one of them was true, then we would immediately know that the other was false. And that is a general rule; if you have a conflict of this sort, and one member is true, then you can infer that the other is false.[6]

But there is a further type of inference you can make: if one of the conflicting statements is *necessary*, then the other one must be *impossible*. Take, for instance, the true conditional 'if two is an even number, then two is not an odd number'. There is a conflict between 'two is an even number', and the negation of 'two is not an odd number'; two cannot be both even and odd, and one of these statements must be false.[7] But we can say more than that: given what numbers are like, it is actually *necessary* that two is an even number. And from that fact, we can infer, not just that it is *false* that two is odd, but that it is also *impossible* for two to be an odd number. Whatever conflicts with a necessary truth is actually impossible, not merely false.[8]

Here is the principle that the opponents of Fate employ, and it is one that the Stoics must grant them. The argument only requires one more principle, namely that true statements about the past are necessary. Whatever is done cannot be undone; the past is immutable and unchangeable, and thus necessary.[9] If Fabius was born at the rising of Sirius, then it is now necessary that Fabius was born at the rising of Sirius; it is no longer possible for him not to have been born just then. But if it is now *necessary* that he was born then, and if there is a conflict between that fact and the proposition that Fabius dies at sea, then this second proposition turns out now to be *impossible*, not merely false. And this applies generally; if divination tells us that something will happen, then any statement to the contrary is not just false, but impossible, since it conflicts with a necessary truth about the past. But in principle, divination should be able to tell us about all of the actions that occur, including all of the actions that we take. And that means that it is impossible for me to do anything but the things that, in fact, I will do; and that means that they are not up to me, after all. Thus divination rules out responsibility.

Let's review the argument once more, before turning to Chrysippus' response:

(i)   if divination is a science, then there are true conditionals of the form 'if p, then q', where p mentions a past event (for example, the birth of Fabius), and q mentions a future event (for example his death).

(ii) in a true conditional of that sort, the denial of the proposition about the future, that is, the prediction, conflicts with the proposition about the past

(iii) true propositions about the past are necessary

(iv) whatever conflicts with the necessary is impossible

(v)   so, any negation of a true prediction is impossible.

If an oracle says I will run for office, given that I was born on a certain day, then it is impossible for me not to run for office. Everything that will happen is necessary, and all the alternatives are impossible. And thus, nothing is 'up to us'.

Chrysippus Responds to the Fabius Argument

Now it is time for Chrysippus' response, again as given by Cicero:

But this is what you [Chrysippus] want least of all . . . you say that even in the case of things that will not be in the future, it is still possible for them to happen. For instance, this gem will never be broken, but it is still *possible* for it to break... And here Chrysippus breaks into a sweat, and hopes that the Chaldeans and other oracles are wrong, and that they will not use that kind of connection to express their theorems, i.e. 'if someone is born at the rising of Sirius, then he will not die at sea'. Instead, he wants them to say 'Not both: someone is born at the rising of Sirius, and that person will die at sea.' What hilarious liberties he is taking, teaching the Chaldean oracles how to express their theorems!

Cicero is bent on making fun of it, but there is a solid point to the response Chrysippus makes: he is denying that divination needs to make use of conditionals. Oracles can make their predictions without claiming that there is any *conflict* between the statement about the past and the denial of their prediction, and thus they do not need to say that the events they predict will happen *of necessity*. Instead, they can proceed by using negated conjunctions of the form 'Not both *p* and *q*', which make no claim about conflict. To say that two things *are* not true together is a weaker claim than to say that they *cannot* be true together. 'Not both: I play the piano and I like to swim': I have said that one or the other is false, but I surely don't claim that there is any *conflict* between playing the piano and liking to swim, or that it is *impossible* to do both—many people do.

Weighing Chrysippus' response:

This response does succeed in defusing the argument as stated. The Stoic belief in divination does not commit them to the necessity of the future, provided that divination does not depend on having its theorems expressed as conditionals. (This is why Cicero's references to the practice of the Chaldean oracles are not really very damaging. It may be that certain non-Stoic oracles misunderstand what divination involves, and so think that they should phrase their theorems in terms of conditionals. But as long as the Stoics do not follow them, then they are not in danger from this argument.) If the theorems of divination are not expressed as conditionals, then they do not express necessary connections.

It is sufficient to observe universal regularities, without making any claims about necessity. But does this settle the issue? To say that

250 ~ *Necessity and Responsibility*

divinatory theorems do not express necessary connections is not to show that there *are* no necessary connections between past and future. Perhaps the oracle is able to observe the regularities it observes, only because they are in fact necessary—that is, whether that necessity is represented in the theorems of their divinatory science, it may be that the science depends for its coherence on the underlying existence of some necessary connections in nature. And if divination depends on the existence of Fate, that is, a network of causes, then it looks as though divination must depend on the existence of necessary connections in nature, unless the causes do not necessitate. The next section will look more closely at whether Chrysippus can split apart causing from necessitating.

Against Fate 2: The Argument that Fate Destroys What is 'Up to Us'

Introduction to Impulse:

The last argument was primarily designed to threaten the Stoics with the unacceptable consequence that all future events would be necessary. This by itself would be an unwelcome result, since the Stoics want to agree with other schools that not all future truths are necessary truths, and not all future falsehoods are impossible. But it is also safe to assume that there is a further point to the argument (though that further point is not made explicitly in that passage): if the future is necessary, then our future actions are not up to us. This is just one instance of a general pattern of anti-Stoic argument, which can be sketched out as follows:

(1) If everything happens by fate, then nothing is 'up to us'
(2) but something is 'up to us'
(3) so, not everything happens by fate.

Cicero presents the Impulse Argument:

Cicero gives us another argument against fate, whose overall structure is of that form, although he does not tell us exactly which of the Stoics' opponents employed it:

They [i.e. the opponents] argued as follows:

(1) If all things happen by fate, then all things happen by antecedent causes;

(2) and, if this applies to impulse, then it applies to whatever is entailed by impulse, and thus it applies to assents as well.

(3) But if the cause of impulse is not 'up to us', then neither is impulse itself 'up to us', and

(4) If this is so, then the things brought about by impulse are not 'up to us', either.

(5) Therefore, neither our assents nor our actions are 'up to us'.

(6) From this, it results that neither praise nor blame nor rewards nor punishments are justified

And since this conclusion is faulty, they think they have provided a powerful argument that not all things happen by fate.[10]

Here there is no mention of necessity, or conflict. The way in which Fate precludes responsibility, on this argument, is not that it makes everything necessary, and so not 'up to us'. Rather, the claim is that things cannot be 'up to us' because of the way that Fate causes them to occur.

Just as the last argument made very careful use of the Stoics' own system of logic, turning their analysis of conditional propositions against them, so too this argument makes careful use of Stoic psychology. From earlier chapters, we recognize the terms 'impulse' and 'assent'; these are the psychological forerunners of any intentional action. More than that; these are the aspects of any action that make it an intentional action, and so make it open to judgment, if it is. All of our actions have many properties. When I drive to the store, there are many things that can be said about my drive—that it occurs on a certain day, in certain weather, following a certain route, that I travel at this or that speed, that my car is this color, and weighs this much. I may make it to the store successfully, or have a breakdown or accident on the way. All of those facts may be useful in some other context, but if we want to judge the praiseworthiness or blameworthiness of my action, what is most important is the impulse that I had in undertaking it. What impression did I have, and what does it say about me that I assented to it? Did I think of the trip as a way to get some alcohol, perhaps, after I have already promised never to drink again? Was I driving to pick up some medicine for a sick neighbor? Those are the issues that count for my moral assessment. Furthermore, those seem to be the issues that are in my control, if any are. I cannot control many aspects of my journey—I certainly cannot control the weather, and there is only so much I can do to prevent my car from breaking down. What is not in my control is not 'up to me', and so I cannot be judged for it—but certainly my own impulses and assents are 'up to me', if anything is.

But, according to this argument, even they are not up to me. For the Stoics claim that everything that happens—absolutely everything—happens by Fate, and thus happens by causes that are sufficient to bring it about. This applies just as much to my having an impulse as it does to the weather during my drive. My impulse may cause me to act, but there are other things that cause my impulse, things that are not 'up to me'. The most obvious of the causes of my impulse is whatever thing caused me to have the impulsive impression that I assented to. Someone brings a cake into the room, and the cake makes an impression on me, it looks like a good thing, like something good to eat. But I didn't cause myself to have that impression. It just came to me, caused by the cake, and caused by the person who brought the cake within my sight. In fact, since fate causes everything, we know that what really caused me to have that impression was fate; fate causing the other person to bring the cake in, fate causing the cake to produce this impression, and so on. How then can it make sense to say that I am responsible for my actions, when I am not even responsible for the very core of them, the impulses that produce them? My actions, and my impulses, are completely determined by fate; thus it cannot be coherent to blame or praise me for them.

Chrysippus Responds to the Impulse Argument:

The response that Chrysippus makes, according to Cicero, is rather complicated, and some of its details are the subject of lively scholarly dispute. But the key move seems to be the one reported below:

Chrysippus has recourse to his cylinder and his cone: they cannot begin to move until given a push, but once that has happened, it is due to their own nature that the cylinder proceeds to roll and the cone proceeds to veer off. 'Whoever shoved the cylinder', he says, 'gave it a start on moving, but did not give it its capacity to roll.' In the same way, the thing that produces the impression makes a sort of imprint and stamp of its image in our mind, but the assent is "up to us". It's just like with the cylinder; there is an external shove, but after that its continued movement is due to its own power and nature.'

Somehow, the analogies of the cylinder and the cone are supposed to show us why our actions are 'up to us', even though everything is caused by fate. The shove that sets the solids rolling is somehow like the impression that comes in from outside, and the shape of the solids is somehow like the 'power and nature' of our minds. Or, more to the point, the *difference* between the cylinder's shape and the cone's shape, and the resulting difference in their movements, is like the *difference* between the power and nature of your mind, say, and the power and nature of my mind. How does the analogy work?

First, we should note something that Chrysippus does *not* say. He does not say that, having received a shove from outside, there was still some further step needed to make the cylinder move. Nor does he say that the cylinder could have received the same shove without the same movement resulting. Given the incoming shove, and given the shape of the cylinder (its 'capacity to roll'), it is already completely determined that the cylinder will roll in a straight line. The same goes for the cone: given a similar shove, and given its different shape, it is already determined that the cone will act as it does, rolling in a veering motion.

In the case of our minds, then, we should draw the same lesson. I saw the cake and had an impulse to eat it; you saw the cake and had no such impulse. Given that I assented when the impression struck me, Chrysippus is *not* denying that my assent was determined. He is *not* claiming that I, with the kind of mind I have (my 'shape'), could have received this same impression and not assented. My assenting, like all other motions and events, happens by fate. However, my assent reflects the 'power and nature' of my mind, that is, its peculiar disposition to assent, just as your not assenting reflects your disposition to assent.

Thus he *is* saying that the impression by itself is not sufficient to determine whether I assent or not, just as the shove by itself does not determine whether the object will roll straight or veer. The impression, by itself, did not *make* me assent, because we know that the impression, by itself, cannot produce that effect. And we know that because when you received the impression, you did not assent.

On the other hand, I was caused to assent, and I was determined to assent, and I was fated to assent. The causes of my assent were two: the incoming impression, and the 'shape' of my mind, that is, its disposition to assent to impressions of that sort (in this case, my sweet tooth, which causes me to assent to the impression that cakes are good to eat).

You, conversely, were caused *not* to assent, and determined not to assent, and fated not to assent, by the incoming impression and the shape of your mind. (It's not as though we are ruled by fate when we give into temptation, but heroically overcome fate when we resist— even the virtuous actions of the Sage are all fated and caused.)

Why does Chrysippus think that he has provided a response to the argument, and what part of the argument is he rejecting? He certainly accepts the first two premisses: all things happen by fate, and all things are caused, and this applies just as much to assents and impulses as to anything else. But he will reject the third premiss. This says, again,

(3) But if the cause of impulse is not 'up to us', then neither is impulse itself 'up to us'.

To begin with, he will deny that the cause of the impulse is 'not up to us'. True, one part of the cause of the impulse, namely the impression, is not up to us. But another part of the cause, namely the assent, is certainly up to us. And indeed, the assent itself is really the much greater part of the impulse. As we saw in Chapter 4, an impulse *is* an assent; it is a motion of the mind towards something. Given that my impulse so thoroughly reflects the character of my mind, it is perfectly legitimate to see it as 'up to me'. The impression just plays the role of a trigger, it provides an occasion for me to manifest the kind of character I have. For some questions of moral assessment, the impression is almost dispensable: what is reprehensible about my character, for instance, is the very fact of my being so easily triggered, whether any particular trigger sets me off or not. For the assessment of the action, though, the impression is not dispensable, since as the analogy of the cylinder and cone shows, the actual movement that is my impulse would not have occurred unless set in motion by the triggering shove from outside. Thus Chrysippus would reject the claim, in the first half of premiss (3), that the cause of the impulse is not 'up to us'; there are two causes, and the impression that comes from outside is by far the less important one.

But furthermore, Chrysippus would reject the premiss as a whole, even if he were to grant its first half. Take the case of the impression—there is something right about saying that it is a cause of my impulse (at least a partial cause), and that it is not 'up to me' (since it comes from outside). Thus there is some truth to the claim that 'the cause of impulse is not "up to us"'. But it in no way follows from that, that the impulse itself is not 'up to us'. Our actions are 'up to us' because they originate from our impulses and assents. And those are 'up to us' because they originate from our character and dispositions, from our minds and the 'shapes' they currently have. True, our impulses are also partly caused by impressions that arrive unbidden. And for that matter, our character and dispositions are partly caused by our past activities, by our education, by our parents, by our society, and so on. Thus it is possible to trace a chain of causation that leads back from our actions, to our impulses, and from our impulses to the external impressions on one side, and to the external causes of our character on the other side. But this should in no way be taken to show that it makes sense to trace a parallel chain of 'up to x's', leading back behind our character to the causes of it external to us. That chain terminates in our characters, in our minds, as they are now, independently of how they got to be that way.

Stoic Compatibilism:

And here we have come to the central claim of Chrysippus' response to the argument. According to the Stoics, my actions, impulses and assents are all caused and determined by Fate, and they are also 'up to me', and these two claims are perfectly compatible with one another. We usually call this sort of a position a 'compatibilist' position, or a 'soft determinist' position. 'Incompatibilists', by contrast, are people who claim that the causal determination of the agent's action is incompatible with his being responsible for it. Incompatibilists may be libertarians, that is, they may argue that we are responsible for our actions, and so deny that our actions are causally determined. Or they may be what are sometimes called 'hard determinists', who argue that our actions are completely determined, and that as a result we are in fact no more responsible for our actions than cogs in a machine.

So Chrysippus agrees that our actions are caused by fate—even our assents and impulses. But our actions are also open to moral assessment, because our actions are caused by the characters we have (however we came to have them), just as the movements of the cylinder and cone are caused by the shapes they have (however they came to have them). External inputs are mere triggers, which determine very little about how we respond. How we respond is really a matter of what kind of moral character we have. When we respond well or badly, our actions are the result of our being good or bad people—and thus our actions are truly 'up to us'.

In order to appreciate the Stoic position, we should look more closely at what it is like to view these issues from the stance of a compatibilist, and how it affects one's ideas about responsibility and causation. Compatibilists must answer the complaints that their view runs counter to our intuitions about responsibility, and that it makes nonsense of moral judgment. The basic compatibilist response is two-fold: first they show why the incompatibilist intuition is misguided, and then they show why the moral assessments that the compatibilist makes are well targeted, after all.

We all have the strong intuition that if an agent is compelled to do F, then the agent is not responsible for having done F. Fair enough—but if you think about the cases in which this rule clearly applies, you will see that they all involve *external* compulsion. And the compatibilist can agree with this—external compulsion is exculpatory on their account as well. But when fate works through the agent's own internal psychology, there is no external compulsion; what makes the agent act comes from inside the agent, and so offers no excuse. Anyone would judge that Fred is not to be blamed for breaking the window if a passing car knocked him into it, whereas Ned is to be blamed for spreading hurtful lies about his friends, if he does it out of malice and spite. As compatibilists, we still make these very same judgments; Fred is not to be blamed, because he was compelled by external forces, whereas Ned is to blamed, because he was not compelled by external forces. What drives Ned to tell such awful lies is the fact that he is such a spiteful and malicious person. No person or thing forced him to tell the lies; he did it because of the sort of person that he is.

Secondly, the compatibilist will argue that when we think about what it means to level moral praise and blame at someone, we should see that an action that was caused by the agent's psychology is *exactly* what we mean to praise and blame. Moral praise and blame should be praise and blame of people's *morals*, that is, their habits, preferences, beliefs, attitudes and overall character. Ned has a malicious character, and enjoys hurting people—that is exactly what is blameworthy in him, and in his actions.

The incompatibilist may say that Ned cannot be blamed for his character, since his character is the product of many factors beyond his control. He is no more responsible for having the character that he does, then he might be for missing an arm or a leg, or being mentally deficient—and surely we do not blame someone for those misfortunes.

The compatibilist will here make two points. First of all, it is true that it would be grossly unjust to blame someone for being mentally deficient, or to level any moral assessment against a person based on their physical or cognitive impairments. But the compatibilist is not suggesting that we should do that. The compatibilist suggests that wicked people are *morally* impaired, and thus *moral* assessment is exactly called for. When I say that Ned is a malicious person, I am describing a feature about him that is in one way on a par with his physical or cognitive make-up; it is a fact about him which he may not be the ultimate cause of, just as he is not the ultimate cause of his height or weight or degree of intelligence. But just as there would be nothing unjust in making *physical* assessment of Ned based on his *physical* condition, or in making a *cognitive* assessment of him based on his *cognitive* condition, so too there is nothing wrong with making a *moral* assessment of him based on his *moral* condition.

Secondly, the fact that the agent is not entirely responsible for his current moral constitution should have no tendency to make us rethink or retract our moral assessment of him. A moral assessment of someone simply is a judgment about their character and morals; a judgment about how they came to be that way would be an *additional* judgment, separate and distinct from the first one. I say that Ned is a malicious person, and you say that his parents made him that way. All well and good, say I; if you would like me to make an *additional* moral judgment about his parents, then introduce me to them—I may well conclude that they themselves are malicious, or cold-hearted, or negligent, and that their bad character had an effect on Ned's. But I certainly will not feel any inclination to retract my judgment of Ned. After all, everything came to be the way it is somehow or another. This car is a lemon; it breaks down frequently and runs poorly when it works. 'But the factory was badly managed', you say. All well and good—perhaps the manager was a lemon, too. But that fact that *he* was a bad manager certainly does not make *this* a good car.

Chrysippus seems to have been a compatibilist of this sort. People's actions are determined by fate. In more detail, we may say that people's actions are determined by their impulses, that is, their assents to impulsive impressions. The impressions come from out-side, and are fated to occur, but they do not compel assent—no matter how persuasive an impression may be, there is no impression that, merely in virtue of what it is like, can compel the assent of every

Necessity and Responsibility ~ 259

agent, no matter what character that agent has. But if a particular agent does assent to an impression, then the assent was fated to occur, and it was caused to occur by the character the agent has—by their beliefs, preferences, desires, and so on—in short, their disposition to assent. Given that they have a certain sort of mind, they will assent to the impression—not only is that a fact about fate, from the cosmic view, it is also a fact about psychology at the local level. We learn this from Epictetus, too: 'It is impossible to assent to what strikes you as false, or not to assent to what seems true; so too it is impossible to keep away from what seems good' (3.7.15). A person who has spent a whole life-time believing that cake is good, that pleasure is good, that honesty does not matter, and so on—this sort of person has a character such that when the impression enters their mind, they will assent to it.

But the assent was not externally compelled—it was compelled by internal factors, by the agent's own character, by their own moral constitution. What more, the compatibilist asks, could be needed in order to make a moral judgment well-grounded and coherent? This person is a glutton for eating the cake, he is unjust for having taken what was not his, he is untrustworthy for having lied about it.

'But it is not his fault that he got that way', says the incompatibilist. Well, I thought we were judging the action of stealing the cake; that action certainly did come from the agent, and in particular from the agent's moral character, and on that ground I blame him for stealing it. If you would now like to examine who is responsible for a different action, that is, the making of this cake-thief's moral character, then I am happy to look into that, too. I think it comes in part from this cake-thief's own past actions, and so I partly blame him for catering to his own bad habits, as well as for this recent theft. I agree, though, that other people are responsible for it, too—indeed, I blame his parents, and I blame his lack of education, and I blame society, too. But I don't blame them for stealing the cake; he did that, and he is still bad for doing it. I blame those *other* agents for a different thing, namely having had a hand in producing a wicked person. The fact that this agent came out blameworthy is a shame and a reproach to the society that had a hand in forming him—the society ought to be reformed so as to foster virtue and honesty in its citizens. I blame the society for being a deficient society, and I blame the person for being a deficient person. (And incidentally, much of my social criticism would be blunted if I had to give up my judgment of the agent—what am I going to blame society for, producing a *blameless* agent?)

That is a brief look at one sort of compatibilist position (others are possible). This one is founded on a semantic view, that is, about the proper meanings of moral terms and their proper targets, and also a psychological view about what constitutes a human character and how it arises. I do not claim that Chrysippus had exactly this view, but I think he had a view of this sort, and I think the view has some merit.

With this in mind, let us return to the passage where Chrysippus discusses his cylinder and his cone. What he showed us there is that the external cause, that is, the impression, is not by itself a sufficient cause of the assent. This goes some way towards supporting the compatibilist position that the action is still 'up to us' in as much as the greater part of its causal origin comes from within the agent. But Chrysippus *did* still concede that the external impression, plus the internal character, were together sufficient to bring about the assent. Together, they form a complete *cause* of the assent. We said that there was a sense in which, even having the impression, I was not *forced* to assent; this followed from what we might call the 'agent-shifting test'; we considered what would happen if a different agent received the same impression, and we found that in many cases that agent would not assent. The fact that I *did* assent is thus plausibly a fact about *me*, that is, it is I who am responsible for the fact that I assented, as we can see from the fact that the other agent did not.

But does the agent-shifting test really show that the impression did not cause *me* to assent? Suppose I'm in a life-boat that can support 300 pounds, and I weigh 250—my weight will stand for my dispositions to assent. You will stand for the impression that comes in from outside; you weigh 100 pounds, and when you jump in the boat sinks, to my deep annoyance. I blame you for sinking my boat. 'But *I* didn't force your boat to sink', you say, 'after all, if you had not been in it, the boat would not have sunk!' True, but somehow irrelevant—when we ask who sank 'my boat', we want to know who sank the boat *that had me in it*! The fact is that, given what I *do* weigh, there was no way for you to jump into my boat, a boat with me in it, without sinking it. Our joint weight absolutely guaranteed that the boat would sink. So too, given my nature, and the nature of the impression, there was no way that I, the person with *my* nature, would not assent to an impression of that sort. It might not force someone else to assent; but given what I am like, isn't it more accurate to say it *did* force me to assent? And furthermore, doesn't Chrysippus have to concede that when we add up all of the causal factors at work here, they made it *necessary* that I would assent? Was it really possible for me not to assent, given the impression and the character that I have?

The definition of Possibility:[11]

To answer that question, we must look at Chrysippus' definition of possibility. He will use that definition in order to claim that even though our assents are caused and fated, it was nevertheless possible for us to assent otherwise than as we did. This claim is based on the definition of what is possible which the Stoics give us in their general account of modality:[12]

P is possible just in case: (1) P is receptive of being true

and (2) P is not hindered from being true by externals.

The first of these clauses ('receptive of being true') seems to be something like a claim about intrinsic coherence or logical possibility; the second involves an assessment of contingent facts, whether in the present or in the future period leading up to the obtaining of P, that might be incompatible with P. So, for instance, it is not possible for me to draw a round square on the blackboard, because 'I draw a round square on the blackboard' is not receptive of being true, even when considered in isolation from all contingent factors; round squares are intrinsically incoherent. But it is not possible for me to draw even an ordinary square on the board, if I am chained up or paralyzed, or if there is no chalk available to me. Even though 'I draw a square on the blackboard' is perfectly receptive of being true, when considered in isolation from such external factors, it is not possible if external factors like chains or paralysis impede the proposition from becoming true.

Plutarch records the following natural objection to the Stoic position; to assess their compatibilism we must see how they answer it. When I assent to an impulse to perform some action, the Stoics agree that my assent was determined and caused by the totality of facts about the content and character of the impression on the one side, and my entire psychological set of dispositions on the other side. Given how the cake looked to me, and given my weakness for cakes, it was determined and caused from all eternity that I should have an impulse to eat it—and so, Plutarch concludes, my assent was necessary, and thus not up to me, and I am not responsible for it.

But this is where the details of Chrysippus' definition of possibility and necessity become relevant. For although the impression and my disposition will combine to cause me to eat the cake, it remains the case that it was possible for me to abstain from eating the cake, by the standards of the Possibility-definition. This says that 'I abstain from eating the cake' is possible, provided that:

(1) 'I abstain from eating the cake' is receptive of being true

and

(2) 'I abstain from eating the cake' is not hindered from being true by externals.

In this case, 'I abstain from eating the cake' is indeed receptive of being true—there is nothing inherently or intrinsically incoherent or impossible about someone's abstaining from eating cake. And neither is it the case that I was hindered from abstaining by external factors. There was no external agent compelling me to eat; no powerful force-feeding machine or gang of cake-pushing ruffians. The only thing that kept me from abstaining—the only thing that made me eat—was my own disposition to find cake attractive; and that is anything but an external factor.

Thus, despite the fact that the combination of the impression and my own disposition is sufficient to bring it about that I will eat the cake, Chrysippus can still consistently deny that it was necessary for me to eat the cake. It was possible for me to abstain from eating the cake; and thus my eating of it was still up to me. It is worth pausing to applaud the extraordinary ingenuity of Chrysippus' stance here, as well as the beautiful systematicity with which he has combined various parts of his philosophical system—the psychology of impressions and assent, the logical definitions of possibility and necessity, the metaphysical theory of causation, and the ethical analysis of responsibility—into a coherent defense of his compatibilism.

But after the applause, it seems to me that we can raise serious problems for Chrysippus by asking whether the notion of 'externals' invoked in the possibility-definition is the same thing as the notion of what is 'external' to an agent's psychology (or whether it will deliver this distinction in the relevant cases). Of course, when considered as part of a general theory of modality, the possibility definition should apply to any proposition whatsoever whose possibility we might want to evaluate, and so should not make any reference to the psychology of agents. Viewed in this light, I take it that we naturally understand the realm of 'external' factors as constituted by the complement of those factors considered as 'intrinsic' by the first conjunct. For example, suppose we are evaluating whether it is possible that some straw should burn, when it is at the bottom of the sea.[13] Into the first conjunct will go our assessment of whether 'this straw is burning' is receptive of truth, or perhaps our assessment of the intrinsic burnability of the subject, straw. Corresponding to either of these renditions will be an examination of the 'external' factors, e.g. additional propositions in the first instance such as 'this straw is at the bottom of the sea', or additional factors like the seawater and its extinguishing properties in the second instance. But however the details go, we will be able to treat any consideration under one or the other of the two headings; what is not 'internal' will be 'external', and vice versa.

If we bring this natural expectation to the case of human action, then Chrysippus' strategy will fail. For if the first conjunct only assesses the abstract fitness of the proposition, for instance, 'I abstain from eating cake,' then the second conjunct will necessarily contain facts about my psychology within its purview, inasmuch as they are 'external' to that proposition abstractly considered. My psychologically determined decision to eat the cake then *does* count as an external impediment, and so it rules out the possibility of my abstaining. It is not external to my psychology, of course, but it is external in the sense of the possibility definition, that is, external to the truth-receptivity of the proposition narrowly considered.

Conversely, if 'external' in the second conjunct means 'external to the agent's psychology'—or at least if it amounts to that in this case, though it is quite baffling what it would amount to in the case of straw—then matters of the agent's psychology will resurface in the first conjunct. That is, we will see that 'I abstain from eating cake' is after all *not* receptive of being true, in light of what 'I' am, that is, in light of my gluttonous dispositions, which are a characteristic part of my soul.

Chrysippus' strategy, in this light, seems to cheat by moving around the dividing-line between 'internal' and 'external'. When he wants to show that a proposition (for example, 'I abstain from the cake') is possible by the first, internal, conjunct, the 'internal' shrinks down to the mere logical coherence of the proposition, considered without reference to my psychological inclinations. Then when he wants to show that it is possible by the second, external, conjunct, the 'internal' expands to include all of my psychology, so that my psychology does not count as an 'external' hindrance.

Or perhaps Chrysippus is not guilty of shifting the landmarks when no one is looking; perhaps the first conjunct always remains focused on a very small central circle of abstract logical considerations, thus excluding the agent's psychology, and the second conjunct always restricts its survey of 'external' considerations to a remote and non-adjacent circular belt, located on the far side of the agent's psychology once again. It's not that he changes his story about what 'internal' means, it's just that there was always a gap between 'internal' and 'external', and the agent's detailed psychological dispositions fall into that gap. And yet, if Chrysippus had made all of this explicit—if he had acknowledged the existence of such a gap in his definition of possibility—then his opponents would have immediately seen that he was begging the question, that is, that he was defending the claim that psychologically determined events are nonetheless not necessitated, by constructing a definition of the possible that systematically excludes considerations of psychology.

The recourse to a specially tailored definition of possibility is not helping. It seems, then, that Chrysippus should concede that Fate does make all events necessary, inasmuch as it causes them all to come about. All of the causes, both those external to the agent (that is, the impression) and those internal to agents (the agent's dispositions to assent), are parts of Fate; and when we add them all up, they necessitate the outcomes. So, Fate makes the future necessary. And in that case, it destroys what is 'up to us'. Another way to diagnose the problem here is to consider the role that the agent-shifting test played in two different arguments; the argument that I am responsible for my assent, and the argument that my assent was not necessitated.

There is nothing incoherent about the agent-shifting test per se.[14] If we want to find out what it is about this plate that is responsible for the fact that a helping of eggs will leave it occupied by ham and eggs, it makes perfect sense to see how this plate differs from plates that do not yield ham and eggs from the same addition.[15] We find out quite directly: it is the plate's possession of ham that makes the difference. Problems only arise when we combine this conclusion with the thought that the plate is in some sense constituted by its current contents, or more generally, when we are unclear about what sort of fact about this plate its possession of ham is. When I say that the addition of eggs to 'this plate' will yield ham and eggs, I am treating the possession of the ham as partly constitutive of the referent of 'this plate'. When I say that it is possible to put eggs on 'this plate' without thereby yielding ham and eggs, I am disregarding its current contents,

266 ~ *Necessity and Responsibility*

and taking 'this plate' to refer to the porcelain purged of the porcine. Either way of talking is separately coherent, and amounts to treating the possession of ham as either an essential part of this plate-of-ham, or an accidental episode in the life of an essentially empty vessel.

What we cannot say is that 'this plate' is responsible for the fact that an addition of eggs will yield ham and eggs (in light of the fact that this plate is a ham-containing plate), while at the same time saying that the addition of eggs does not force 'this plate' to contain ham and eggs (in light of the fact that if it didn't contain ham no such contents would result)—that clearly involves an illicit shift in the referent of 'this plate'. Perhaps Chrysippus is innocent of any parallel confusion, but I strongly suspect otherwise. First I am responsible for my assent, because 'I' am this bundle of dispositions to assent. But then the impression does not force me to assent, because 'I' would not assent if I had different dispositions.

And even if a coherent collection of distinctions can be marshaled to his rescue, I want to claim that reflection on the agent-shifting test will inevitably lead from the conception of the agent as constituted by their internal nature and dispositions, to the conception of an agent shorn of dispositions, an abstract agent not identified with their detailed psychology. We will see more of this line of development in the next chapter.

In the end, it would have been wiser for Chrysippus to agree that my assent is necessitated as well as being determined and caused. Once he has accepted the compatibilist stance that consists in saying that I can be responsible for my actions, even if I am determined to take them and caused to take them, it seems perverse to become squeamish about saying that I am necessitated to take them as well. Why strain at necessitarian gnats, while swallowing causal camels? Of course, we begin the chapter by noting that it was an assumption shared by the Stoics and their opponents that necessity is destructive of moral assessment; I cannot be praised or blamed for what I was necessitated to do. But once we have seen the rationale that underlies Chrysippus' compatibilism about caused actions, it seems that anyone who finds that view congenial would also find compatibilism about necessitated actions acceptable. Chrysippus had nothing to lose by taking the next step. Conversely, if his opponents would have been scandalized by compatibilism about necessitation, it seems unlikely that they would have been comfortable with compatibilism about causation, either. So the doctrine that Fate causes but Fate does not necessitate turns out to be an unstable and unsatisfying sort of compromise; a clear examination of it shows that it is far too much for one group and far too little for the other.

NOTES

1. *DL* 7.23 = *SVF* 1.298 = LS 62E = IG2 II–1.
2. See Bobzien's comments on the 'General Causal Principle', Bobzien (1998a), 39 and 'Fate Principle', Bobzien (1998a), 56.
3. Signs from birds e.g. *Iliad* 8.245, 12.201, 12.822, etc.; birds and a snake, *Iliad* 2.308; significant sneeze in *Odyssey* 17.541; omens from the liver e.g. Euripides *Electra* 827–829.
4. Cicero *de Divinatione* 12–15 = *SVF* 2.954 = LS 38E.
5. I follow a standard Stoic procedure in eliminating the double negative 'not not trustworthy' (*DL* 7.69 = *SVF* 2.204 = LS 34K2 = IG2 II-3, though note that LS fail to translate the crucial claim that 'not: not: it is day' asserts 'it is day').
6. Remember that the conflict obtains between the antecedent of the conditional and the *negation* of the consequent. (In the conditional sentence 'if it is day, it is light', the antecedent is 'it is day', and the consequent is 'it is light'.) So if the antecedent is true, it is the *negation* of the consequent that is false; thus the consequent itself is true, as we expect from a conditional.
7. Once again, eliminating the double negative in 'not: two is not an odd number'.
8. Another way to look at it: for a proposition P to be possible, there must be some case in which it could be true. And that means there must be some case in which its being true would not conflict with anything else true in that case. But a necessary truth Q is true in every case, and we're supposing that P conflicts with Q. Thus in every case, there would be something true, Q, with which P would conflict if it were true. So P must be false in every possible case, i.e. P is impossible.
9. Aristotle quotes with approval a couplet from a fifth-century tragedy by Agathon which says 'of this alone even the god is deprived: to make undone whatever things have been done'. (*Nic. Ethics* 1139b11).
10. Cicero *de Fato* 40 = *SVF* 2.974 = LS 62C = IG2 II–90.

11. Here I rely on the reconstruction of Chrysippus' compatibilism in Bobzien (1998a), though I diverge from her assessment and verdict. Her book is the best source for a full discussion of this material; for a slightly more tractable presentation of her findings, along with fuller accounts of my criticisms of Chrysippus, see Brennan (2001).

12. *DL* 7.75 = *SVF* 2.201 = LS 38D = IG2 II–3, and see Bobzien (1999), 112–115 for extensive discussion.

13. Alex Aphr. *In A. Pr.* 183 = LS 38B.

14. I here repeat a few paragraphs from Brennan (2001).

15. I agree with comments in Bobzien (1998a), 270 on the ubiquity and validity of this 'underlying mode of reasoning'.

16

The Lazy Argument

The Lazy Argument is designed to attack determinism by showing that it makes nonsense of planning, deliberation, and effort. If the argument is a good one, then it shows the Stoics, and us, that we cannot both believe in determinism, and still understand our own actions in the way we always have. But our understanding of our own actions is deep-rooted and heart-felt, and our commitment to determinism fairly speculative and insecure; thus if faced with the choice between them, we will abandon our belief in Fate. Or that, at any rate, is how the Lazy Argument is intended to steer us away from Stoicism.

The Stoic response—attributed explicitly to Chrysippus by Cicero—is to reject the soundness of the argument. The Lazy Argument does not show us the incompatibility of Fate and ordinary goal-directed behavior, and thus we need not choose between them. We should look at the argument first, and then at Chrysippus' reply, before turning to our own thoughts about what the argument succeeds in showing.

One argument is called by the philosophers the 'Lazy Argument', because if we give in to it, then we will never do anything in life. Here is how it is propounded:

(1) If it is fated that you will recover from this disease, then you will recover whether you call in a doctor or not;

(2) So too, if it is fated that you will *not* recover from this disease, then you will *not* recover whether you call in a doctor or not;

(3) but one or the other *is* fated;

(4) thus it accomplishes nothing to call in a doctor.[1]

The moral of the Lazy Argument is completely general: if everything is fated, then nothing you do matters. Events will carry you along to your fate no matter what you may do or not do. And since you will get whatever you would like to get in life, or not get it, quite independently of whether you exert any effort to get it, then there is no reason for you to exert any effort to achieve your goals. If you enjoy exerting effort for its own sake, then you may, of course, but if like most of us you are primarily interested in getting a good job, or leading a happy life, then you face something like Newcomb's Problem.

This is a modern puzzle beloved of philosophers, in which our normal rules for how to make choices seem to give us unclear or contradictory guidance. This modern puzzle comes, like many ancient puzzles, in the form of a story. You are approached by a team of brainy-looking people in lab-coats, and the scientist in the lead is holding two boxes. One of them is a medium-sized metal cash-box, whose lid is closed. The other is a small plastic box containing a one-thousand dollar bill, plainly visible through the clear sides. The lead scientist tells you that she and her team of researchers have been studying human psychology for decades, and yours in particular for years, and have become very good at predicting how people will behave. They have come to give you the metal box, and whatever is in it, but first you must decide whether you also want to take the thousand dollar bill. You may have the thousand dollars and the metal cash-box, or the cash-box without the thousand dollars. There's just one other point you should know: the team of scientists perform this sort of experiment quite often, and before each time they decide whether or not to place a million dollars in the cash-box, based on their prediction of how the person will behave. In those cases in which they predict that the person will *not* choose the thousand dollars, they put the million dollars in the box. If they predict that the person *will* choose the thousand dollars, then they do *not* put the one million into the metal box. They have already arrived at a prediction about how you will choose, and put the money in the box—or not—accordingly. Would you like to choose now?

Most of us feel pulled in two ways here. If I am going to get the metal box no matter what, and I can also have the thousand dollars for the asking, then why not take the thousand? But on the other hand, these people are very good at predicting my behavior. If I take the thousand, then that means that they will probably have predicted that I take the thousand. And that means that they will not have put in the million dollars. That's not good. Whereas if I don't take the thousand, then they will probably have predicted that, too, and so there will be a million dollars in the metal box. What would I rather do, take the thousand and get an empty metal box, or pass up a measly thousand and get a whole million dollars? Furthermore, these people have been running this experiment for a while, and checking the results of their predictions. The people who took the thousand, didn't get the million, and the people who passed up the thousand got the million—that's how it's been, in a large number of past cases, with few if any exceptions. Given that record, it seems much more likely that I will get the million if I pass up the thousand—and doesn't it make more sense for me to do the thing that is more likely to get me the million?

Philosophers disagree about how one should choose. More importantly—since cases like this don't arise too often—they disagree about how one should think about the choice, and what facts and rules one should take into consideration. The most common response to the problem, and the one which strikes me as most sensible, is to act in the way that gives you the better pay-off no matter what the scientists do. In the case of Newcomb's Problem, that means taking the thousand dollars. We can see this most easily if we put the possible outcomes into the form of a matrix:

	Scientists put in million	Scientists don't put in million
You take thousand	$1,001,000	$1,000
You don't take it	$1,000,000	$0

I don't know whether the million is in there, but if it is, then taking the thousand gives me a better outcome than not taking it, and if it is not in there then taking the money gives me a better outcome than not taking it. What makes it hard to see this is the thought that my action *now* can influence how the scientists have *already* decided. If my choice now could alter whether the money is or is not in the box, then it would no longer be clear that I should choose the thousand. But my choice cannot alter the facts that way. The money is either in the box or it is not in the box, already, and there is nothing that I can do right now to alter that fact. So it is rational to take the thousand.

The Lazy Argument presents a sort of Newcomb's paradox, with Fate as the team of psychologists. Suppose that you want a good job, but (like most of us) find the effort of trying for one very disagreeable. If you try for the job, you may get it, or not, depending on what Fate grants you, but in either case you'll sweat a lot. If you don't try, then once again you'll either get it or not, but at least you won't sweat. In this story, making an effort to get the job is like passing up the $1,000 dollars that is clearly visible in the box. Not trying—taking the lazy way—is like taking the $1,000 dollars. Most of us think that we will get the job only if we work for it, and not get it if we do not—that is, that we will get the big pay-off only if we pass up the little pay-off. But here as in the Newcomb case, that simply is not true. Fate has already decided, eons ago; the money is in the box, and the job is in our future, quite independently of what we do right now:

	Fates grants job	Fate doesn't grant job
You don't try	good job and no sweat	no job and no sweat
You try	good job and sweat	no job and sweat

It is not up to you what Fate does. But no matter what it does, you get a better pay-off by not trying than by trying. So it is only rational not to try. If the theory of Fate is true, then it is rational to be lazy. But we know that it is crazy to be lazy; so the Stoics must be wrong about Fate.

In the case of Newcomb's Problem, the crucial claim is that my actions now cannot affect the presence of the million dollars in the box. In the Lazy Argument, the crucial claim is that there is no connection between my action and what Fate has already decided. This is the point that Chrysippus attacks.

This argument is rejected by Chrysippus. For certain things, as he says, are 'simple', whereas others are 'connected'. A simple one is, e.g., 'Socrates will die on that day'; whether he does something or not, his day of death is determined. But if something is fated in the way that it is fated that Oedipus will be born to Laius, then one cannot also say 'whether or not Laius has intercourse with a woman'. For this matter is connected, and 'co-fated'— Chrysippus calls it this, because what is fated is *both* that Laius will sleep with his wife, *and* that he will beget Oedipus with her. It's as though someone said 'Milo will wrestle in the Olympics'; if someone responded 'so he'll wrestle whether or not he has an opponent', then he'd be wrong. Milo's wrestling is 'connected', since there is no wrestling without an opponent. So this whole class of fallacious arguments can be rejected in the same way. 'You'll recover whether or not you call in a doctor' is fallacious, for whether or not you call in a doctor is just as much fated as whether or not you recover. As I said before, these two are what Chrysippus calls 'co-fated'.[2]

The Lazy Argument claims that fated events will occur no matter what we do; Chrysippus rejects this claim. There are still necessary connections between events; there's no wrestling without a partner, and no procreation without intercourse (at any rate, this looked fairly solid in Chrysippus' day). So it is false that Milo will wrestle, whether or not he has a partner, and false that Laius will have a son, whether or not he has intercourse. Nothing about Fate interrupts the normal pattern of causal relations between events of different kinds; if you want to wrestle, you still need a partner, and if you want to recover, you are still advised to call in a doctor.

If laziness causes you to neglect a necessary step, then the outcome you want will not occur. Thus, says Chrysippus, it is surely *not* rational to be lazy, even if everything is fated.[3] Even if the outcome is determined, you had better make a determined effort to attain it.

I want to raise two problems for Chrysippus' response to the Lazy Argument. The first is about how the connections between co-fated things can have the right sort of influence on my behavior. The second is about how my knowledge that things are 'co-fated' helps to blunt what I take to be the real force of the Lazy Argument.

Chrysippus tells me that if I am going to recover, then I still have to call in a doctor. And he tells me that if I am fated to recover, then I am also fated to call in a doctor. I very much hope that I will recover, and so I hope that I am fated to recover. If I believe Chrysippus, then I can see why I won't recover without calling in a doctor, and so I also hope that I am fated to call in a doctor. But if I am fated to call in a doctor, then I am fated to do it whether, for example, I walk to the telephone now or not. It may be plausible to think, given the kind of disease I have, that if I do not call in the doctor, then I cannot recover. But it is surely implausible to suppose that if I do not walk to the telephone right now then I cannot call in the doctor. Perhaps I'll phone him later. Perhaps I will not make any phone call, because I am fated later to write him a note. Or perhaps I will neither phone nor write, but as I am lying asleep in bed a large brick will come crashing through my window. The remaining fragments of glass in the panes will be arranged in a pattern that sketches out the letters 'Dr. Cohn'. When I am wakened by the noise of the crash, I will see the letters in the broken window and be so surprised that I will cry out 'Dr. Cohn!' in a loud voice. The doctor, who has never previously come to my part of town, will have been accidentally dropped at the corner by an inebriated cab-driver, and when he hears my cry he will come to my house to investigate. That's not impossible, after all. And some things that occur by Fate occur in even stranger ways—for everything occurs by Fate, according to the Stoics, and some things do occur in very strange ways.

Or take the example we get in a different text, again attributed to Chrysippus:

If it were said that Hegesarchus the boxer will come out of the ring without taking a single punch, then it would be absurd for someone to suppose that Hegesarchus would fight with his guard lowered, on the grounds that he is fated to come off without taking a punch. For the original statement was made on account of how good he is at guarding himself against punches.[4]

Chrysippus wants it to seem absurd that Hegesarchus would drop his guard, or that some third person would expect him to drop his guard, just because it is fated for him not to get hit. The boxer should know, and the spectator should know, that there is still a necessary connection between not getting hit, and keeping your guard up: if you want to come off without taking a punch, you have to keep your guard up! Thus our desire for outcomes, combined with our knowledge of what it takes to bring those outcomes about, will still give us guidance about what we have to do to bring them about.

The trouble with all of this is that it will almost never be the case that I find myself contemplating a choice between performing and not performing an action which I know to be necessary to a later occurrence. Suppose I am Hegesarchus, entering the boxing ring: shall I put up my guard? Well, surely I cannot know that my putting up my guard *now* is the event without which I will not escape from the ring untouched. For it is just as easy for Fate to bring this about by having my opponent struck by lightning. Or perhaps I am fated not to take a punch, and fated to put up my guard. But am I fated to put up my guard *this* way, by thinking about it and deciding to raise my arms? Perhaps I am fated to put up my guard only after I stand here for a while pondering, when a passing bird drops a twig on my head, which jars me out of my perplexity into unthinkingly raising my arms.

Thus Chrysippus' use of co-fated things that are joined by a necessary connection suggests a solution to the problem of deliberation, but the solution will not in fact work. He would have to be able to trace a chain of necessary co-fated events all the way back to the agent's point of deliberation, such that it would be clear to the agent that unless they do this now, there is no way for that to happen then. And this he cannot do.

One might respond that I can at least act on probabilities. It is surely more probable that I will reach the doctor by phoning his office than by crawling into bed; it is more probable that Hegesarchus will avoid getting punched by keeping his guard up than by standing in the ring pondering the Lazy Argument. And if I can identify an action that will increase the likelihood of the outcome I desire, then I have reason to undertake it.[5]

But this brings us back to Newcomb's Problem. Arguing that I should perform the action that experience shows is more likely to produce the desired outcome is rather like arguing that I should pass up the thousand dollars on the grounds that, in the past, most of the people who passed it up got the million dollars. It may be that on the basis of past trials, there is an *extremely* high probability that I will get the million only if I pass up the thousand—it may even be that in the past, not a single person who took the thousand got the million. But if the big event is already settled—if the money is already in the box, or not, before I make my choice—then considerations of probabilities are out of place. Nothing I do now can increase or decrease the likelihood of the money's being in the box. So, too, if Fate has already decreed, eons in the past, that I will recover, then nothing I do now can alter that fact. Of course my recovery requires certain necessary preliminaries, and if I could somehow avoid taking them, then my recovery would not follow. But I cannot avoid taking them, since they too are fated. It really does not matter what I decide to do now; if I am fated to recover, then I am also fated to do whatever is necessary to my recovery. If I am fated to recover, then it is either necessary for me to call in a doctor, or it is not. If it is not necessary for my recovery, then there is obviously no point calling in the doctor; but if it is necessary for me to call him in, then given that I am fated to recover, I must be fated to call him in. If I'm fated to call in the doctor, then it is either necessary for me to use the telephone or not. If it is not necessary, then there is no point in using the phone; but if it is necessary for me to use the phone, then given that I am fated to recover, and thus fated to call in the doctor, I must be fated to use the phone as well. So it doesn't matter whether I pick up the phone or not; I'll call in the doctor, and recover, some way or another. Or, if it does matter that I will pick up the phone, then I am fated to pick up the phone whether I reach out for it now or not. And so on.

There is a second general problem with Chrysippus' introduction of co-fated events as an answer to the Lazy Argument. The original argument is best understood as a complaint about there being something in my future—let's call it 'the big event'—over which I have no control. Chrysippus' response is intended to make it look as though the big event is in my control after all. But its real effect is to show me that things are worse than I had thought; along with the big event, there is another event, the co-fated one, which is also not in my control. To see this, imagine being strapped into an experimental rocket-sled, which is mounted on a metal rail. You cannot unstrap yourself, nor can you turn off the rocket, or dislodge your sled from the rail. The metal rail terminates one hundred meters in front of you, in a massive and impenetrable brick wall. Now Chrysippus tells you about your fate: just inside of the next hour, the rocket will fire, and you will be propelled down the track at blinding speeds, and crushed to death against the brick wall. Somewhat alarmed by this news, you ask, 'then am I fated to be crushed against the wall no matter *what* I do during the next hour?'

Chrysippus, all suavity, replies as follows: 'Nothing of the sort! It is ridiculous to suppose that you are fated to be crushed against the wall *no matter what you do* during the next hour. Quite the opposite— you will be crushed against the wall at the end of the hour *only* if you cross the ninety-meter mark during the last fraction of a second in that hour. If you don't cross the ninety-meter mark, then of course you will not come to the end of the track (it's mounted on a *rail*, you see).'

You then ask the obvious question: 'Well, am I *going* to cross the ninety-meter mark a little before the next hour is up?'

And Chrysippus replies, 'Why of course! Your crossing the ninety-meter mark is *co-fated*, you see. You are fated to slam into the wall at the end of the hour, and fated to cross the ninety-meter mark slightly before that.'

You continue, 'So am I fated to cross the ninety-meter mark at that time, no matter *what* I do between now and then?'

Chrysippus replies, without a trace of irritation (he is a Stoic, after all), 'You're making the same mistake again. Of course you are not fated to cross the ninety-meter mark *no matter what you do*. Who ever said that? You will cross the ninety-meter mark, only if you cross the eighty-meter mark at a slightly earlier time. And, to forestall your next question, you are of course fated to do that, too.'

This conversation is not going anywhere, because the parties have something different in mind in talking about 'what the agent does'. The person strapped in the sled has a conception of what actions are available to him given his circumstances: he cannot untie his straps, for instance, but he can move his left big toe, he can wiggle his eyebrows, he can sing a song, and so on. Contemplating the next hour of his life, he can imagine this list remaining constant, or perhaps changing, if his circumstances change; perhaps a strap will loosen so that he can move his left shoulder, ever so slightly. Now he has in mind a list of all the things of that sort that he may be able to do in the next hour, and with reference to that list he wants to know the following from Chrysippus: is there anything on that list such that, if he does that, or refrains from doing it, then he will not be hurtled down the track to his death? And the answer to that question is surely 'No.'

Chrysippus, however, counts a great many more things into the list of 'what the agent does'.[6] He is counting something like crossing the ninety-meter mark as something that the agent does, so that he can say that if the agent does not do *that*, then the agent will not strike the wall. But being propelled across a point on a track by a rocket to which one is strapped hardly counts, in my book anyhow, as something one *does*. It seems to be a classic case of something that is done *to* you. Chrysippus seems to be glossing over the difference between actions that are really our *own*, that is, ones that we *do* in some rich sense, and events that merely happen to us.

We may think about the first premise of the Lazy Argument as though it says something potentially ambiguous:

(1) If it is fated that the big event will occur, then it will occur no matter what I do.

Chrysippus takes this in the following way:

(1C) If it is fated that the big event will occur, then there is no event, prior to the big event, such that its occurrence is a necessary precondition for the big event.

And he has an easy time showing the falsehood of this claim: there are many prior events that are necessary for the big event. But the reason that this response is so unsatisfying is that the person who posed the Lazy Argument meant something different by it, like:

(1L) If it is fated that the big event will occur, then there is no action I can take to prevent it.

The notion of an 'action I can take' is an admittedly vague one, and I do not know how the original proponents of the Lazy Argument would have made it sharper. But I am fairly confident that they meant something that Chrysippus failed to understand. Whatever we mean by 'an action I can take', it surely excludes being propelled past the ninety-meter mark by a rocket-sled. And yet the thing that Chrysippus needs to show us, and fails to show us, is that the preliminary co-fated events are different from being carried past an earlier mark on the track. The proponent of the Lazy Argument focuses on the fact that the later event is fated, and that this seems to take it out of our control. Because they are fated, my recovering or not, or Laius' having a son or not, seem to be more like things that happen to us than like things we do. The request to be shown an earlier event that determines them is a request to be shown that my recovery is really my action, something I can do or at least contribute to bringing about. Instead, we are just given another event that happens to us.

Now there is one way of putting this complaint that would at least draw the lines of battle clearly, even if it would not settle the issue. This would be for the proponent of the Lazy Argument to put their premiss as follows:

(ID) If it is fated that the big event will occur, then there is no event, prior to the big event, such that its occurrence is a necessary precondition for the big event, and it is not determined to occur also.

In a sense this is something like what we want: we want to be shown that the rocket will not fire if we wiggle our toes, and that it is not determined whether or not we will wiggle our toes. But of course to say that it is not determined whether or not we will wiggle our toes amounts, in this context, just to saying that the wiggling or non-wiggling does not happen by Fate. If we ask Chrysippus to show us that some earlier action does not happen by Fate, then he will reject the request out of hand; he claims that everything happens by Fate.

Furthermore, if this is all that the Lazy Argument amounts to—a request to be shown that every fated event depends on some earlier event that is not fated—then it may seem that it is not much of an argument. It turns out to be a thinly disguised denial that an action that is fated can really be our action, and from our earlier discussion of compatibilism we know that Chrysippus denies this. It may at first appear to do more than that, because of the incorporation of two actions, for example, the recovery and the calling the doctor. But when we see why the proponent of the Lazy Argument is unsatisfied with Chrysippus' treatment of the earlier event, then we see that the same complaint could have been lodged against the first event without further fanfare: if I am fated to recover, then my recovery is not really my own action. The detour through the doctor adds nothing new.[7]

Of course, the same diagnosis will be leveled *against* Chrysippus by the proponent of the Lazy Argument. Chrysippus puts us on a sled headed for a brick wall; we don't really do anything, we are simply fated to have things done to us. He *seems* to make some room for genuine human action by introducing these co-fated events. It *looks* as though my recovery is in my control, because it depends on my calling a doctor, and that looks as though it is in my control. But it isn't in my control, any more than the recovery itself; the doctor is just another point on the fixed track. It's just more fated events, from the farthest-distant future up to the next breath I take. I want to be shown that there is an action that I can take which will affect the future. If by 'an action I can take' I mean an undetermined, unfated one, then I may be asking Chrysippus for something he was never willing to grant to begin with, but I am still putting my finger on why his response to the Lazy Argument does not get to the real problem. Or it may be that those of us who find Chrysippus' refutation unsatisfactory have in mind a sense of 'an action I can take' which does not beg the question against him by demanding something undetermined. In either case, the Lazy Argument has at least shown me what is at stake in saying that everything is determined.

We have looked at two objections to Chrysippus' response to the Lazy Argument. The first objection involves the question of planning and deliberation. I have some desires for the future. Chrysippus can show me that for any future event I desire or fear, there is some prior event that is linked to it necessarily, such that if the earlier event does not occur, the later one will not occur. The trouble is that I can never know, of some particular action I am contemplating, that this action is necessary to the attainment of my future end.[8] It is just as possible for fate to bring about the future event by having me abstain from this action as by having me perform it. But then my desire for the future outcome can never give me any reason to perform a particular action in the present, or abstain from performing it, either—and at this stage Newcomb's Problem tips the balance towards making me lazy.

The second objection in some ways acts as a supplement to the first one, by supposing that Chrysippus could after all show us a train of events, reaching from the future towards the present, which would each be linked by connections whose necessity is obvious to us. If that sequence does not terminate in an action which is somehow really and truly in our control—if every earlier step is necessary and sufficient for the later step and every earlier step is already determined—then it still seems that there is no reason for me to take any action. For the only actions that I can take now amount to deciding whether I should whistle or hum as I hurtle down the track; there is no action I can take that will change the outcome. And this too makes me Lazy.

The Lazy Argument shows a powerful conflict between Chrysippean fatalism, and our ordinary understanding of deliberation. As Aristotle observed, not everything is a possible subject for deliberation. We do not deliberate about what we believe to be impossible, or what we believe to be necessary; when we deliberate, we do so with the thought in mind that the thing still may turn out either way, that its future truth or falsehood is not yet fixed.[9]

Thus if someone comes to us and asks our advice, we have the right to expect that they are not wasting our time by making a show of deliberating over what is in fact a foregone conclusion. If someone tells us that they are ill, for instance, and want advice about whether or not to call in a doctor, then it is a presupposition of this deliberation that the calling of the doctor is not fixed, that is, that it is neither true already that the doctor will be called nor true already that the doctor will not be called. About matters that are already settled, it is possible to inquire or investigate, but not deliberate—one might as well deliberate about whether 327 ought to be a prime number or not.

So the Lazy Argument invites us to join a deliberation over whether or not to call in a doctor. If the parties to that deliberation now learn that the resolution of the illness *is* fixed, that is, that it is already the case that the patient will recover, or that it is already the case that the patient will not recover (though they may not know which), they can then validly infer that there is no reason to call in the doctor. For if the resolution of the illness is already fated and determined, then so are all of the necessary preliminaries to the resolution of the illness.[10] If, for instance, the patient is going to live, and if this is fated, then if there are any events previous to the patient's recovery that are necessary for its occurrence, then these must already be fated as well. But ex hypothesi, the calling in of the doctor is not fated. So it is not among the necessary preliminaries to the resolution of the illness. There is no necessary role for it in the unwinding of the events that will lead to the resolution of the patient's illness—the doctor may be called in, or not, without any effect on the necessary preliminaries to the resolution of the illness. It

The Lazy Argument ~ 283

really is pointless to call in the doctor. Let's recast this version of the Lazy Argument in a more explicit form:

(1) We are deliberating about whether to call in a doctor
(2) If we are deliberating about whether to call in a doctor, then it is not yet fixed and fated that we will call in a doctor, or that we will not call in a doctor
(3) The resolution of the current illness, whether the patient will recover or die, is already fixed and fated.
(4) If the resolution of the illness is already fixed and fated, then so are all of the necessary preliminaries to that resolution.
(5) The calling in of the doctor is not fixed and fated.
(6) So, the calling in of the doctor is not one of the necessary preliminaries to the resolution of the illness.

The upshot is not merely that we cannot tell whether the doctor is needed or not, or that for all we know the doctor won't make a difference. On the present construal of the Lazy Argument, we may conclude more than that: we have demonstrated that calling the doctor is not necessary. The outcome—recovery or death—is already fated, and so are all of its necessary antecedents, and the doctor's presence or absence is not among them.

Now it is an assumption of this argument that there are necessary connections between events, and that in particular some events that are fated to happen later may depend on the occurrence of earlier events. It is exactly because the resolution of the illness—the recovery or death, whichever it will be—has necessary preconditions which are themselves fated, that we can tell that the doctor's involvement is utterly pointless, if it is open at all, as the context of deliberation presupposes. If the resolution of the illness is fated, then so are all of the co-fated necessary conditions—it simply turns out that the doctor's involvement is not among them. That is all part of the structure of the Lazy Argument.

Thus it is a piece of the grossest impertinence for the Stoics to think that they are discovering a blunder in the Lazy Argument when they point to the existence of co-fated events. The fact that some events are co-fated with others is not a Stoic revelation that explodes the Lazy Argument as a fallacy—quite the opposite, the existence of co-fated events is a common premiss accepted by both sides, and built into the very structure of the Lazy Argument. The advocates of the Lazy Argument are granting that whatever is necessary to the fated resolution of the illness is co-fated along with that resolution—that's exactly why we can tell that the doctor isn't necessary to the resolution of the illness, if it really is still a subject for deliberation whether we should call him in or not. If the Stoics harp on their co-fated events, and insist that the calling in of the doctor is one of them, then this merely shows that there is no real deliberation possible in the question of the doctor—indeed, no real deliberation possible in any situation, if the Stoic claim of universal determinism is true.

The Stoics will presumably deny this—they will reject (2) in the argument above, which claims that deliberation presupposes openness. But since that is the real point of contention—not this business of co-fated events, whose existence is granted by all sides to the dispute—that is where their real work lies in trying to defuse the Lazy Argument. And unfortunately, there is no evidence that the Stoics ever took up this challenge, of trying to show us how we can make sense of deliberation without openness.[11]

I think the Lazy Argument is a very powerful one, and I think that Chrysippus' introduction of 'co-fated' events is a rather surprising and disappointing failure on his part. What disappoints is not so much that he did not solve all the problems, as that he seems to have crucially failed to understand the original complaint.

NOTES

1 *de Fato* 28–29 = LS 55S = IG2 ii–84.
2. *de Fato* 30 = SVF 2.955, 956 = LS 55S = IG2 ii–84.
3. Given Cicero's mention of 'simples', e.g. Socrates' dying on a certain day, one might think that the Stoics still face an amended Lazy Argument: if my recovery is 'connected', then it is not rational for me to be lazy, but I can never *know*

whether an event is simple or connected, and so I can never *know* whether it is a case in which Laziness is justified or not. Even this fallback would tend to cast doubt on the rationality of action. But I suspect that the Stoics did not think that any event was simply fated in this way; even Socrates' death is connected to a web of causal preliminaries. There are not two different classes of events, i.e. the simply-fated and the fated-in-connection; the point about Socrates' death is merely intended to illustrate by contrast what the Stoics meant by saying that things are fated in connection with other things.

4. Eusebius *Praep. Evang.* 6.8,265d = *SVF* 2.998 = LS 62F = IG2 II–93.

5. I think this is something like Bobzien's defense of Chrysippus at Bobzien (1998a), 225–226: 'For a non-futile action it is sufficient that there is a chance that the action matters for the outcome in that there is a probability that it is a necessary condition for triggering or preventing a prospective cause from being active and thus furthers a certain envisaged result. And I can see no reason why this should not have been all Chrysippus was after.' I'm not sure exactly how this defense works, however, because I am not sure how to understand the references to 'a chance' and 'a probability'. If that simply means, 'some positive, non-zero chance/probability', then the difficulty returns that for any action, both doing that action and not doing it will be equally non-futile. It may be that going to the phone now is the necessary condition that triggers and thus furthers; or it may be that not going to the phone now is the necessary condition that triggers and thus furthers; there is some probability in each direction (epistemic, as Bobzien notes). But if inaction is never any *more* futile than action, then why not be lazy? If the suggestion is that there is *more* probability in one direction than the other, then it seems to me that the considerations from Newcomb's problem return; relative probabilities are mis-applied if the agent's choice cannot alter the outcome.

6. I don't mean this as a claim about his official philosophy of action, according to which being moved in this way would certainly *not* count as a 'thing that I do'. But part of the point of the Lazy Argument is exactly to show the Stoics that the co-fated events, which at first glance *seem* like fully voluntary actions (and so among the 'things that I do') are in fact fundamentally more like things that are done *to* the agent. It is not so much that Chrysippus would count crossing the ninety-meter mark as 'something that I do', as it is that, given his view of fate, the events which he *does* count as 'things that I do', e.g. my calling in the doctor, or raising my guard, turn out to be more like being carried across the ninety-meter mark.

7. Compare to this the complaint that Aristotle makes, that if future events were already determined then '. . . there would be no need to deliberate or take trouble (thinking that if we do this, this will happen, but if we do not, it will not)', *de Int.* 18b31–33, trans. Ackrill. Here too, Aristotle's reference to two actions seems to me to obscure the thought that captures our ordinary presupposition of indeterminacy, and is denied by the determinist. There is no difficulty for the determinist in agreeing to the parenthetical biconditional: there are many

pairs of events such that if you do this, then this will happen, and if you do not do it, it will not. The real point of contention is not that point, but whether both events are already determined, or neither is yet determined. For some reason, indeterminists like Aristotle and the author of the Lazy Argument seem to think that they can make the consequences of determinism more vivid and threatening by drawing our attention to an earlier event; is it because prior to being shown the connection we can imaginatively grant that some distant future event is determined, while still naively assuming that more proximate events are not?

8. As one bit of useful jargon would have it, Chrysippus can show me that some *type* of event is a necessary precondition, but he can never show me which *token* event is the necessary one, or (in most cases) that any token event *could* be uniquely necessary.

9. See Aristotle *De Int.* 9 18b32; *Nicomachean Ethics* III.3.

10. The axiom employed is only this: if F(p) then if N($p \Rightarrow q$) then F(q), i.e. if it is fated that p, then if necessarily , if p then q, then it is fated that q. We could support the argument with a fancier tensed version, but it would come to much the same thing. E.g. F(p@$t2$) then if N(p@$t2 \Rightarrow q$@$t1$) then F(q@$t1$), i.e. if it is fated that p should occur at some later time, and p's later occurrence necessitates q's earlier occurrence, then it is fated that q should occur at the earlier time.

11. An anonymous reader for the Press objected here that deliberation is no harder for the determinist than for the indeterminist. 'Given our imperfect knowledge of the future, we can typically only know that there exists an action such that it is the thing that I'll do. Does this knowledge make deliberation impossible? Does it require that determinists have a different account of deliberation in a non-open world? No, for the truth of indeterminism means that we know the same thing—that there is some action that I'll perform later today.' This fails to distinguish deliberation from discovery; if there is already a fact in place about what I will do, then I cannot deliberate about it, only set out on a fact-finding mission to try to discover what is already true about what I will do—like trying to measure a physical constant that has been fixed since the big bang. And that is simply not what we take ourselves to be doing in deliberation; whether rightly or wrongly, we deliberate with the thought that what we will do is as yet not merely unknown to us, but genuinely unsettled, undetermined—that there is as yet nothing *to* know.

17

The Evolution of the Will

In many respects, a book about Stoic ethics should not need to include a discussion of Fate. The Stoics did not adopt their theory of universal determination in order to achieve any particular ethical goal, or in order to solve any particular ethical problem. Nor does the theory of Fate have any drastic consequences for their ethical views in general. Quite the opposite, they spent most of their time arguing that their views on Fate did *not* have the vast ethical consequence that critics claimed—that one could continue thinking about human action, both prospectively and retrospectively, pretty much as one always had, despite the fact that everything is fated.

However, there are several reasons why I have thought it important to spend nearly one quarter of this book discussing fate. First there is the fact that many students of Stoicism have thought that the doctrine of Fate *was* crucial to Stoic ethics, and so I could not provide a clear view of Stoic ethics without setting this mistake to rights. Second, one of the themes of this book has been the marvelous ingenuity with which the Stoics constructed their system as a whole, and the degree of theoretical interconnectedness and cohesion that marks the Stoics as philosophers of the first rank. This is clearly brought out in the number of issues that were connected to the Stoic view of Fate. They were able to tell an amazingly coherent story about Fate and its relation to physics, to logic, to the psychology of action, to moral responsibility, and so on. Here again, part of the lesson to be learned from the Stoics is that no one can hope to do justice to any of these topics without doing justice to all of them. One cannot have an adequate view of logic without thinking about its potential connections to determinism. Nor can one have an adequate view about moral responsibility without thinking about causation in general. We must constantly be thinking systematically.

But the best reason for discussing fate in a book of this sort is the fact that the Stoic theory of fate did come, over the centuries, to have an immense impact on the way that other philosophers talked about such topics as free will and moral responsibility. Even if the Stoics argued strenuously that their views on fate had little impact on their own views on ethics, there is no doubt that their views on fate played an immensely important role in the development of many other ethical systems, and in the creation of what we take to be the problem of free will as we understand it today. Whether we are engaged in the more abstract discussions that focus on general issues of causality and laws of nature, or the more concrete debates over how society should deal with wrongdoers, we are taking part in a discussion that has evolved over many centuries, and one whose evolution was crucially affected by the Stoic theory.

I end this section with consideration of one instance of this evolution. As Susanne Bobzien has shown, the ancient debate over moral responsibility is carried out in very different terms from the modern one, and makes very different assumptions. Modern thinkers are inclined to accept something like the following principle of moral responsibility:

(CDO) An agent is only responsible for an action if that agent Could have Done Otherwise.

For example, Fred broke the window; but was he responsible for breaking the window? If Fred was knocked into the glass by a passing car, then Fred is not responsible for breaking the glass, because Fred could not have done otherwise. Given where he was standing, how

The Evolution of the Will ~ 289

fast the car was moving, how much Fred weighs, how thick the glass was, and so on, there was no way for Fred *not* to break the glass. Thus he is not responsible for its being broken. On the other hand, if Fred walked up to the glass with a hammer, and calmly and deliberately struck the glass with the hammer, when it was perfectly open to him to refrain from striking it, then Fred is responsible for breaking the glass. He chose to break it; he didn't have to. He could have done otherwise, and for us that makes all the difference.

The trouble with this analysis comes when we look deeper into Fred's psychology. If Fred was drugged, or hypnotized, and broke the glass because of the drugs or hypnosis, we will be inclined to think that he could not have done otherwise, and so is not responsible. On the other hand, if he is an adolescent out for kicks, and merely likes the sight and sound of glass breaking, then we feel once again that he could have done otherwise, and hold him responsible. If he recently escaped from a mental institution where he is being treated for a pathological desire to break glass, and he was acting on that patho-logical desire, then we may feel somewhat nervous about whether to say he could have done otherwise or not (we may want to know more about how he generally reacts to the presence of unbroken glass, how typical or atypical this behavior is, and so on).

But how should we draw the line between the kid who breaks glass for kicks, and the mental patient who suffers a compulsion? Both of them, after all, had a desire to break the glass, and broke it while acting on that desire. In the case of the kid, we say that the desire is part of what makes him responsible: if he had not wanted to break the glass, but banged on it to wake up someone in a burning building, then we would feel differently about the breakage. In the case of the mental patient, we feel some inclination to say that the desire makes him *less* responsible. But why? What's the difference between the two desires? Why does one of them make Fred more responsible, and the other make Fred less responsible? (If we say that the desire becomes pathological once the person cannot control it anymore, then we have not made anything clearer; whether the agent could have controlled it or not is exactly what is in question.) And in general, when an agent has a desire to do something, and acts on that desire, then does it make sense to say that they could have had that very desire and still acted otherwise? Is there some tiny agent within the agent who can stand apart from all of his own desires and consider them in a completely neutral way? Is that what we need to preserve the idea that agents are fully responsible for some of their actions?

None of these questions arises in the ancient context, because they adopted a different criterion for moral responsibility:

(AA) An agent is only responsible for an action if the agent Acted Autonomously.

Here, the central question is whether the agent was the cause of the action, or whether something else other than the agent was the cause of the action. This is a different criterion from the CDO criterion above. The question is not 'could the agent have done something other than what he did?', but rather 'did the *agent* do it, or did something other than the agent do it?' If the car pushed Fred, then it was not Fred who was responsible, but the car (or its driver). However, if the agent was fully informed about the situation, and acted on his own desire, without being compelled by some other external force or factor, then he is responsible for his action—even if it is the case that, given his beliefs and desires at the time, there was no way for him to do anything other than what he did.

There is an old French phrase that—like many French phrases—gives elegant expression to a bad idea: *tout comprendre, c'est tout pardonner*. To understand everything is to forgive everything. When we rush to judge others, it is because we do not fully understand what led them to act as they do. If we came to understand all of the psychological forces in play, then we would no longer blame individuals for their actions.

To accept this maxim is to accept an artificial choice: we can either have an adequate theory of psychology, or an adequate system of moral assessment, but not both. Insightful psychology must lead to toothless morality; or if we choose to make substantive moral judgments then we must turn a blind eye to psychological complexity. We should not accept this choice. An adequate theory of moral assessment must accommodate the fact that sometimes people are to blame, and that forgiveness is not always merited. But an adequate psychology must strive to make all human actions explicable, and explicable in such terms that when we understand all of the forces in play, we can see why the agent acted as they did, and could not have acted otherwise.

The ancient view does an excellent job of avoiding the false dilemma. Ancient psychological theories always strove for complete explanatory power: understanding an agent's actions means seeing that given the beliefs and desires they had, they could not have acted otherwise than as they did. On the other hand, ancient moral theories were richly judgmental—only too judgmental, it may sometimes seem. Actions are wrong, and agents are wrong to perform them, exactly because the actions come from the agent's desires, and the desires themselves are wrong and culpable. (Indeed, as we saw in the case of the Stoics, the presence of culpable desires in the agent's mind renders all of their actions culpable, even when they are not acting on the vicious desire itself!) What makes the agent responsible for their actions is that the actions stemmed from the agent's psychology, not from anywhere else. It is true that, given those beliefs and desires, the agent could not have acted otherwise; but the action is still the *agent's* action, because it came from the *agent's* beliefs and desires. If something outside the agent's psychology had been the source of the action—a passing car, for instance—then the agent would not be responsible. But the mere fact that the agent could not do otherwise, given their actual psychological state, does nothing to extricate them from responsibility for the things that they actually did. Autonomy, not the ability to do otherwise, is the issue.

I think Bobzien is right to draw our attention to this difference in conceptions of moral responsibility, but I also think that a slight shift of emphasis can help us see how this historical difference arose. If we think of the two positions in Bobzien's terms, as a contrast between autonomy and the ability to do otherwise, then it becomes natural to ask when the debate shifted, and why. Who was it who first started worrying about the ability to do otherwise, if no one had worried about it before? Why did people come to find the agent's autonomy no longer sufficient for responsibility, if they had found it sufficient before? Such questions would lead us to look for evidence of an historical shift in the debate, to discover what caused people to transfer their interest from the one topic to the other.

I think these historical investigations would be misguided, however, because I think the contrast between the two conceptions is somewhat obscured in Bobzien's formulation. People were always interested in the ability to do otherwise—just as much in antiquity as today. And people have always been interested in the agent's autonomy, and still are today. What has changed, instead, is the conception of the agent with respect to whom these other distinctions are made. And that change in the conception of the agent is one that we can trace in history, running right through the middle of the Stoics.

In Bobzien's terms, the ancients were interested in the agent's autonomy from external forces, that is, whether the agent or something outside the agent was the original source of the causal chain that led to the action. But the reason that the ancients made autonomy necessary for responsibility is because they felt that external forces and factors hinder the agent *from doing otherwise*. That is, what is important about the agent's autonomy from external influence is that it leaves the agent free to do otherwise, so far as external factors are concerned. If I am tied to my chair, or locked in my room, then I am not responsible for remaining in my room; external forces prevent me from doing otherwise. On the other hand, if I am not tied or locked or otherwise hindered from leaving my room, then I am responsible for staying in my room. I am free to do otherwise, so far as external factors are concerned; that is what it means to say that I am autonomous.

Of course, so far as my psychology goes, it may be that I am not capable of doing otherwise. My beliefs and desires may be such that I am psychologically compelled to stay in my room—given what I want and what I believe, it is not possible for me to do otherwise. But in antiquity, that is no threat to responsibility, because I am acting as an autonomous agent, unhindered by anything outside me.

The Evolution of the Will ~ 293

If we now contrast this with the modern view, it should be clear that the difference is best seen as a difference in where I draw the boundaries of my self, or draw the boundaries around agents in general. Moral responsibility now requires that I be autonomous even from my own beliefs and desires—that even my own psychology leaves me free to do otherwise. And this is a natural evolution of the ancient view, if we imagine a shrinking of the self, so that desires that were once thought of as internal to the agent come to be seen as external to the agent. We can get a picture of the whole evolution if we imagine each agent in terms of a geometrical point, surrounded by a ball, surrounded by the world at large. In antiquity, the agent was the whole thick ball of desires, beliefs, inclinations, tendencies, predispositions, and so on. The only thing external to him was the world at large—other people, animals, inanimate objects, and so on. But when we exclude the desires from the agent's self, we begin to shrink the agent down to a geometrical point, that is, the 'ego' or 'will'. Genuine responsibility requires me to be completely free, autonomous, and unhindered in my choice—I must be capable, so far as everything external goes, of doing the opposite of what I do. But now that even my own desires are external to my point-like self, it follows that I must be capable of doing the opposite, even while I have the very same desires and beliefs that I do have. And it is not clear that such an idea is coherent, much less consistent with a fully explanatory psychology.

Thus the proper contrast between ancient and modern debates is not a contrast between autonomy and the freedom to do otherwise. Instead, it is a contrast between a psychologically rich and complicated self, whose autonomy consists in its ability to do otherwise, so far as the world outside the whole psychology goes, and an abstract and point-like self, whose autonomy consists in its ability to do otherwise, even so far as the agent's own desires and preferences go. Or rather, the desires and preferences are no longer conceived as being the 'agent's own', since they belong in the shell of psychology that is external to the point-like self.

In these terms, I think we can see some of the historical reasons why the self began to shrink, from a thick ball of psychological complexity, to a vanishingly small point of abstract will. One source of this evolution is the Platonic and neo-Platonic doctrine of the eternity of the soul, and its reincarnation in successive human bodies. Already in the *Republic* and *Phaedo*, Plato had suggested that the lower parts of the individual's soul—the parts responsible for appetitive and spirited desires—are not essential to the agent, but only arise when a unified and simple rational soul is dropped into a physical body. When I am a separate soul, existing between incarnations, I do not have any bodily desires, only my desires for knowledge, truth, and union with God. It is when I am dropped into a body that I come to desire food and all the rest—and that is also when I become confused about the nature of my own true self. My desire for food, for instance, is incredibly persuasive, as is my pleasure in getting the food I desired; both of them make me think that I am this whole, embodied animal, and that these desires and satisfactions are mine. But, according to Plato, this is not so; the real me is much smaller. The real me is a rational soul, that takes on bodies at certain times in its eternal career, and acquires bodily desires only as a result of its association with bodies. Ethical and spiritual progress involves my coming to see that my bodily desires and pleasures are not an accurate guide to who I really am. As I come to see that I am only a rational soul, I also come to consider many of my desires—especially my desires for bodily satisfactions—to be external impositions, and encumbrances:

The body provides us with thousands of distractions because of the nurture that is necessary for it, and if diseases befall it then they hinder us from our search for the truth. And it fills us full of all sorts of lusts and desires and fears and illusions and nonsense, so that, as they say, truly no sort of wisdom of any kind arises for us from the body. Wars, conflicts, and fights arise from no other source than the body and its desires—for all wars occur for the acquisition of possessions, and we are compelled to acquire possessions for the sake of the body, when we are enslaved to its maintenance.

(*Phaedo* 66b–d)

In this passage a great swath of our ordinary psychology—our desires for food, sex, physical comforts and possessions—is relegated to the

The Evolution of the Will ~ 295

outside of the agent proper, and the desires for these things are treated as a source of compulsion, necessity, and slavery.

This extreme alienation of the agent from his own bodily desires was not adopted by most of Plato's immediate successors—it is not even clear how consistently Plato espouses it. Certainly Aristotle and Epicurus are both willing to treat an agent's bodily desires as full citizens in the individual's psychology. Thus when they admit those desires back into the sphere of the agent, they remove them from the list of possible external compulsions, and thus remove them from the list of potential exculpating factors. Acting on the desire for food is not being *externally* hindered or compelled; that desire is internal to the agent. Thus, so far as external things go, one could still have done otherwise (though so far as one's entire psychology goes, one could not). Thus, when an agent acts from his desire for food, he has acted autonomously. It was the agent himself (including his desires), not anything else, that caused him to act.

The more extreme view of the *Phaedo* was revived by the neo-Platonists, starting with Plotinus in the early 200s AD, and made its way through them into the early Christian Church Fathers, Augustine most of all. But meanwhile, a second philosophical development was leading to the shrinking of the self: the Stoic doctrine of assent. Now as we have seen, the Stoics did not think that I as an agent am something distinct from my desires. Quite the opposite; they identified the agent with his mind as a whole, and this in turn with his disposition to assent to various impressions, which is the same thing as his disposition to have particular beliefs and desires. Thus on Chrysippus' view, if my action stems from my assent, and this in turn from my disposition to assent, then it is fully my own action. Hindrances from outside of my psychology impair my autonomy, of course, in as much as they make me incapable of acting otherwise than as I do. If the external world hinders me from doing otherwise, then I am not responsible for my actions. But even actions that are entirely up to me, acts for which I am fully morally responsible, are still compelled by my disposition to assent, and the fact that someone with my disposition cannot do otherwise does not exculpate me in the least.

When we read Epictetus, it may seem that a change has occurred; and here the mere appearance of a change in time leads to a real change, as a misunderstanding of Epictetus became influential. Chrysippus is quite clear about the fact that impressions come from outside, that they are not up to the agent, and that they are not desires. We do not have a desire unless and until we assent to an impression; that assent then constitutes the desire. Thus the desire, that is, the assent, comes from within us, and comes from our psychology, since this simply is our disposition to give or withhold assents to impressions. But in Epictetus, this picture is given a different emphasis. The emphasis on the fact that our assent is unconstrained, and the emphasis on our ability to scrutinize incoming impressions, makes it look instead as though we are able to hold our own desires at arm's-length. If we confuse the incoming impressions with nascent or incipient desires, and suppose that our faculty of assent is able to approach each new impression with an absolute freedom either to assent to it or to suspend its assent, then it looks as though we are completely unconstrained, even by our own desires.

This misimpression is abetted by a certain unclarity in Epictetus' formulation. Epictetus clearly thought, along with Chrysippus, that our assent is determined by our overall psychology. If an impression arrives that, so to speak, fits into our pattern of desires and beliefs, then we will assent to it. The impression itself does not compel us, or necessitate our assent (since someone else might receive the same impression and not assent). But given the sort of disposition to assent that we have, it is not up to us not to assent. I believe, for instance, that two is an even number; that means that I have a disposition to assent to the impression that two is an even number, when it arises. The freedom of my assent, on Epictetus' view, does not consist in my ability to suspend assent from what I believe, as though I could now entertain the impression that two is an even number and refuse to assent to it. My psychology as a whole necessitates my assent; given my beliefs, it is not possible for me not to assent to this impression. Rather, the freedom of my assent is simply the fact that, when I get an impression which my psychology compels me to assent to, there is no way that a force *external* to my psychology could prevent me from assenting to it. We have looked at this sort of passage already:

Man, you have a prohairesis that is by nature incapable of being hindered or compelled.... I will show you this first from considerations of assent [to non-impulsive impressions]. Is anyone able to hinder you from consenting to what is true? Not a one. Is anyone able to compel you to accept what is false? Not a one. Do you see that in this area you have a prohairesis that is unhindered, uncompelled, and unimpeded? Move over to desire and impulse, and it is no different.[1]

For just as it is impossible to assent to what seems false to you, or dissent from what seems true, so too it is impossible to abstain from what seems good to you.[2]

What is the cause of our assenting to something? That it seems to us to be the case. So, it is not possible to assent to what seems not to be the case. Why? Because this is the nature of the mind, to consent to what is true, and be dissatisfied with what is false, and suspend about things that are unclear ... So when someone assents to the false, you know that he did not *want* to assent to something false (for every soul is unwillingly deprived of the truth, as Plato says), but rather something false *seemed* true to him. Move over to actions— do we have anything in the practical case like true and false? We do; what we should and shouldn't do, what is profitable and unprofitable, what is mine and what is not mine, and the other things like that. 'So isn't it possible that something could *seem* profitable to someone, but that he would not choose it?' No, it is not possible.[3]

What is misleading about these passages is that they interpolate an extra stage of 'seeming' into the orthodox two-stage account of impression and assent, and this talk of 'seeming' is dangerously ambiguous. Suppose I receive an impression that two is an even number. Given my many past exposures to this and related impressions, and given the assents I made in the past and the disposition that I developed thereby, I will assent to this impression—I cannot do otherwise. The freedom of my assent does not consist in any ability to do otherwise *now*; given my disposition, that is, my prohairesis, I cannot do anything but assent. But my assent is still free, according to Epictetus, because no external force can hinder me *from* assenting. But where in this process is there a place for 'seeming'? Given how

298 ~ *The Evolution of the Will*

Epictetus uses it here, he must mean something very strong by that phrase, such that whenever something seems to me a certain way, I assent to it, straight off. But 'seeming' in this strong sense is really nothing other than assenting; to respond to an impression by saying 'that seems true to me' in this sense is exactly to assent to the impression. To respond to a practical impression by thinking 'that seems good to me', or 'that seems like the thing to do' is exactly to have a practical assent, that is, an impulse.

There is another sense of 'seeming' though, in which one can say that something seems a certain way to you, without thereby assenting to its really being that way. When it is half-way in the water, the oar 'seems' to be bent, but of course I do not assent to the impression that the oar is bent. It isn't bent, it only seems that way (or it merely seems that way, or just seems that way). Where should we put this sort of 'seeming'? Inasmuch as it bears no direct relation to assent, it ought to be part of the impression. Perhaps this sort of seeming is part of what characterizes some impressions as more plausible or persuasive than others—for example, that oar really *seems* bent to me, though I currently do not assent to its being bent.[4] But impressions of this sort, no matter how plausible or persuasive, are still a very different thing from beliefs and desires.

So there is a sense in which one can say, for example, 'that impression seems true to me' and merely refer to an impression without assenting to it, and there is another sense in which to say that is to make a report of your assent to it, that is, of your belief. So too, there is a sense in which you can say 'that cake looks good to me' and merely refer to an impression, and another in which you have just reported a desire for the cake. In the first sense, the 'seemings', that is, impressions, come from outside, and they are not up to the agent, and they are not beliefs or desires. In the second sense, the 'seemings', that is, assents, come from the agent's psychology, and they are beliefs and desires.

If we are not very careful to keep these senses separate, then we may start to combine different features of the two kinds of 'seeming' into a very unorthodox, un-Stoic entity. This would be a sort of impression/desire that the agent can have but not act on, can feel and

The Evolution of the Will ~ 299

yet scrutinize. Like a desire, it engages the agent's psychology, fitting with their preferences and dispositions. But like an impression, it comes from outside the agent, so that moral responsibility demands that it not hinder the agent from acting otherwise. Here we have moved a step closer to the thought that real moral responsibility requires that the agent be unconstrained even by his own desires.

And corresponding to this monstrous un-Stoic impression/desire hybrid, there will also be a monstrous un-Stoic faculty of assent. My assent is free, on the orthodox view, for two reasons: when I assent to the impression that two is even, then my assent is unnecessitated in the Chrysippean sense, in that the impression by itself is not sufficient to make me assent. Someone with a different psychology would not have assented, and this is sufficient to show that my assent was up to me, that is, came from my psychology, and not from outside. My assent is also free in the Epictetan sense, in that no external force could cause me to withhold my assent, or to assent to the contradictory. Both Chrysippus and Epictetus agree that the actual impression that I have, plus my actual disposition to assent, are sufficient for the assent; given this impression, and given my psychology, I cannot do otherwise than assent. Chrysippus adds the thought: but the impression by itself is not sufficient, since another psychology would have done otherwise; so the assent is up to you, and thus you are responsible for the action. Nothing external can force you to have the assent you have. Epictetus adds the thought: and nothing external can prevent you from having the assent you have, since the impression plus your psychology are *sufficient* conditions for the assent.

It looks, then, as though when I assent there is nothing external that can either force me to assent or prevent me from assenting. Thus I am free to assent or not to assent, so far as any external influences that may be at work. But of course, this is a completely misleading summation of the state of affairs, if we take it to mean that when an impression comes in, it is completely open to me either to assent or not to assent. Both Chrysippus and Epictetus would deny this. Whenever an impression comes in, it meets a mind that has certain dispositions to assent and lacks others, and given those dispositions it is fully determined whether I will assent or not. This mistake is only made worse if we blend in the further confusion based on the ambiguity in 'seeming', and suppose that even when I feel a 'desire' it is still completely open to me both to assent to it or not to assent to it.

Combine this with the wholly orthodox view that each agent is most essentially his faculty of assent, and it comes to seem that I am essentially something different from my desires, and that they belong to the world outside of me. It follows that for me to act in a fully unhindered way, that is, so that I am capable of doing otherwise so far as the outside world goes, I must not be hindered even by my desires. Even if I act on a desire, and no matter how compelling the desire may be, moral responsibility requires me to be able to do otherwise. And the doctrine of assent, as misunderstood above, seems to provide me with the ability to do otherwise; no matter what 'desire' comes into my mind, I am free to assent to it or not. Having shed my desires as external, my self has shrunk to a point-like faculty of assent, the free and unconstrained will.

Add to this the fact that Epictetus himself sometimes sounds a great deal like the Socrates of the Phaedo. In this, once again, he is being faithful to his Stoic antecedents, but his expressions are suggestive of the neo-Platonic future:[5]

Nature is an extraordinary thing, and 'a lover of animals', as Xenophon said. At any rate, we cherish and take care of our bodies, the most disgusting and filthy things of all—for we couldn't bear to take care of our neighbor's body, even for a mere five days. Just think what it's like—getting up at dawn to wash someone else's teeth, and after he has done his business you have to give him a wipe down there. What is really extraordinary is the fact that we love such a thing, given how much upkeep it requires each day. I stuff my paunch. Then I empty it. What could be more tedious? . . . But I must serve God. That's why I wait, and put up with washing this wretched little body, and giving it fodder, and sheltering it.[6]

[genuine students of Stoicism should say:] 'Epictetus, we can no longer bear to be bound up with this little body, feeding it and watering it and resting it and cleansing it, and associating with people of this sort because of it. Aren't all of these things indifferent, and nothing to us? And death is not a bad thing, is it? And are we not among God's relations, and did we not come from there? Let us go back to where we came from; let us be released from these bonds that are attached to us and weigh us down . . . ' Then it would be my job to say: 'Men, wait for God. When he gives the signal and releases you from service, then you will be released. But for the meanwhile, put up with dwelling in this place where he has stationed you . . . Stay here, and do not depart without reason.'[7]

You are a little soul, lugging around a corpse, as Epictetus used to say.[8]

Here again we see the conception of the agent in the process of shrinking to exclude the body and its desires, and this alienation leads to the reclassification of large portions of the agent's psychology. What was internal when it was *my* desire becomes external when it is my *body's* desire. The true self, the real me, is a rational soul, which will be most clearly revealed only after it is freed from the body. The boundary of 'external hindrances' advances inwards; when I act from my desire for food, this action is no longer fully up to me, but is symptomatic of the way that my body, which is not me, hinders my eternal soul, which is the real me.

The story of the historical evolution of the modern problem of free will is of course much more complicated than this—indeed, there is no single modern problem of free will, but a group of interrelated ones, and each of them has its own complicated origin. But many of the central concepts and controversies arose from the Stoic system, and can be traced back to doctrines that the Stoics held, or attacks that their opponents launched against them, or misunderstandings that arose as Stoicism was blended into the revival of Platonic philosophy that provided the intellectual underpinnings of Christian theology.

NOTES

1. *Discourses* 1.17.21–24.
2. *Discourses* 3.7.15.
3. *Discourses* 1.28.1–7.

4. Assent, unlike persuasiveness, is an all-or-nothing affair; some impressions may be more persuasive than others, but one either assents with one's whole mind or one does not. Still, this raises the question what it means to say that some impressions are more persuasive than others, or more plausible. The question is especially clear in a case where I assent to neither of two impressions, but find one more persuasive nevertheless (e.g., the oar in water *seems* bent, though I don't believe it is; the oar in water doesn't even *seem* to have legs and arms, and I do not believe it does). I think the answer can be put in two roughly equivalent ways. First, we may say that the persuasive impression is qualitatively more similar to impressions that I have assented to in the past—even though I fully believe the oar is not bent, it gives off an impression much like the impressions that I have received in the past from things I believed were bent. Second, we may say that although assent is an all-or-nothing affair, it nevertheless arises from a state of mind that involves a great deal of complexity. Our overall disposition to assent is composed of a great many dispositions to assent to impressions with various characters, corresponding primarily to impressions we have encountered in the past. My lack of assent to the impression that the oar is bent is the result of an interaction between my disposition to assent to the impression that things that look like that are bent (a disposition relative to visual appearances, as it were), and my disposition not to assent to the impression that such objects as oars would bend under these conditions (a disposition relative to impressions of the stability and persistence of objects and their properties), and other sorts of dispositions, considered as modules in my overall disposition to assent. There are several references in Stoicism to things called '*aphormai*', i.e. 'starting points', which may well have been something like these modular, defeasible dispositions to assent (cf. e.g. *DL* 7.76 = *SVF* 2.201 = IG2 II–3; *Origen de Princ.* 3.108 = *SVF* 2.988; *Anecdota Graeca* Paris. 1.171 = *SVF* 3.214; *DL* 7.89 = *SVF* 3.228 = IG2 II–94). Put in these terms, the mistake is to suppose that the resultant all-or-nothing assent is anything more than the result of a mechanical integration of these different particular dispositions—in particular, there is no further faculty that surveys the particular dispositions and then awards the overall victory to one or another on some further basis. The weights are loaded into the two pans, and one side goes down; there is not a further mechanism for *deciding* which should predominate.

5. There is nothing here that is new; as I have argued before, Chrysippus himself had identified human beings with their souls as distinct from their bodies. And Cleanthes before him had written in what sounds like a Platonic vein:

> A human being is a weak and vulnerable thing, in need of ten thousand kinds of assistance, like food and shelter and the rest of the attention to the body. And the body stands over us like some sort of bitter tyrant, demanding its daily exactions, and if we do not provide for it by washing it and anointing it and clothing and feeding it, then it threatens us with diseases and death. (*SE AM* 9.90 = *SVF* 1.529).

The Evolution of the Will ~ 303

Another text says that Cleanthes said that only the soul was the human being (Epiphanius *ad Haeres*. 3.2.9 = *SVF* 1 Cleanthes 538); unfortunately, this text also attributes to Cleanthes the view that the good and the honorable consist in pleasures, a piece of such flagrant nonsense that it seriously reduces the evidential value of the text as a whole.

6. *Epictetus* fragment 23.

7. *Discourses* 1.9.12–17.

8. Marcus Aurelius *Meditations* 4.41

On the background of theology and cosmology, see Furley (1999), Mansfeld (1999b), White (2003) and Algra (2003).

On all aspects of determinism, the state of the art is Bobzien (1998a). Shorter and more accessible treatments can be found in Hankinson (1999), Brennan (2001), and D. Frede (2003).

On the will, see Kahn (1988), Mansfeld (1991), Bobzien (1998b), Inwood (2000), Brennan (2001).

Conclusion

18

Taking Stock

We have surveyed a considerable portion of the Stoic system, beginning with their psychology and epistemology, then spending the central portion of the book on the core topics in ethics, and devoting the final portion to the theory of Fate. It is time to sum up, point some morals, and draw some conclusions.

I

What it means to be a Stoic ought to look different now than it did in the opening chapter, when we considered the various caricatures of Stoicism available in literature and popular culture. Some of the charges should now seem unfair and misguided. In particular, I think that the Stoics turn out to have a much more interesting view of the emotions than anything that is summed up by talk of 'being stoic' or 'acting stoically'. The Stoic rejection of emotions has nothing to do with striking a fearless pose while shivering in your shoes; a cosmetic concealment of deep feelings is not what they were after. But neither did they insist on the utter eradication of emotions for the reasons we might have thought, for example, that emotions are disturbing, or unmanly, or likely to be a bad bargain of painful over pleasant. In fact, their brief against emotions has very little to do with how they feel, and everything to do with wanting to get a clear view of what is really valuable in life, with wanting to avoid mistakes about what is really good and bad, mistakes that get encoded in beliefs and then expressed in actions.

The claim that it is possible to eradicate emotions—that it is even possible, as Hume puts it, to 'exult in the midst of tortures'—also turns out to be much more interesting than it first seemed, inasmuch as it is based on a deep view about the structure of all human motivation, and the indispensable role of assent. The Sage is not just good at the gritting of teeth; instead, what might seem like evils to us simply don't seem that way at all given the Sage's value orientation. Physical affliction cannot make a mark on his soul unless he assents to some belief about it—that is true about the Sage, and no less true about the most craven among us. The difference between the courageous and the cringing lies in our thoughts, that is, whether we think physical affliction is bad; and, with no such inclination to think that anything bad is happening, the Sage undergoing torture does not need to work at trying not to feel dejected.

Far from shallow machismo, then, the Stoics have a deep and powerful conception of psychology, of what it is to be a rational creature, and to be moved only by beliefs. No wonder that Hume ridiculed them; his psychology and theirs are poles apart. For Hume, beliefs are a lot of idle chatterers, commenting on the proceedings but incapable of initiating action or setting the limbs in motion. For that, he thinks, one needs brute passion, the felt push and pull of sensual dynamics. For the Stoics, it is these sorts of things that are intrinsically inert and impotent. How could a mere physical sensation produce any action, unless one assented to a belief about its value? Plutarch is hinting at an even larger debate than he knows about when he remarks:

What is the subject most argued about by Chrysippus himself and Antipater in their disputes with the Academics? The doctrine that without assent there is neither action nor impulsion, and that they are talking nonsense and empty assumptions who claim that, when an appropriate impression occurs, impulsion ensues at once without people first having yielded or given their assent.[1]

With only a little modification, this could describe the fault-line that still divides the moral psychology of Humeans from that of Kantians and other rationalists. On the whole, I am inclined to think the Stoics are wrong here; in the light not only of evolutionary theory but of developmental psychology, it seems to me that the motivational dynamics of adult human beings cannot be as radically different from the motivation of other animals, and human children, as the Stoics would make it be. But this debate is not easily settled, and the Stoic position is far from silly.

II

Both in the ethical theory proper and in the theory of fate, there is a pervasive unclarity about the extent to which the Stoics want to revise our practice as a result of revising our attitudes and values.[2] Seeing things as fated, and see them as indifferent, must be intended to play some role in curbing one's efforts and reactions; but how do the details go?

IIa

The theory of indifferents is supposed to alter my reaction to my current state. I am meant to see my lameness as an indifferent thing, not a bad thing, to see my wealth as an indifferent thing, not a good thing, and so on. And this is meant to moderate my reactions to my current fortunes. It should also have some effect on how much I should do to pursue, for instance, some food. The Stoics want to revise our practice to some extent—they want me to care less about food, pursue it less intently, and care less about my success or failure in attaining it. On the other hand, they do not want to advocate a complete revision of our practices—for example, that I should cease to eat, cease to think it important whether others eat, or even conduct myself vis-à-vis food in an unconventional way.

IIb

The theory of determinism is also supposed to alter my reaction to my current state. Seeing my current health as the dictate of providence is intended to moderate my reaction to it, to make me content with it. If I accept events as necessary, I will live moderately and harmoniously. But this line of thought, too, makes it unclear how much I should do, for example, to save my sick child from dying. The Lazy Argument *is* a problem, not just at the level of dialectical fencing, but when I have expended a certain amount of energy to save my child, and am wondering whether to expend a further quantum. My persona as father urges me to do whatever is up to me to attain the natural state of the child's health; on the other hand, Musonius is telling me to accept the child's death as necessary and inevitable and so live more harmoniously.

IIc

We see the same problem if we consider reservation. This too seems designed to induce moderation and produce consolation, but how and how much and up to what point are all left unclear. If I pursue food, I should do so with reservation, that is, with the thought that I will get it unless something intervenes. But how large of an intervention should I see as decisive evidence that I'm not meant to eat? If my bread falls on the floor, may I pick it up, or should I take it that Zeus is sending me a message? If we're out of bread, should I run to the shop, or should I decide that fate has interceded to show me it wasn't meant to be? Or if I don't pick up the bread, or don't run to the shop, am I just failing to exercise the proper diligence in selection?

At this stage the apologist for ancient philosophy may point out what was already said in the beginning of this book: that ancient ethical theories were designed to help agents reflect on how to live and what to value, and that unlike modern ethical theories they were not obsessed with explicit algorithms for solving practical dilemmas. Adopting the Stoic system will lead to fundamental changes in values and understanding; whether that will lead to a trip to the shop on some occasion can only be determined by the practical wisdom of the perfected Stoic agent; it cannot be determined in advance. The apologist for the Stoics may add that you won't get a great deal more help from the Aristotelians, either.

But I find that only mildly helpful. You can *say* that the lack of mechanical cut-off points shows the ineliminable role for particular judgment, but that's only to acknowledge that the system goes alarmingly quiet at some crucial moments. So too with the general comparison to other ancient philosophical schools; this only shows something that we can all agree—that Stoicism may not be *worse* than Aristotelianism in dodging hard questions, or deferring them to the Sage.

Here is a quote from Dr. Johnson, in which he parodies an ethical view that bears enough resemblances to Stoicism to make the criticism apply. It's from his novel *Rasselas*, about a fictional prince of Abyssinia who goes on a quest to discover the secret of happiness.

Rasselas went often to an assembly of learned men, who met at stated times to unbend their minds and compare their opinions. . . . [One of the wise men begins to discourse].

'. . . The time is already come when none are wretched but by their own fault. Nothing is more idle than to inquire after happiness, which nature has kindly placed within our reach. The way to be happy is to live according to nature, in obedience to that universal and unalterable law with which every heart is originally impressed; which is not written on it by precept, but engraven by destiny, not instilled by education, but infused at our nativity. He that lives according to nature will suffer nothing from the delusions of hope, or importunities of desire; he will receive and reject with equability of temper, and act or suffer as the reason of things shall alternately prescribe. Other men may amuse themselves with subtle definitions, or intricate ratiocination. Let them learn to be wise by easier means; let them observe the hind of the forest, and the linnet of the grove; let them consider the life of animals, whose motions are regulated by instinct; they obey their guide, and are happy. Let us therefore, at length, cease to dispute, and learn to live; throw away the encumbrance of precepts, which they who utter them with so much pride and pomp do not understand, and carry with us this simple and intelligible maxim, that deviation from nature is deviation from happiness.'

When he had spoken, he looked round him with a placid air, and enjoyed the consciousness of his own beneficence. 'Sir', said the Prince with great modesty, 'as I, like all the rest of mankind, am desirous of felicity, my closest attention has been fixed upon your discourse. I doubt not the truth of a position which a man so learned has so confidently advanced. Let me only know what it is to live according to nature.'

'When I find young men so humble and so docile', said the philosopher, 'I can deny them no information which my studies have enabled me to afford. To live according to nature, is to act always with due regard to the fitness arising from the relations and qualities of causes and effects; to concur with the great and unchangeable scheme of universal felicity; to co-operate with the general disposition and tendency of the present system of things.'

The Prince soon found that this was one of the sages whom he should understand less as he heard him longer. He therefore bowed and was silent; and the philosopher, supposing him satisfied, and the rest vanquished, rose up and departed with the air of a man that had co-operated with the present system.

(*The History of Rasselas, Prince of Abyssinia*, ch. 22)

Some parts of the picture simply do not apply to Stoicism—especially the suggestion that an untutored reliance on animal instinct will provide an adequate guide to conduct. But the Sage's inability to give a detailed, substantive answer to Rasselas' question is certainly à propos.

III

Another kind of deferring occurred throughout our discussion of ethics. This happened whenever it became clear that the Stoics were basing an unintuitive claim about our good, or our end, or what is befitting for us, on a deep claim about human nature, about the kinds of things we are. Frequently this new and deeper view about human nature involved a perspective that was bound up with an entire world-view, with a view about our relation to the whole of nature, or to Zeus. It is because of the kind of predominance that soul has in us that indifferents are indifferent; it is because of our relation to Zeus that following nature is our end. On the one hand, interpretive considerations make it clear that the Stoics want to ground their most characteristic theses this way. Sometimes the testimony makes their intentions explicit. At other times it becomes clear that we face an interpretive choice between attributing to the Stoics a facile, flat-footed and unpersuasive argument based on uncontroversial premisses—the sort of premisses to which an Epicurus or an Aristotle could subscribe—or an interesting, powerful, and intriguing argument, based on controversial premisses, but premisses to which the Stoics are committed in any case, for example, the existence of Zeus, the cohesive unity of the cosmos, the universal pervasiveness of reason, and so on. And so we get a better account of the ethical theory—a more exegetically faithful account and a more philosophically satisfying account—by following their lead in making the ethical picture depend to a large extent on the non-ethical picture. I find it very persuasive that, if we bore the relation to Zeus that they suggest we bear, health and food really would form no part of our good. But the gain in conditional plausibility comes at a cost in non-conditional plausibility; the question of whether we should really believe what they say about ethics has been deferred to the question of whether we should believe what they say about the cosmos.

IV

One of the most resilient misconceptions about Stoicism involves the idea that fate's dominion ceases at the soul's circumference, that our souls are like an 'inner citadel' that fortune's siege-machines cannot assail.[3] Here are two passages that have been taken as evidence of this sort of view:

When a dog is tied to a cart, if it wants to follow it is pulled and follows, making its spontaneous act coincide with necessity; but if it does not want to follow it will be compelled in any case. So it is with human beings, too: even if they do not want to, they will be compelled in any case to follow what is destined.[4]

Lead me, Zeus and Destiny, wherever you have ordained for me. For I shall follow unflinching. But if I become bad and am unwilling, I shall follow nonetheless.[5]

When we are told both that everything is fated, and also that our souls are somehow free, it seems natural to conclude that there is a sort of causal fire-wall separating inside from outside, insulating the soul within from the ineluctable causal nexus without. The dog's body may be fated to move, but its mind is still free to cooperate or not. Or at least, however it goes for dogs, our human minds are free to think, choose, decide and react however we want, and the mental events are not fated, not caused, and not destined—surely that is the point of Stoicism, to counsel virtue through resignation, and to give us the freedom to cooperate with the dictates of fate.

But we have seen ample evidence that this simply was not their view. There is, to begin with, the repeated affirmation that every-thing, without exception, happens by fate and as the result of ante-cedent causes—and the arguments used to bolster this claim are just as applicable to mental events as to extra-mental events.[6] Further-more, there is the fact that their account of the soul makes it simply another parcel of matter in a material world—a part of the cohesive and coherent *pneuma* that constitutes the cosmos. Had they wished to purchase it some exemption from causation, they might at least have made it of a different stuff, or no stuff at all. Consider, too, the care with which they elaborated the causal connections between the soul and the rest of the world, working in both directions. The theory of perception tells us how the objects around us impose a physical alteration on our impressionable souls; the theory of impulse tells us how our souls reach out to change the world in turn. This last point, about the causal connections running from my mind out into the world, shows that it will not help to claim that all external events are fated while all mental events are free.

Suppose that a proponent of the inner citadel interpretation denied that causation and fate were meant to encompass all events—perhaps they might argue that the Stoics had in mind only external events when they said that all events are fated and caused. Still, they must also agree that some mental events really are the causes of physical events in the world, as the theory of impulse claims; when I act on an impulse to raise my arm, my arm raises, the air in the room shifts, the front legs of my chair carry a greater weight, and so on. To say that the chair-legs' bowing, like all other external events, was fated from all past time, and caused by an unbroken chain of antecedent causes, is to say that whatever caused that event was just as much the result of antecedent causes, just as much fated to happen, as the event itself. And that means that my internal impulse was fated to occur. That is the price of saying that all external events are fated, and that internal events cause external events—the fixed and determined status of the events down-stream must inevitably flow up-stream to the earlier events that caused them.

This 'upstream argument', as we might call it, shows the determination of an extremely large class of mental events: namely, any mental event that has any effect on the external physical world, either directly or at any degree of indirection. It is important to notice this inevitable inward constriction of the alleged causal firewall. The range of allegedly free mental events is going to get squeezed and squeezed—first nothing that directly causes a determined event, then nothing that indirectly causes one.

Perhaps this argument does not show that all mental events are part of the causal nexus, but what might be left? Well, maybe the desperate defender of the firewall interpretation would say that we at least have left free to us our *passive reactions* to events. We will sometimes have a free and undetermined choice between mental event A and mental event B, so long as neither option has any downstream effects on the external world. Maybe we can't freely choose whether to walk to the store or stay home, but we can freely

Taking Stock ~ 317

choose how we feel about what has already happened to us. And in fact, I think something like that view explains why interpreters of this school are so eager to embrace the dog-and-cart simile: it looks like a model where we can choose to embrace fate or resist fate, since neither the embrace nor the resistance has any consequences on whether we are dragged by the cart.

But, whether I embrace or resist must be causally idle not only with respect to whether I am currently being dragged or not, but also with respect to any *future* choices I may make that might affect the external world; also with respect to any moans and groans I might make now or later; also with respect to any possible sign that I could give to another human being which would indicate whether I had embraced or resisted. Indeed, the causal firewall has been constricted so far that its advocates will have to concede the following: they are free to embrace fate or resist it, but only in ways that would leave it inscrutable to any possible observer whether they had in fact embraced fate or resisted it. So, from the fact that a person drags their feet while being dragged by the cart, we cannot tell whether they embraced fate or resisted it; from the fact that they cry aloud and curse the gods we cannot tell; from the fact that they keep getting drunk at every opportunity and sobbing incoherently we cannot tell. It may be that somewhere within their causal firewall they are making all the right Stoic choices, free from the determination of fate. But in fact, no one else could ever know, and they themselves could never realize it in a way that led to any change in their external behavior. They may be free and happy in there, but that can have no effect on whether they say 'I'm free and happy!' or 'woe is me that ever I was born!' Those external effects are determined, and so whatever mental events are causally connected to them receive no shelter from the alleged causal firewall.

But this also undermines our ability to identify the sort of life we think is enviable. What about Socrates? He was never down-cast, never troubled, always tranquil: now *that* was a life worth living! Or was it? For to describe Socrates' life as it appears in the historical record is only to describe the external features—the genial counten-

318 ~ *Taking Stock*

ance, the unhurried gait—and these were all destined, these all took place outside the charmed circle. Even his words, his arguments, his conversations, were all fated to happen just as they happened. If there was a free soul somewhere in there, its freedom only extended to mental events that were unrelated to the smile, the swagger, and the speeches. We cannot know what his allegedly free, internal life was like—all we can know is that it had no causal connection to the words of good assurance that he uttered on his deathbed, to the steady hand with which he lifted up his final cup. Perhaps he was happy, or perhaps he lived a life of constant frustration and turmoil, a life of mental anguish and crippling timidity. Perhaps the really enviable life was had by someone else—by one of his prosecutors, for instance, or a skulking whiner, or a snarling predator. We cannot know which life is the really worthwhile life to imitate—though in fact there is no point in trying to imitate another person in any case, since anything we could attempt to imitate would be simply another observable, external behavior. Both the behavior we observed and our own attempts to imitate it would thus be destined and determined. There is, in other words, no living room left in the inner citadel— no possibility of making free decisions that affect the course of our life, or of the lives of those around us. The inner citadel seems to promise us freedom, but in fact it gives us no freedom to *do* anything.

My point here is that there is no way to develop a stable and attractive interpretation of Stoicism from the thought that external events are fated and internal events are not fated. Instead we should accept the straightforward reading of the evidence, according to which the mind's assents, impulses, and judgments are just as much a part of the causal nexus as any external events are. We may not find the resultant picture of human life any more pleasant or desirable— the complaints I alleged against the inner citadel view are generally paralleled by complaints against the universal determinist interpretation that I have espoused in the previous chapters. But it is certainly better—more accurate, more faithful, and less ad hoc—as an interpretation. It has the further advantage that it bears its undesirable consequences more clearly on its face. The inner citadel view, by contrast, appeals to many casual readers, by seeming to promise a desirable approach to life that it can never really deliver.

It is the goal of most great philosophers to produce a system that is just as unified, just as coherent, just as comprehensive, as the object that they study, namely, the entire world, both natural and human. It is the general fate of these glittering constructions to collapse into fragments, and be quarried piece-meal by later readers for the odd insight or helpful thought. We should not shrink from being intellectual scavengers, ourselves. The original system-builder's systematic pride would bid us to take or leave the philosophy as a whole, but this is advice we are not obliged to follow—for who, faced with that choice, could choose anything but to leave all systems strictly alone? Still, as we are picking over the bits to be preserved, we should keep in mind two things: first, that the failure of past systems should not blunt our ambition to build anew; and second, that we should not limit ourselves to filching the odd architectural detail, the minor finial or boss. Sometimes the features most worth preserving are exactly the broad outlines, the structural and architectonic connections between parts. After the Parthenon fell, Westerners profited from seeing the details and decorations that Elgin and others brought back. But much more influential was the basic plan, now mirrored in banks and courthouses around the Western world. In studying Stoicism, we can find all sorts of small phrases and images that are attractive and easily taken away. But we can also learn from the interconnectedness of the whole system, even when we can no longer support or embrace the system as a whole.

NOTES

1. Plutarch *Sto. Rep.* 1057A = *SVF* 3.177 = LS 53S; trans. LS.
2. I noted this problem in Brennan (2000a); Barney (2003) also has some good thoughts along these lines.

3. Hadot (2001). The image comes from Marcus Aurelius 8.48: 'Remember that your mind becomes unconquerable when it turns to itself and is content with itself, not doing anything it does not wish to do, even when its refusal is irrational. How much more so, then, when it forms its judgment in a rational and circumspect manner? That is why our mind is a citadel when it is free of the passions, for the human being has nothing more impregnable than it into which it can flee and thereafter remain unplundered.'

4. Hippolytus, *Refutation* 1.21 = *SVF* 2.975 = LS 62A = IG2 II–92. Translation modified from LS.

5. Epictetus *Encheiridion* 53 = *SVF* 1.527 = LS 62B. Translation from LS.

6. For instance, the argument from bivalence that Chrysippus uses at Cicero *de Fato* 20 = *SVF* 2.952 = LS 38G = IG2 I–15.

REFERENCES

Algra, K. (2003) 'Stoic Theology' in Inwood (2003), 153–178.

Algra, K., Barnes, J., Mansfeld, J., and Schofield, M. (eds.) (1999), *The Cambridge History of Hellenistic Philosophy* (Cambridge: Cambridge University Press).

Annas, J. (1990) 'Stoic Epistemology' in Everson (1990), 184–203.

—— (1993) *The Morality of Happiness* (Oxford: Oxford University Press).

—— (ed.) (2001) *Cicero: On Moral Ends* (Cambridge: Cambridge University Press). With a translation by R. Woolf.

Arnold, E. (1911) *Roman Stoicism* (London: Routledge and Kegan Paul).

Barney, R. (2003) 'A Puzzle in Stoic Ethics', *Oxford Studies in Ancient Philosophy* 24, 303–340.

Blank, D. (1998) *Sextus Empiricus: Against the Grammarians, Translated with an Introduction and Commentary* (Oxford: Clarendon Press).

Bobzien, S. (1998a) *Determinism and Freedom in Stoic Philosophy* (Oxford: Oxford University Press).

—— (1998b) 'The Inadvertent Conception and Late Birth of the Free-Will Problem', *Phronesis* 43, 133–175.

—— (1999) 'Logic: The Stoics' in Algra et al. (1999), 92–157.

Bonhöffer, A. (1968) *Die Ethik des Stoikers Epictet* (Stuttgart: Frommann).

—— (1996) *The Ethics of the Stoic Epictetus*, trans. W. O. Stephens (New York: Peter Lang).

Boudouris, K. J. (ed.) (1994) *Hellenistic Philosophy* (Athens: International Center for Greek Philosophy and Culture).

Brennan, T. (1996) 'Reasonable Impressions in Stoicism', *Phronesis* 41(3), 318–334.

—— (1998a) 'The Old Stoic Theory of the Emotions' in Sihvola and Engberg-Pedersen (1998), 21–70.

—— (1998b) 'Demoralizing the Stoics', unpublished; delivered at a meeting of the Boston Area Colloquium on Ancient Philosophy.

—— (1999) *Ethics and Epistemology in Sextus Empiricus* (New York: Garland).

—— (2000a) 'Reservation in Stoic Ethics', *Archiv für Geschichte der Philosophie* 82 (2), 149–177.

—— (2000b) Review of Algra et al. (1999) *The Cambridge History of Hellenistic Philosophy*, in *Bryn Mawr Classical Review*, 2000.09.11

—— (2000c) Review of Blank (1998) in *Classical Review* 50 no. 2, 432–434.

—— (2001) 'Fate and Free Will in Stoicism', *Oxford Studies in Ancient Philosophy* 21, 259–286.

—— (2002) Review of Sorabji (2000) in *Philosophical Books*.

—— (2003) 'Stoic Moral Psychology' in Inwood (2003), 257–294.

Brittain, C. and Brennan T. (2002) *Simplicius on Epictetus Handbook*, 2 vol. (London: Duckworth).

Brody, B. A. (ed.) (1989) *Suicide and Euthanasia* (Dordrecht: Kluwer).

Brunschwig, J. (ed.) (1986) 'The Cradle Argument in Epicureanism and Stoicism' in Schofield and Striker (1986), 113–144.

Brunschwig, J. and Nussbaum, M. (eds.) (1993) *Passions and Perceptions: Studies in Hellenistic Philosophy of Mind* (Cambridge: Cambridge University Press).

Burnyeat, M. F. (1983) *The Skeptical Tradition* (Berkeley: University of California Press).

Cherniss, H. F. (ed.) (1976) *Plutarch: Moralia*, vol. XIII (London: Heinemann; Cambridge MA: Harvard University Press).

Cooper, J. M. (1989) 'Greek Philosophers on Suicide and Euthanasia' in Brody (1989), 9–38.

—— (1996) 'Eudaimonism, the Appeal to Nature, and "Moral Duty" in Stoicism' in Engstrom and Whiting (1996), 261–284.

Craig, E. (ed.) (1999) *Routledge Encyclopedia of Philosophy* (London: Routledge).

Dillon, J. and Long, A. (eds.) (1988) *The Question of 'Eclecticism'* (Berkeley: University of California Press).

Dorandi, T. (1999) '2. Chronology' and '3. Organization and Structure of the Philosophical Schools' in Algra et al. (1999), 31–62.

Edwards, P. (ed.) (1967) The Encyclopedia of Philosophy (New York: Collier Macmillan).

Engberg-Pedersen, T. (1990) *The Stoic Theory of Oikeiosis* (Aarhus: Aarhus University Press).

Engstrom, S. and Whiting, J. (eds.) (1996) *Rethinking Duty and Happiness: Aristotle, the Stoics, and Kant* (Cambridge: Cambridge University Press).

Everson, S. (ed.) (1990) *Epistemology.* Cambridge Companions to Ancient Thought 1 (Cambridge: Cambridge University Press).

Frede, D. (2003) 'Stoic Determinism' in Inwood (2003), 179–205.

Frede, M. (1983) 'Stoics and Skeptics on Clear and Distinct Impressions' in Burnyeat (1983), 65–93. Repr. in Frede (1987), 151–176.

—— (1986) 'The Stoic Doctrine of the Affections of the Soul' in Schofield and Striker (1986), 93–110.

—— (1987) *Essays in Ancient Philosophy* (Minneapolis: University of Minnesota Press).

—— (1994) 'The Stoic Conception of Reason' in Boudouris (1994), 50–63.

—— (1996)'Introduction' in Frede and Striker (1996), 1–28.

—— (1999a) 'On the Stoic Conception of the Good' in Ierodiakonou (1999), 71–94.

—— (1999b) 'Stoic Epistemology' in Algra et al. (1999), 295–322.

Frede, M. and Striker, G. (eds.) (1996) *Rationality in Greek Thought,* (Oxford: Oxford University Press).

Fritz, K. von (1970) 'Epictetus' in Hammond and Scullard (1970).

Furley, D. (1999) 'Cosmology' in Algra et al. (1999), 412–451.

Gill, C. (2003) 'The School in the Roman Imperial Period', in Inwood (2003), 33–58.

Hadot, P. (2001) *The Inner Citadel* (Cambridge MA: Harvard University Press).

Hammond, N. and Scullard, H. (1970) *The Oxford Classical Dictionary* (Oxford: Clarendon Press).

Hankinson, R. (1999) 'Determinism and Indeterminism' in Algra et al. (1999), 513–541.

—— (2003) 'Stoic Epistemology' in Inwood (2003), 59–85.

Hicks, R. D. (ed.) (1925) *Diogenes Laertius: Lives of Eminent Philosophers* (London: Heinemann; Cambridge MA: Harvard University Press).

Hooker, B. (2000) 'Moral Particularism: Wrong and Bad' in Hooker and Little (2000).

Hooker, B. and Little, M. (eds.) (2000) *Moral Particularism* (Oxford: Oxford University Press).

Ierodiakonou, K. (ed.) (1999) *Topics in Stoic Philosophy* (Oxford: Oxford University Press).

Inwood, B. (1984) 'Hierocles: Theory and Argument in the Second Century AD', *Oxford Studies in Ancient Philosophy* 2, 151–184.

—— (1985) *Ethics and Human Action in Early Stoicism* (Oxford: Oxford University Press).

—— (1999) 'Rules and Reasoning in Stoic Ethics' in Ierodiakonou (1999), 95–127.

—— (2000) 'The Will in Seneca the Younger', *Classical Philology* 95, 44–60.

—— (2003) *The Cambridge Companion to the Stoics* (Cambridge: Cambridge University Press).

Inwood, B. and Donini, P. (1999) 'Stoic Ethics' in Algra et al. (1999), 675–738.

Irwin, T.H. (1986) 'Stoic and Aristotelian Conceptions of Happiness' in Schofield and Striker (1986), 205–244.

Kahn, C. (1988) 'Discovering the Will: from Aristotle to Augustine' in Dillon and Long (1988), 234–259.

Kamtekar, R. (1998) '*Aidos* in Epictetus', *Classical Philology* 19, 136–160.

Kaufmann, W. (1967) 'Nietzsche' in Edwards (1967), 504–514.

Kavka, G. (1985) 'The Reconciliation Project' in Zimmerman and Copp. (1985).

Lloyd, A. C. (1978) 'Emotions and Decision in Stoic Psychology' in Rist (1978), 233–246.

Long, A. A. (1967) 'Carneades and the Stoic *telos*', *Phronesis* 12, 59–90.

—— (1970) 'The Logical Basis of Stoic Ethics', *Proceedings of the Aristotelian Society* 71, 85–104. Reprinted in Long (1996), 134–155.

—— (ed.) (1971) *Problems in Stoicism* (London: Athlone Press).

—— (1974/1986) *Hellenistic Philosophy. Stoics, Epicureans, Sceptics* (1974, London: Duckworth; repr. 1986 London/Berkeley/Los Angeles: University of California Press).

—— (1982) 'Soul and Body in Stoicism', *Phronesis* 27, 34–57. Reprinted in Long (1996).

—— (1988) 'Socrates in Hellenistic Philosophy' *Classical Quarterly* 38, 150–171. Repr. in Long (1996), 1–34.

—— (1989) 'Stoic eudaimonism', *Proceedings of the Boston Colloquium in Ancient Philosophy* 4, 77–101. Repr. in Long (1996), 179–201.

—— (1996) *Stoic Studies* (Cambridge: Cambridge University Press).

—— (1999a) 'Stoic Psychology' in Algra et al. (1999), 560–584.

—— (1999b) 'The Socratic Legacy' in Algra et al. (1999), 617–641.

—— (2002) *Epictetus: A Stoic and Socratic Guide to Life* (Oxford: Oxford University Press).

Long, H. (ed.) (1964) *Diogenis Laertii Vitae Philosophorum* (Oxford: Oxford University Press).

Lutz, C. E. (1947) 'Musonius Rufus: "The Roman Socrates" ', *Yale Classical Studies* 10, 3–147.

Mansfeld, J. (1991) 'The Idea of the Will in Chrysippus, Posidonius, and Galen', *Boston Area Colloquium in Ancient Philosophy* 7, 107–145.

—— (1999a) 'Sources' in Algra et al. (1999), 3–30.

—— (1999b) 'Theology' in Algra et al. (1999), 452–478.

Mitsis, P. (1993) 'Seneca on Reason, Rules, and Moral Development' in Brunschwig and Nussbaum (1993), 285–312.

—— (1999) 'The Stoic Origin of Natural Rights' in Ierodiakonou (1999), 153–177.

Mutschmann, H. and Mau, J. (eds.) (1961) *Sexti Empirici Opera, vols. II and III Adversus mathematicos* (Leipzig: Teubner).

—— (1962) *Sexti Empirici Opera, vol. I Pyrrhoneae hypotyposes* (Leipzig: Teubner).

Nussbaum, N. (1994) *The Therapy of Desire* (Princeton: Princeton University Press).

Oldfather, W. (1925) *Epictetus: The Discourses, Manual, and Fragments*, 2 vol. (Cambridge MA: Loeb Classical Library).

Pembroke, S. (1971) 'Oikeiôsis' in Long (1971), 114–149.

Préchac, F. (ed.) (1972) Seneca *de Beneficiis* (Paris: Les Belles Lettres).

Reynolds, L. (ed.) (1965) Seneca *Ad Lucilium epistulae morales* (Oxford: Oxford University Press).

Rist, J. M. (1969) *Stoic Philosophy* (Cambridge: Cambridge University Press).

—— (ed.) (1978) *The Stoics* (Berkeley: University of California Press).

Rowe, C. (1995) 'Ethics in Ancient Greece' in Singer (1995), 121–132.

Sandbach, F. H. (1975) *The Stoics* (London: Chatto and Windus).

—— (1985) *Aristotle and the Stoics* (Cambridge: Cambridge Philological Society).

Schofield (2003) 'Stoic Ethics' in Inwood (2003), 233–256.

Schofield, M. and Striker G. (eds.) (1986) *The Norms of Nature: Studies in Hellenistic Ethics* (Cambridge: Cambridge University Press / Paris: Editions de la Maison des Sciences de L'Homme).

Sedley, D. (1999a) 'Stoicism' in Craig (1999).

—— (1999b) 'The Stoic–Platonist Debate on *kathêkonta*' in Ierodiakonou (1999), 128–152.

—— (2003) 'The School, from Zeno to Arius Didymus' in Inwood (2003), 7–32.

Sharples, R. W. (1996) *Stoics, Epicureans, Sceptics: An Introduction to Hellenistic Philosophy* (London: Routledge).

Sihvola, J. and Engberg-Pedersen, T. (eds.) (1998) *The Emotions in Hellenistic Philosophy* (Dordrecht: Kluwer).

Singer, P. (ed.) (1995) *A Companion to Ethics* (Oxford: Blackwell).

Sorabji, R. (1993) *Animal Minds and Human Morals* (London: Duckworth).

—— (2000) *Emotion and Peace of Mind: From Stoic Agitation to Christian Temptation* (Oxford: Oxford University Press).

Stockdale, J. (1993), *Courage Under Fire: Testing Epictetus's Doctrines in a Laboratory of Human Behavior* (Stanford: Hoover Institute).

Striker, G. (1983) 'The Role of *oikeiôsis* in Stoic Ethics', *Oxford Studies in Ancient Philosophy* 1, 145–167. Reprinted in Striker (1996a), 281–298.

—— (1986) 'Antipater, or the Art of Living' in Schofield and Striker (1986), 185–204. Reprinted in Striker (1996a), 298–315.

—— (1991) 'Following Nature: A Study in Stoic Ethics', *Oxford Studies in Ancient Philosophy* 9, 1–73. Reprinted in Striker (1996a), 221–280.

—— (1996a) *Essays on Hellenistic Epistemology and Ethics* (Cambridge: Cambridge University Press).

—— (1996b) 'Plato's Socrates and the Stoics' in Striker (1996a), 316–324.

White, M. (2003) 'Stoic Natural Philosophy' in Inwood (2003), 124–152.

White, N. (1979) 'The Basis of Stoic Ethics', *Harvard Studies in Classical Philology* 83, 143–178.

—— (1985) 'Nature and Regularity in Stoic Ethics', *Oxford Studies in Ancient Philosophy* 3, 289–306.

Woolf, R. (2001) [Cicero's De Finibus] see Annas (2001).

Zanker, P. (1995) *The Mask of Socrates* (Berkeley: University of California Press).

Zimmerman, D. and Copp D. (eds.) (1985) *Morality, Reason, and Truth* (Totowa New Jersey: Rowman and Allanheld).

INDEX OF CITATIONS TO
ORIGINAL TEXTS

INDEX OF CITATIONS TO *SVF*
(*STOICORUM VETERUM FRAGMENTA*)

SVF 3.15:	151	*SVF* 3.473:	227
SVF 3.29:	132	*SVF* 3.476:	227
SVF 3.37:	132	*SVF* 3.478:	227
SVF 3.39:	152, 201	*SVF* 3.493:	180, 181, 200
SVF 3.67:	199	*SVF* 3.494:	180, 181, 200
SVF 3.91:	111	*SVF* 3.495:	181, 200
SVF 3.96:	133	*SVF* 3.496:	181, 200
SVF 3.97:	133	*SVF* 3.498:	180
SVF 3.107:	133	*SVF* 3.501:	199, 200
SVF 3.112:	80, 133	*SVF* 3.510:	181
SVF 3.117:	132	*SVF* 3.513:	180
SVF 3.124:	112	*SVF* 3.516:	181
SVF 3.169:	110, 181	*SVF* 3.528:	199
SVF 3.171:	110, 111	*SVF* 3.557:	199, 200
SVF 3.177:	320	*SVF* 3.560:	180, 181, 199, 200
SVF 3.178:	168, 201	*SVF* 3.561:	200
SVF 3.179:	168	*SVF* 3.564:	112
SVF 3.183:	168	*SVF* 3.613:	200
SVF 3.191:	113, 200	*SVF* 3.617:	34
SVF 3.211:	199, 200	*SVF* 3.627:	199, 200
SVF 3.214:	303	*SVF* 3.661:	181
SVF 3.228:	303	*SVF* 3.665:	112
SVF 3.262:	201	*SVF* 3.686:	228
SVF 3.284:	180	*SVF* 3.699:	227
SVF 3.313:	168	*SVF* 3.728:	228
SVF 3.314:	200	*SVF* 3.730:	199
SVF 3.315:	200	*SVF* 3.743:	229
SVF 3.323:	200	*SVF* 3.752:	133
SVF 3.340:	168	*SVF* 3.763:	199, 230
SVF 3.397:	111		
SVF 3.401:	111	*SVF* 3. Archedemus 8:	61
SVF 3.409:	111	*SVF* 3. Diogenes 17:	168
SVF 3.414:	111	*SVF* 3. Diogenes 44:	201
SVF 3.416:	111	*SVF* 3. Diogenes 45:	201
SVF 3.432:	111	*SVF* 3. Antipater 57:	201
SVF 3.462:	227	*SVF* 3. Antipater 66:	20

INDEX OF CITATIONS

TO LONG AND

SEDLEY'S *HELLENISTIC PHILOSOPHERS*

INDEX OF CITATIONS TO IG2

(INWOOD AND GERSON, *HELLENISTIC*

PHILOSOPHY, 2ND EDITION)

GENERAL INDEX